Stars in my Eyes

The author relaxing at home
(Photograph by Felicity Haze).

Stars in my Eyes

To Joanna.

KEN JOHNSTONE

_Best Wishes
Happy Gardening_

May 2004

The Pentland Press
Edinburgh – Cambridge – Durham – USA

First published in 2001 by
The Pentland Press Ltd
1 Hutton Close
South Church
Bishop Auckland
Durham

Email: manuscripts@pentlandpress.co.uk
sales@pentlandpress.co.uk
Web: www.pentlandpress.co.uk

ISBN 1-85821-827-6

Typeset in: Plantin 12 on 15
by Carnegie Publishing
Carnegie House
Chatsworth Road
Lancaster

www.carnegiepub.co.uk

Printed and bound by
Antony Rowe Ltd
Chippenham

Also by the same author:

Mistress of Monterey (Francombe Printers, 1993)
Triple Triumph (Francombe Printers, 1994)

*With my thanks for all their help to
Ken Millichap, Peter Jones, John Robson,
Ronnie Cogan and Veronica Squires*

Contents

Illustrations

Foreword

MY NICK-NAME for the sole owner of Kenneth Johnstone Associates is 'Splashy'. This comes from his habit of splashing fantastic ideas all over the place but only soaking the right people!

He is an oddly exciting Graham Greene character who has organized the great El Alamein Nights for Monty and Churchill; introduced All-In Wrestling to TV and nearly got fired by Associated-Rediffusion for having such crazy ideas; insured Winifred Atwell against hi-jacking; floated life-jackets off the North African coast for Uffa Fox; tried to import snow flakes for a ski-run on Hampstead Heath; and introduced golf buggies to the UK.

J. L. Manning
The *London Evening Standard*

CHAPTER I

In Town Tonight

It was my somewhat hilarious appearance in the BBC's popular show *In Town Tonight* that started it all.

I had just returned from a journey across Canada and I had ended up spending a few months at Kitimat, a new town being created on the edge of the wilderness in northern British Columbia. It was run by Alcan and situated on a fjord to which ships would in time bring bauxite from Jamaica to be processed into aluminium. Conditions were certainly stark. Entry was only permitted to those who worked there and a few families.

Intent on seeing this brave new community for myself, I got permission in Vancouver for a visit and eventually got fixed up to stay as a member of the fire brigade. I don't mind admitting that there were times on a call-out in the middle of the night when I was hanging on the back of the engine with the semi-arctic wind whistling up the back of my ill-fitting fireman's trousers, when I prayed that at least enough of the fire would be left burning on our arrival so that I could warm myself!

On my return to London I was at once invited to appear on *In Town Tonight*. Felicity Kendal and Sir Donald Wolfit, the actor, were also on the programme. The interview with John Ellison was a great success and as I was being faded out to the background music of Eric Coates' 'Knightsbridge March' and the familiar cry 'Carry on London!', an oversize fireman's helmet, produced courtesy of the BBC's prop department, gradually obscured me from view.

The telephone calls started long before I left the studio at Maida Vale. Old friends were on the line. There was also a message asking me to call at an office in Kingsway. On arrival there next day I found it to be the headquarters of the new Associated Rediffusion (AR-TV). I was interviewed by Bill Gillette, Programme

Controller, who asked me to attend a production meeting later in the week.

As a result, I virtually found myself Head of Sport at ITV and with only three months left before it was on the air!

Of course the BBC had a long and distinguished track record in broadcasting sport and they had most sporting events tied up either for radio or TV. It was, you might say, a pretty daunting task. There was also a kind of loyalty to the BBC on the part of many sporting bodies and in Peter Dimmock and Paul Fox the Corporation had a hugely successful partnership aided by a great team. Added to this we would only be transmitting as a station on Monday to Friday, which precluded sharing the feast of weekend sporting events, and there was virtually nothing planned. It was still the time of black and white TV, of course.

The offices at Kingsway House in the Strand were being rebuilt and there was a constant cacophony of noise. Sometimes meetings had to be abandoned as voices were drowned under the racket of electric drills. Even spending a penny became hazardous and ladies often had to resort to the nearest tube station or hotel. My only outside staff was a solitary cameraman, Bill McConnel, who was superb, despite having lost a leg during the War.

Government plans for commercial television in competition with the BBC were highly controversial. They were announced on 13 November 1953. The contractors were to draw their revenue from advertisements of not more than six minutes for each hour of broadcasting. The new TV output would be under strict control and would start in London, followed by Birmingham. To face the competition the BBC were to get a licence fee of £3, up from £2. My slot was to be called *Cavalcade of Sport*.

CHAPTER II

Cavalcade of Sport

So THERE I WAS IN KINGSWAY HOUSE in London's Strand. At last! The days were whizzing by. I had the feeling that I was now very much on my own trying to put together the first ever ITV sports programme. And the vultures were outside – waiting.

Bill Gillette, beset with his own problems as Programme Controller, gave me what time he could and lots of encouragement, but shortly after the opening of ITA he unfortunately left the company with dramatic suddenness. This was a tremendous 'smack in the eye' for me – he was an enthusiast and great to work for. He understood me and I am bound to say that at times, without him, I felt almost rudderless.

Other sections were busy grappling with their own problems and our Outside Broadcasts – which in the BBC was such a strong fortress – had to cope with all manner of technical problems. The Head of OBs – using the BBC vernacular – was an ex-RN Commander, Robert Everett, who tried to manage manfully in a world new to him. Stephen MacCormack, formerly of the BBC, took over as Controller of Programmes, but I was left to work on my own. Anyway, I felt that I had to get out and about and very much follow my own instincts.

Racing was certainly not my cup of tea, but I suddenly found myself courted by important people in the racing industry. Lunching at the Dorchester and having breakfast at the residences of at least two members of the peerage found me a trifle embarrassed by their attention as, apart from anything else, we were, after all, Monday to Friday and could not cover weekend racing.

A full-time racing man was drafted in later, but I had already made good connections with Hurst Park and Jack Knights who ran Windsor where mid-week night-time horse racing, which I

3

arranged to be televised, proved popular. But quite soon after our launch, the BBC announced its then biggest Outside Broadcast contract worth £20,000 (good money in those days) a year for exclusive television, telefilm and telerecording rights of racing at Kempton Park. The agreement included sound rights and was to last four years. Peter Dimmock, the quite brilliant Head of Outside Broadcasting, BBC, announced: 'Our relations with major sporting events are very cordial indeed and we have not yet announced our long-term agreements.' Privately he intimated to me that we might get a share of the Test Matches, but this was more in a spirit of fun, for I found that what he was offering me was virtually the tea interval!

I think some consternation was caused in their ranks and also, I might add, with Associated Rediffusion directors when, following the announcement of BBC sports plans and under strong pressure from the media, I intimated that we, too, had ambitious sporting plans and some of the press promptly wrote these up as firm arrangements which, I am afraid, set a number of alarm bells ringing. I had said that these were some of our plans and that we also hoped to take viewers behind the scenes at a number of sports from polo to tennis and that a number of race meetings were being negotiated, including Sandown Park and Hurst Park, which was a fact.

For *Cavalcade of Sport*'s first show I worked away like a beaver arranging for a 'Parade of All the Champions', including even Foxhunter in the studio. There were over forty champions of sport present. It was Thursday, 29 September 1955. Leslie Ayre, TV correspondent for the *London Evening News* reported the next day: 'What is to the viewer's advantage – and most fascinating to observe – is the determined show of enterprise by each side, a sort of taking the viewer by the lapel and whispering "See what clever boys we are!" '

He went on, '*Cavalcade of Sport* weighed in heavily with a parade of big name sporting stars. There seemed to be regiments of them – cricketers, speed men, racing personalities, athletes, boxers, show-jumping types, footballers, cricketers, etc. – and their names were rattled off like a roll of drums.

'*Sportsview* countered on the same evening with a demonstration of mobility, with Peter Dimmock sitting in the studio with fingers crossed in the hope that the technicians would bring it off. In the main they did – the phone conversation with Pat Ward in the *Ile de France* and the picture interview with Angela Ward in Manchester – but they lost the picture of Erica Batchelor from Wembley.

'*Cavalcade* whipped in with a phone call to Randolph Turpin ...' (This may have included a bit of ad lib by Tony Van den Bergh in the studio.)

Later Vic Oliver in *This is Show Business* (BBC) also brought in sport when he said, 'I hear Chris Chataway has read the news in 3 minutes 58 seconds flat!'

Forgive me if I now digress somewhat, but I should like to take you back in time. I shall never forget London on the morning of 20 July 1951. I happened to be in the West End and arriving by Underground I had to struggle up the stairs; on reaching street level, I was almost bodily lifted by the struggling mass of humanity. It was the day of the big fight between Randolph Turpin and Sugar Ray Robinson for the Middleweight Championship of the World. The West End had come to a complete standstill, literally jammed with heaving humanity.

Sugar Ray had indeed captivated the public's imagination. He trained at the Star and Garter hostelry at Windsor near the castle and commuted to and from London in a vast pink Cadillac he had shipped over from the Continent. His party was large and colourful and included the manager, trainer, sparring partners, masseur, barber and a dwarf who acted as a kind of court jester. Oh, and there was also a personal golf professional.

To an austere Britain this was refreshing and just the occasion to raise a cheer with all the hype and magnetic presence of the World Middleweight Champion himself. The media loved it all.

The one o'clock weigh-in on that day was to take place at Jack Solomons' famous gymnasium in Windmill Street just off Piccadilly Circus. Hence the solid mass of people through which the police would somehow have to push their way to get Sugar Ray and his party up to the door which led by a narrow staircase to the gymnasium and which, I might add, was one of the most heavily guarded entrances in all London on that morning.

As the day wore on the excitement spread across the nation and I realised of all sports, boxing alone could bring this incredible buzz, and that in presenting two men in the confined space of a ring, it was absolutely ideal for television. And to be at the fight that evening in the amazing atmosphere at Earl's Court when Eugene Henderson, the referee, finally awarded the verdict to Turpin with the crowd going mad, complete strangers hugging one another and dancing in the aisles, the fight broadcast to the nation and the whole place erupting – this was for me further proof that boxing was made for television – and the reverse.

Little did I then realise that I would become a regular and, I might add, welcome visitor up that narrow staircase in Windmill Street, past the ever vigilant 'Sailor', the doorman, and into the office of Jack Solomons who, removing his seemingly ever-present cigar, would cordially greet me thus: 'Hello, Ken, my son!' Within days of getting to work at ITV I was in touch with him and took a leading part in bringing him into our camp. This was a big coup.

Jack was undoubtedly one of the top boxing men in Europe. He was about fifty-five when I first met him. Fighting and fish had been his main interests. Not only was he born in a basement room beneath a Petticoat Lane fish shop, to be later in business as a fish merchant, but when he was about thirty he joined in with three others to purchase the lease of an old disused church in Devonshire Street, Hackney which they rather grandly called The Devonshire Club. Jack, eventually running the place himself, put in a front man as promoter and soon the venture really took off with Jack as manager and matchmaker.

By 1937 he had joined Sydney Hulls senior, then Britain's leading promoter, as matchmaker for the supporting bouts at the big Harringay Arena Tournaments. He also began working with promoter John Muldoon on several Royal Albert Hall shows and it was here that he first met Sam Burns, who was to become his General Manager and with whom I later had an excellent association.

Jack had a great advantage over other boxing promoters because soon after the War he had made an arrangement with Mike Jacobs and the International Boxing Club in America which ensured that all the American fighters who came over here would be solely under his promotion. This arrangement held good for a number of years, much to Jack's advantage, until Jarvis Astaire brought over Jimmy Carter, a former World Lightweight Champion and this encouraged other promoters to disregard it also. In fact the flood gates opened.

The opening of ITA was on 22 September 1955 and was not lacking in drama off the screen. The BBC went on the air half an hour earlier than usual to counter ITA's opening speeches from the Guildhall. The death by fire of Grace Archer in their popular BBC radio feature, *The Archers*, was timed for maximum drawing power away from our opening.

The six minutes of advertising on television long awaited by the snipers proved tasteful enough, the first being for SR Toothpaste.

We had boxing in the programme from Shoreditch Town Hall, where Lew Lazar fought Terence Murphy in an eight-rounder. The fact that one of the first ads was for Mackesons Stout and the shot on TV immediately following was of Terence Murphy spitting in a bucket was just one of those things!

The 'Discoveries' type of show was popular. There was a novel twist in which Ralph Reader introduced a programme called *Chance*. In this first show Pat Kirkwood introduced her discoveries and Ralph compered. In subsequent shows a star would introduce his or her own discoveries. It was a good twist and when originally Bill Gillette had discussed the format of our opening I had enthusiastically voted for the inclusion of Ralph's 'Chance' rather than other forms of 'Discovery' items. It went down well.

Getting on the air from scratch after only a few months of non-stop preparation was, I believe, an achievement. The press reception was mixed. Under the heading 'A Sticky Wicket for *Sports Cavalcade*', Peter Black wrote in the *London Evening News*:

Independent TV is batting on a sticky wicket. The BBC has immeasurably superior network facilities: ITV is obliged for the moment to rely upon interviews.

It is thus following BBC's *Sportsview* in the direction where *Sportsview* itself is weakest. What it must do – and the problem is far easier to state than to resolve – is find something better than interviews.

It once seemed wonderful to see these modern heroes actually smiling at us, but *Cavalcade of Sport* emphasised – as *Sportsview* is emphasising – that once the novelty has worn off they are inclined to be dull.

Whether they straddle a horse, kick a ball, hit a ball, punch a nose, walk, run, jump, row or swim the interviews fall into a similar pattern ending with the commentator saying that he is sure that we will all join in wishing them luck!

Well, there I was with only dear Bill McConnel and his magic camera quite apart from a limited budget. But I knew I had to get more action. Sir Stanley Rouse, then Secretary of the Football Association, came to my rescue. He arranged for me to have the use of QPR's ground at Shepherd's Bush for outside camera rehearsals and I got in touch with Bill Fallowfield, the then Secretary of the Rugby League, with the result that I was able to include Rugby League action in my *Cavalcade of Sport*.

What really happened was that two teams of Rugby League players came down each week from Leeds by coach. They ran out onto the pitch and played twelve minutes each way. Meanwhile, to form 'a crowd', we were out earlier in the day inviting in housewives out shopping, nurses with some time off, stray visitors, truant schoolboys, people who had lost their way, sailors on leave ... we even gave them coffee. They sat together watching the game and we then moved them to watch from another angle in order to indicate 'another section of the crowd'. Building the excitement became an art.

Sir Arthur Elvin, who owned Wembley, was very encouraging to me. For instance, when the visit of Russia's amateur boxers was confirmed for Wembley it was obtained exclusively by me for TV coverage. But this glittering prize was mine for only twenty-four hours. I remember sitting on the steps at Wembley one night after leaving Sir Arthur, looking up at the stars and in particular one up there which was my favourite – 'I've done it,' I told it. 'My first exclusive!' But came the morning and the news that ITA (Independent Television Authority) said that it had to be shared with the BBC. It was, I suppose, a national event – Great Britain v Russia.

Peter Waterman discussing moves with Georges Carpentier whilst Trevor Wignall, Daily Express *Sports Editor, looks on. Taken at the Savoy Grill, London, after they had appeared with me in a* Cavalcade of Sport TV programme.

But Sir Arthur was always supportive. I continued to be on his 'Special Guests' lists for such events as the Cup Final, where one got special treatment along with 'the wise and the good'. I must say, going to Wembley for a superb lunch, then the game in the best seats and then tea in such a rarefied atmosphere made for a good day out.

I started a series called *Where Are They Now?* which, of course, included live studio interviews, but with flash-backs, and this created considerable interest. The first of these featured Georges Carpentier, the former Light-Heavyweight Champion of the World, who had fought Siki and Jack Dempsey. He was recognised worldwide as a suave, debonair sportsman of huge personality known as 'The Orchid Man'. He starred with Sally O'Neil in *Hold Everything* made by Warner Brothers in Hollywood. Now he ran his own night club in Paris. He was a terrific draw. Taxi men recognised him at once. When I took him for lunch at the Savoy

Grill, some of the kitchen staff apparently took turns to peep at him from the doorway. This was unheard of! Our TV interview, interspersed with some stills of him in action, was a great success and got a big press.

Then there was Kay Don, who, on 9 July 1931, had set a speedboat record of 110 m.p.h. in Italy in his boat, 'Miss England II'. That interview was backed by excellent flash-back material and went down very well.

I became very friendly with Donald Campbell, who appeared on the show, and dined out several times with him and his wife, Tania Byrne, the cabaret artist. He was, of course, the 34-year-old son of the late Sir Malcolm Campbell. He had broken the World Water Speed Record himself on Ullswater in July of that year. He made two runs over the lake in his turbojet hydroplane, 'Bluebird', at an average speed of 202.32 m.p.h., but sadly he was to be killed later when it exploded.

I might add that Stirling Moss, who had won his first Grand Prix beating World Champion Fangio in the British Grand Prix on 17 July 1955, was a fascinating subject in a series that was very well received.

Leslie Ames, the Test cricketer, was another subject and then I got the idea of bringing Stewart MacPherson into the series. His had, after all, been the most popular voice on the air. With his distinctive trans-Atlantic accent and crisp phrasing he was regarded as the fastest voice on radio and a huge success. His boxing commentaries in those days before television were so fluent and colourful, and his partnership with a former referee, W. Barrington Dalby, who gave the inter-round summaries, so popular that on one famous occasion Hugh Dalton, then Chancellor of the Exchequer, delayed his Budget broadcast for an hour rather than interrupt the transmission of the MacPherson commentary on a Freddie Mills fight.

Stew originally came to London from his native Winnipeg entirely on spec. He got a job in a shoe shop in London, but got fired for constantly chewing gum. He had, however, given a little help with the editorial for an ice-hockey programme and was able to get a trial as a would-be radio commentator on the game. This proved so successful that it wasn't long before he was doing regular sports broadcasts on ice hockey, skating, cycling and boxing.

When the Second World War broke out, the BBC abandoned outside broadcasting. Too old to join up, Stew despondently returned to his native Winnipeg to become sports editor of a local radio station: but a few months later he received a cable to join the BBC's reporting unit.

He arrived back in London just in time for the Blitz and was assigned to the RAF; he filed a notable account of a bombing raid over Cologne and then switched to the ground war as the invasion began. He had the ability to find off-beat features behind the front line, but his best reports included covering the Canadians at Dieppe and at the Battle of Arnhem.

In no time after the War, it seems, his voice had also become famous in entertainment in this country. *Twenty Questions* and *Ignorance Is Bliss* were popular regular shows. He compered the Royal Variety Command shows and toured the country with a *Twenty Questions* show and this, in addition to his popular boxing and Boat Race commentaries and his own national weekly newspaper column, really put him in the big time.

He was demanding high fees as a freelance broadcaster and, although he was a star of a then non-visual medium, his rimless glasses, square-jawed features and tall rangy build were so often featured in the press that he was a truly big national personality. His flamboyant style, including a magnificent Bentley car, was well known, but in 1949, when he was one of the busiest and best-known broadcasters in Britain, Stewart Macpherson suddenly decided to give it all up and join a radio station in Minneapolis – a city of only half a million people.

His farewell performance in Britain was at a 'Royal Command Radio Party' given by King George VI for the staff at Windsor Castle. Members of the Royal Family were devoted admirers of his work. His sudden departure was attributed to his wife, who missed the countryside and life generally of the mid-west and soon after their return they were back in Winnipeg in their beloved Canada.

It was certainly a nostalgic moment for Stew when I met him on his arrival at Heathrow. He had readily agreed on the telephone to my invitation to him to come over. I left him to make some visits of his own and first thing next morning we met to work out his appearance with me that evening – it was great to be even momentarily partnering him on TV.

He had not been back in London for years, it seemed, since his sudden decision to leave and this was quite a coup for me. We had an excellent press and everything went like clockwork. He was obviously very excited about it all. There was considerable reaction by the public and the switchboard was kept busy for some days afterwards.

One further aside on his spectacular return. One very famous hotel wasn't too sure about the booking. 'You mean THE Stewart Macpherson?' they queried nervously about the request for a reservation prior to his arrival. Apparently there had been some fun and games with residents' shoes – they used to be left at night outside bedroom doors – but I never knew the truth of it.

All the *Where Are They Now?* episodes were very well received. Another of them was my interview with Floyd Paterson. As Middleweight Champion at the Olympics of 1952 when he represented the USA, he established himself as a world-class sportsman and on becoming professional had those epic battles in the ring with Sonny Liston.

Ingemar Johansson, whom I also welcomed to London, knocked Floyd down seven times in one fight. They were to meet three times and despite these vicious contests, they remained close friends. The Swede was always impeccably dressed, extremely well mannered and was to appear in the movies, do modelling and be very successful in business in his own right.

For Outside Broadcasts I developed a good connection at Streatham Ice Rink. Their team, nearly all Canadians, got used to doing interviews on the spot for us, introducing the game and so on. I had to go after other weekday sports such as cycle racing and some athletics, though being weekday only was always a restriction.

I made a good friend of Derek Ibbotson who on 19 July 1957 recaptured the mile record for Britain in 3 minutes 57.2 seconds. The first four men on that day all broke the magic four minutes. Derek, who was from Huddersfield, took on and beat the Olympic champion, Ron Delany of Ireland, and the new world 1,500 metres record holder, Stanislav Jungwirth of Czechoslovakia, in front of a television audience of ten million viewers – I hasten to add not all ITA! He broke the tape eight-tenths of a second faster than Australian John Landy's record of 1954. I used him quite often on TV.

It is worth noting that on 13 August 1957 the BBC announced a revamp of its radio programmes in a bid to stem the drift of its audience to television. Evening audiences for radio had declined by a million to 3.5 million. Eight years previously an average nightly audience had been eight million. But television had then been in its infancy with transmissions just beginning to spread beyond London. With the development of commercial television, six million people were estimated to watch BBC and ITV each evening. Radio planners fought back with earlier starts to the Light Programme, plus hourly news summaries.

When Chris Brasher arrived at his house in London from the 1956 Melbourne Olympic Games, having won the 3,000 metres Steeplechase Final, we were there to welcome him home as he met members of his family.

Derek Ibbotson being interviewed by the author for Cavalcade of Sport.

One morning Jack phoned me and asked if I would look after two of his guests that evening at a big fight. They turned out to be glamorous Hollywood star, Debbie Reynolds and the famous crooner, Eddie Fisher, of 'I want to be loved by you' fame. What made it all the more exciting was that they had just arrived in London with the world's press in full pursuit because of their rumoured engagement. Sitting next to Debbie at the ringside with her snuggling up to me and grabbing my arm when the fighting got a bit fierce and saying 'Oh, Ken – I can't look any more' made for a pretty exciting experience. I don't mind admitting my thrills that evening came more from outside the ring than in it! We talked about the film *Singin' in the Rain.* 'Gene Kelly was a real charmer and lovely to work with,' she told me. 'His timing was unbelievable and in that marvellous dance in the rain there were surprisingly few retakes.' It seemed to me that we never stopped talking when afterwards I joined them for dinner at The Ivy. She told me how she had first met Sinatra and when we chatted about her part in *Show Boat* I was able to tell her of the old Mississippi steam boat I had lived aboard at Kitimat.

Debbie now owns her own hotel in Las Vegas where she exhibits movie memorabilia, much of it being purchased by her from MGM when they sold off its warehouses full of costumes and furniture. She married Eddie, of course, and they have a daughter, Carrie Fisher, who is an actress, and a son, Todd, who says, 'Some people, if they're looking for their mother go first into the kitchen. For mine, I just go to Vegas!'

Eddie and Debbie were to end their marriage in 1959 and he later married Elizabeth Taylor.

Debbie's memorable quote was, 'I stopped making movies because I don't like having to take my clothes off!'

There was intense rivalry at this time between Jack Solomons and Harry Levene. Harry would phone me if he discovered that I had been out to lunch with Jack and speculate good humouredly how we had got on. It all seemed childish at times for I also sometimes lunched with Harry himself. His family had been killed in a bombing raid during the War and he appeared at times to be quite bitter. He had managed his first professional boxer when he was still a teenager. He managed the Bagatelle Restaurant in

London's Mayfair – a very classy joint – had a flat in Park Lane and was always impeccably turned out. But he was almost hypnotised by the 'fight game' as he called it.

Mickey Duff worked for him, helping his promotions, doing odd jobs, selling the tickets and assisting at weigh-ins. He was always cheerful and helpful and appeared to eat, drink and sleep boxing. Mickey was quite a bright young man. The son of a rabbi in Bournemouth who had come over from Cracow in Poland when Mickey was only nine, he concealed his love of the fight game from the family by using not his own name of Morris Prager, but that of Mickey Duff. Actually, he was born Monek Prager. His father married four times. Mickey and he became bitterly estranged. However, he was to become a top boxing promoter in the 1960s and 1970s and guided such as John Stracey, Lloyd Honeyghan and Alan Minter to world titles in the States. He owns homes in Florida and Israel, still loves his boxing, but insists, 'Frankly I am not now in it for the money!' He has been a manager and promoter in the game for fifty years and it seems to sit lightly on his soul. His business empire was later said to stretch from the Kray Brothers on one hand to Frank Bruno in pantomime at the other. There was the much-publicised investigation into boxing in 1984 in which there were suggestions that Terry Lawless, Mike Barrett, Jarvis Astaire and he were operating a cartel against the interests of boxers, but in the end the British Boxing Board of Control exonerated them all.

Still on the boxing theme. Rocky Marciano over in the States was not only a World Champion, but he had become an accomplished performer on television. I thought that if I could get a young boxer with a big future and groom him for TV appearances, it would be an added attraction for *Cavalcade of Sport*. Certainly the BBC had no such arrangement.

Freddie Mills had become a great enthusiast for *Cavalcade of Sport* and a good friend of mine. He was always ready to help. His great fight – one of the greatest ever seen in this country – with Gus Lesnevich at White City for the Light-Heavyweight Championship of the World on 14 May 1946 had established him as one of our 'sporting greats'. He loved television, was a real showman at heart and I used him whenever I could, but, as I explained to him, I was looking for one of the new young breed whom I could train for studio spots. Freddie, being Freddie, readily understood.

Whereas Rocky was already established on top of the boxing world, the young man I selected had not yet won any titles as a professional. He was Peter Waterman. Peter was a product of the famous Caius Boxing Club held in the Nine Elms Baths, Nine Elms Lane, Battersea. Here the cap and mufflered queue would wait patiently, usually in the cold, for the balcony to open where for 2/6d they would be entertained to an evening of educated fisticuffs. Under the gas lighting the hard wooden seats provided a grandstand view of some of our finest young amateur boxers either in training or in inter-club bouts. There were some fascinating characters, among them big, blonde Basil Kew. On the night he scored his shock KO in the first round over Henry Cooper, now former British Heavyweight Champion, his crazy dance of joy round the ring ended with him slipping and falling flat on his face.

It was clear that pale, slim, slit-eyed Peter Waterman had real style and substance and therefore it was no surprise when he quickly disposed of four opponents to win the South-West Divisional Championship and go on to gain national honours as an amateur. The devoted committee men and enthusiastic working members of the club produced some splendid boxers and Peter, on becoming their Youth Welterweight Champion, successfully going through the divisions to become ABA Welterweight Champion and going on to represent England in the Olympic Games at Helsinki, was obviously a big favourite and a fine advertisement for the club.

His first fight as a professional earned him £15 with his manager, Jarvis Astaire, taking nothing from it, though he was entitled to 25 per cent of every purse after training and travelling expenses had been deducted.

Ambitious Waterman, though, had no intention of protecting his good looks. He was known as a rock 'em, sock 'em kind of fighter. The son of a Cockney railwayman, he had five sisters and two brothers – one of them, Dennis, went in for the stage and TV with big success - and he went to the Henry Thornton

Grammar School, Clapham, where he studied French, German, Mathematics, Art and even the violin.

He shared a flat with Peter Jones in West Norwood, London. Peter was London Sales Manager for a national company of home electrical appliances, had been Hon Secretary of Caius Boxing Club and became a steadying influence on the young Waterman. Peter, however, had a string of girlfriends come to the flat, but Peter Jones was able to guide him in such a way that he began reading T.E. Lawrence, Winston Churchill or Thurber, quite apart from his painting. Peter Waterman had worked in the Antique Department at Fortnum and Mason and then as a salesman in a haberdashery shop in Balham owned by his manager, Jarvis Astaire, and had done his National Service as a clerk in the RAF. Now he formed himself into a limited liability company and his future seemed good. He was very personable with clear enough diction and came over well on television. I took him over to Paris where we jointly did some commentating from the Palais de Sport. He also ran a coaching series on TV for youngsters.

Peter began to appear regularly on ITV and his 21st birthday TV party included many well-known sportsmen. Jack Solomons for one did not agree with glamorising fighters. 'They are animals,' he once told me. 'They should be treated as such.'

It was a fact that the glitzy world of show business began to affect Peter – after all he was only twenty years of age – and he began to believe the compliments made to him. I remember one enthusiast for the fight game, or at least the fighters, was a dashing blonde called Sally Weston whom we somehow thought was related to Garfield Weston the big entrepreneur at that time. Once at the Thomas a' Becket, Harry Levene, the old and hugely experienced promoter, was watching the boxers in training. He also observed Peter being less than friendly to two former fighters. Some time later Harry strolled over to where Peter was stretched full length on the massage table. Harry told him, 'I like you, Waterman.'

'Thank you, Mr Levene,' replied Peter.

Harry continued, 'You know why I like you, son? You're the nastiest bastard I've met since the days of Jock McAvoy!'

Peter Jones later told Waterman, 'That was what is known as a back-handed compliment.'

He was living in a world of hard paymasters in which he was more or less a commodity.

L. Marshland Gander, writing in the *Daily Telegraph* at this time, referred to ITV and BBC 'sharing the best transmission of the week, namely Pirie's running victory over Zatopek' and described it 'as packed with excitement, suspense and drama as anything yet seen'. So sport did represent good viewing!

Incidentally, I know that it is hugely out of time and context, but it may be of slight interest to mention here how all this was being done on the thinnest of shoestrings, as they say. Financial details of what the BBC spends on sport have always been notoriously difficult to find, but in his year of retirement, Sir John Birt, the departing Director General, told the parliamentary Culture, Media and Sport Select Committee, 'We are now spending more than £150 million a year on sport.'

This was the year 2000, of course, but way back when I was Head of Sport at ITV, the budget was by comparison so infinitesimal it would make one blush to write it down.

I went to Manchester to see Peter fight Roger Facquier of France. It was the twenty-ninth fight of his professional career and he chased the Frenchman so hard around the ring, throwing such a wide repertoire of punches, that the fight was stopped after three rounds. It was nine days before Christmas 1955. Sammy MacCarthy, another bright British hopeful, had unfortunately been knocked out that evening and I insisted on giving up my first-class sleeper on the London train to him. I have good reason to remember it. On reaching London, I was so tired when driving off that I inadvertently grazed the side of another car. A firm of solicitors, on hearing of this, insisted on attending to the ensuing case themselves without charge. It transpired they were fans of *Cavalcade of Sport*!

There were some great young characters around in the game at that time. Terry Spinks (the first British Boxer to win an Olympic medal in twenty years), Dave Charnley, Sammy MacCarthy, Joe Lucy among them. Joe had the licence of the Thomas a' Becket pub in the Old Kent Road where upstairs on the first floor there was a private gym which could be used by invitation only.

One evening I was up in this gym, together with the London agent of John Huston, the famous film director. We were watching

Alan Pompey, a young coloured boxer, work out. He had been spotted by Huston taking the part of a boxer in a film and as it was felt he might have a future, Kid Berg had come along to look the boy over. Suddenly we were joined by John Huston himself. He had just completed *Moby Dick* over in Ireland for Warner Brothers, starring Gregory Peck as Captain Ahab and not long afterwards in came the then William Hickey, columnist of the *Daily Express*, accompanied by three others. One was a dark-haired girl who, on throwing back the hood which shielded her face, could be seen to be strikingly beautiful. Her escort was a tall handsome young Englishman. Sworn to secrecy, we were told that these two young people were the couple then being hunted all over the world.

They were, in fact, young Jimmy Goldsmith and Isabel Patino, the young daughter of the Bolivian tin millionaire, and they had eloped. The other guy was a private detective who at once took up his position at the door. They were obviously madly in love, though quite why they were in a room over a pub down the Old Kent Road with half the world searching for them I would never know, though I believe that John Huston had made secret arrangements to meet them and this was, after all, probably the most unlikely place for them to be spotted.

Jimmy was half Jewish. The Patino family had said that they did not marry Jews and Jimmy's family had replied famously, 'We do not marry Red Indians!'

His father was Frank Goldsmith, Conservative MP for Stowmarket in Suffolk, who had owned hotels, among them the Carlton in Cannes. Jimmy's story is, of course, quite incredible. There was his £8,000 horse-racing betting coup at Eton – later his takeover battles, asset-stripping, his running fight with the magazine *Private Eye* which christened him 'Golden-balls' and, of course, his multiple women. He became one of the richest men in the world. Chatting with him that evening one could see he was obviously restless with energy, his eyes flashing with excitement.

Suddenly they were ready to leave. Their romantic dash would continue worldwide until finally they would marry in Scotland, but even then only after a dramatic chase. I will never forget her hauntingly beautiful face. Sadly she was to die in childbirth with her daughter, also named Isabel. Jimmy was almost inconsolable.

He looked after the little girl and never went out partying for six years.

The daughter, now in her mid-forties, lives in Spain and has a £50 million fortune which she inherited from her grandfather.

He had, though, a strange relationship with women. He married his French secretary, Ginette Lery, though it did not last long for he left her to live with Lady Annabel Vane Stewart, the former wife of Mark Birley, who had named the famous London night club, Annabel's, after her. Not long after marrying Annabel, Jimmy's attention turned to a French journalist and until his death he resided in homes looked after both by her and Lady Annabel, who also has a splendid home in Richmond, Surrey.

He flung himself into business affairs. For six years he slaved away building up businesses and was always intrigued by high finance. He launched Cavernham Foods and was involved in very aggressive takeover battles with Jim Slater as a business associate. He obtained a major shareholding, for instance, in the famous store, Fortnum and Mason.

He criss-crossed the world in private jets to his various estates. He had eight children by three wives and a mistress. His son and heir, Zac, says of him, 'I miss my father. He knew how to make decisions. Politicians now are so emasculated, they're such wimps.' He has a younger brother, Ben, and he says of his sister, Jemima, 'She's a magnet for the cameras. There's only a year between us, so we're always either fighting or incredibly close.' He is a great admirer of his brother-in-law, Imran Khan. 'He's honest and he is strong,' he says.

The children have a share in the £1.5 billion Goldsmith inheritance. Zac runs a magazine, the *Ecologist*, together with his uncle, Teddy Goldsmith. I don't think that it's a seriously commercial venture. The trouble with children, particularly the sons of very successful people, is that they often have this overwhelming challenge to do well themselves. Zac can be alarmingly switched on. 'Do you think we need a new political party?' he asks. 'We could call it the Classic Conservatives!'

Zac, a gangling, well-meaning, if naive 23-year-old, is the second of Lady Annabel Goldsmith's three children by Sir James – Jemima, who is 24, Ben 17 and Zac.

James Goldsmith had, indeed, a dynamic, tempestuous life and not surprisingly in the nature of his character, he was a big casino gambler. But probably his most incredible undertaking came about in the final stages of his life when, having become a Euro MP in France, he set up his own Referendum Party to contest the 1997 General Election, spending a fortune on fielding candidates, none of whom was successful. He was tragically suffering from cancer and died soon afterwards. It was his last grand but sad and painful ego trip.

There was much malice shown towards him in his life, but he wanted in his own way, and with his own money, in this last campaign of his to ensure that the facts of the loss of sovereignty were made known so that the general public was in a position to respond. He saw it as a service to the nation – a counterweight to the massive propaganda financed by the European institutions and their allies.

But to get back at last to that night at the Thomas a' Becket. After they left we discussed the young boxer's potential and later John Huston, Kid Berg and his lovely wife came over to my flat in Belsize Park. There, over drinks, we chatted about films. How boxing had figured quite often – Max Baer, Primo Carnera and Jack Dempsey in *The Prize Fighter and the Lady*; Georges Carpentier and Sally O'Neil in *Hold Everything* for Warner Brothers; Joe Louis in *The Spirit of Youth*. But we soon got on to Humphrey Bogart. John reckoned that Katherine Hepburn and Humphrey were the greatest of all female and male screen stars. He laughed when he recalled a film correspondent's piece on Humphrey which read, 'He runs the gamut of emotions from A to B.'

John recalled directing him for Warner Brothers in *The Maltese Falcon* with Mary Astor and Peter Lorre. 'This was his first big break, of course. *Treasure of the Sierra Madre* was another superb film; and again *The African Queen* with Katherine Hepburn. For a guy with so many disparate roles, be carried them off superbly,' he told me, adding, 'but *Casablanca* made Bogart and Bogart made *Casablanca*.'

No-one bar Orson Welles had made a more impressive debut as a film director than John. *The African Queen* was, I think, his greatest. He and his father, Walter, both won Oscars. What a character! Behind his grizzled eminence lay his early life as a screenwriter, gambler and general hell-raiser with several failed marriages. One of his hobbies was hunting with the Galway Blazers, of which he was joint master. He loved Ireland.

It was a marvellous evening for me – the grand finale being when we pushed back the furniture and Huston, who loved boxing, and Kid Berg, in their shirtsleeves, squared up and did two or three minutes sparring. How they loved it. Kid Berg was, of course, the former Junior World Welterweight Champion. He had won his title at the Albert Hall in London in 1930 and was affectionately known then as 'The Whitechapel Windmill'. He fought everywhere and everyone.

If I may pick up on the Waterman story again. I went to Rome with Jarvis Astaire and Peter and his 'camp.' Jarvis was very good company. He was about thirty-two at the time. He told me he always had this fascination for boxing, even as a kid. He had been barely twenty when he ran his first charity boxing show at the Hammersmith Palace Theatre. It was held in aid of the Soldiers Sailors and Airmen Families Association. He got involved in the world of business even as a young man through the entertainments industry which drew him like a magnet. He was later to represent Dustin Hoffman, the *Johnny Carson Tonight* show and the great Muhammad Ali.

His first wife Phyliss died tragically in 1974 and as a result he was inspired to involve himself more than ever with the Variety Club and other great efforts for charity. Early in 1981 he married Nadine Hyman, a beautiful French divorcee. Their five years of happiness were to be cut short when she died only five and a half weeks after being diagnosed as suffering from cancer. He does not, however, carry Fate's blows on his sleeve and he has always greeted me with a buoyant cheerfulness.

Later, with the passing of his father-in-law, he and his brother-in-law became joint managing directors of Mappin and Webb and then came the purchase of the vast chain of chemists shops under the banner of Lewis and Burrows. By the early 1970s he was to become a multi-millionaire.

I remember once some years later a chance meeting in a cinema queue in London when he introduced me to Marcia Williams,

Harold Wilson's secretary when he was Premier. There were unfounded rumours of a romance.

We were in Rome because Peter was to fight the Italian, Marconi, for the European Championship. It was a soft, warm, Mediterranean type of evening and the fight held in the open in the Olympic stadium drew a fashionable but noisy crowd. The Romans proved very partisan and though he obviously out-pointed Marconi, Peter had to accept a drawn decision. The Italians had an unpleasant habit as you left the open-air arena down one of the tunnels of leaning out above you and belabouring you with rolled-up newspapers.

He was next scheduled to fight Wally Thom for the British Welterweight Championship when it was suddenly announced that Thom was unfit and that Kid Gavilan of Cuba would be available if accepted by Waterman's handlers. I thought this to be an alarming substitution. Kid Gavilan was really big time and had, until recently, been the Welterweight Champion of the World. But the substitution was accepted by Jarvis Astaire.

Peter was naturally excited at the idea. 'Of course I respect his ability as a boxer. He is right there at the top – probably knows more about boxing than I will ever learn,' he told me. This was typical of his then relaxed outlook, but as Reg Gutteridge wrote at the time, 'If it means fighting street-corner style, that will suit Peter. He just hates losing!'

That was, in fact, so true. Peter went into that fight with a determination that was staggering – he caused a sensation by defeating Gavilan on a points decision. Jack Solomons wasn't too pleased. Next day all hell broke loose. Peter Wilson in the *Daily Mirror* denounced the verdict. Ben Green, the referee, never again got a professional engagement and had to resort to refereeing wrestling.

One morning I got a call from Geoffrey (later to be Sir Geoffrey) Cox, Editor of the Independent Television News, a very kind man. Would I go that evening to the Festival Gardens at Battersea to interview Elizabeth Taylor just before the 9 o'clock News? It was the first showing of Michael Todd's *Round The World In Eighty Days* and it was to be followed by an open-air banquet with food brought in from around the world.

Elizabeth Taylor was, of course, married to Mike Todd who directed the film – which was to gross thirty-three million dollars and win many awards, and was destined to break the all-time box office record held by *Gone With The Wind* and by Cecil B De Mille's remake of *The Ten Commandments*. I was to join the party at the Charing Cross Embankment for the trip upriver. I kept an evening dress at the office and was able to finish what I was doing and be in time to get through the crowds to see the film preview and be down at the Embankment to go on board.

It was certainly a crew of celebs – the boat was a floating party. I kept trying to concentrate on what I was to say on TV, but it was difficult. A.E. Matthews, the famous Shakespearean actor, kept trying to ply me with drinks – all of which I politely refused – and for one hectic moment I struggled at the head of a gangway

My TV date with Elizabeth Taylor. (Camera Press, *London*)

trying to keep him from falling down, assisted by two members of the Crazy Gang. Fortunately we all regained our balance. Eventually, stone sober, I arrived at Battersea. I had less than thirty minutes before the interview. I found the TV crew and we sorted out positions. I was obviously nervous and trying to keep a clear head. After all, I was not a film buff and here I was about to go on peak TV viewing time for several minutes to interview one of the world's greatest film stars – and on a big night for the film world quite apart from the viewing public.

David Niven and Cantinflas, who was a great success, Trevor Howard, Robert Morley and Shirley MacLaine, all duly arrived and suddenly there was Elizabeth Taylor walking towards me. The first thing you notice are her wildly attractive eyes. When they are on you, you can feel your knees beginning to buckle. She is extraordinarily beautiful.

What could I say?

Not 'Welcome to London,' for God's sake – it's her home town!

But she put me at ease right away, even repeating my name - 'Hello, Ken.'

First I congratulated her on receiving the British Film Academy Fellowship Award and after the initial congratulations about the show my first cue was to ask after her husband, Mike Todd, who was unfortunately ill in bed at the Dorchester. I can't really remember what was actually said during the interview though, of course, she did most of the talking – suddenly it was all over and just to make it one incredible night for me, she kissed me ever so gently on my cheek.

Apparently ITN were pleased with how I had handled it.

Incidentally, studio interviews were not assisted in those days with the use of slick auto-cues. I remember once interviewing Yolando Pompey, the Trinidadian boxer, on the air when the whole of what was in use as an auto-cue apparatus suddenly exploded with pieces of it raining down on us.

I have one press cutting dated 5 June 1956:

What a wonderful thing this television is. Tomorrow, for instance, more people will have a bet on a horse than any other day in the year.

People who don't know the difference between selling plates and a classic contender will be putting on their bobs and half-crowns. In the old days Mum used to ask the milkman what he thought; or she would take a list of runners and stick a pin in one name. Television has changed all that – no need for guesswork now!

Tonight on *Cavalcade of Sport* we shall see the Derby covered more fully probably than ever before.

I asked Ken Johnstone, who is introducing and presenting this programme, if he was going to name a specific animal as his choice to win the first prize of £17,500. He was cautious. 'Too many people might resent failure,' he said.

Still on the subject of 'the horses', I went up to see Mirabelle Topham, the owner of Aintree and a former Gaiety Girl. Reputed to be something of a tartar, she was charming. We got along famously. She even insisted on presenting me with a new television set to mark the occasion. The resulting piece for *Cavalcade* about the history of the Grand National, which I produced and presented, was very well received.

Another press cutting in the *Evening News* dated Wednesday, 2 November 1955 was headed 'Discoveries':

Discovery No 1
Did you notice intelligent use of lighting in the production *Downbeat*; and the unselfconscious use of studio equipment with cameras and monitor screens in full view? And, surprisingly, the director responsible for it all, Dick Lester, is only 23. [Absolutely brilliant, too – author's note.]

Discovery No 2
A girl singer in *Youth Takes a Bow* named Bassey from Cardiff makes the blues really something. Someone should sign her up right away! [I know how good she was and I told her so that evening – author's note.]

Discovery No 3
That fight commentators are still sure that they have to talk all the time – even though the viewer can see! And that they still use that

phrase about someone's fist spelling 'Dynamite'. [Point taken – author's note].

My innovative idea of putting wrestling on TV had been so successful that I then decided that snooker was made for TV. My idea was for Joe Davis, the World Snooker Champion, to be 'at home' to a group of sportsmen. We staged it at the Albany Club in Savile Row in London's West End. June, his delightful wife, was on camera to welcome everyone, then Joe joined some of the guests in play and gave a fascinating exhibition spot himself. Jockeys, footballers, cricketers, boxers, rugby players – most sports were represented and Percy Fender, Captain of the Surrey cricket team, found a marvellous commentator for me. He was Ted Lowe, possessor of a lovely soft voice who went on to do regular TV commentaries before retiring only in 1999.

Mind you, sitting in the studio doing the link-up I worried a bit about the cue line, 'And now we go over to the Albany Club, where Joe Davies has his snooker balls on the table.' It was a great success, though, and became a regular weekly part of my *Cavalcade*.

Joe's brother Fred came along once or twice to join in and later through *Pot Black* on the BBC and the Embassy World Championship he was treated very much as a star and many of his fans were women; but he was always motivated by the huge success of Joe, who was, of course, a legendary figure, the undefeated World Champion. He was twelve years older than Fred. Both were extremely affable and it was always a joy to be associated with them, either individually or together. It is amazing that one family should have produced two such outstanding brothers in one sport. Joe told me that he never coached Fred, who had actually learned his trade on a miniature table given to him as a Christmas present.

Joe had retired in 1946 and the way was therefore cleared for a new champion. Fred was, in fact, the only player to beat his brother in competition on level terms and this he did four times. By 1969 the new era of the pro game had begun. It became almost compulsive viewing on TV and in 1985 drew the highest figure of viewers at midnight ever recorded. Then the game became over-saturated on television.

Earlier I had decided to get some assistance as I had been

entirely on my own and maintaining, I might add, a mighty work schedule, sometimes meaning very little sleep – I had a call from a sports enthusiast and actor, Kent Walton, who was keen on doing commentaries on football, in particular, though we had few of those to do being Monday to Friday, but he had an unusual clipped kind of mid-Atlantic voice and he was certainly very persuasive. I took him on as a reporter. Kent's wife, Lynne, was a very sweet person. I only discovered later that she had been married to Leslie Grade, Lew's brother, before she met Kent.

I was able to help Kent further when one day Leslie Mitchell, our senior announcer who was, of course already nationally known, asked me if I knew of someone to front a new pop programme. 'Try him,' I said indicating Kent. Thus he was able to front up, introduce and compere the successful *Cool for Cats* show.

After a number of phone calls I met Peter Bridges, who was well versed in tennis, being a referee at Wimbledon. I arranged for him to come in to see to our contracts and administration generally and help in our future arrangements at Wimbledon. He was friendly with Fred Perry and, through him, I had several trans-Atlantic phone calls with the great man.

A welcome arrival was Johnnie Robson. He had been very active in my Scout Troop in Newcastle upon Tyne and was now a reporter on the *North Shields Gazette*. I phoned him and offered him a job. He did not hesitate to come and at once fitted into the job of helping me.

I arranged with Danny Blanchflower to help out where liaison was necessary with the world of football. Danny had, of course, been first with Barnsley before coming to Spurs via Aston Villa. He had a lovely droll sense of humour. He told us how, when he was in the Northern Ireland team, they made their first appearance at Wembley Stadium. In previous years apparently, they had been side-tracked to the provinces, but nobody had objected as they thought it better to play before a packed provincial crowd rather than a half-empty Wembley. 'Most of us,' said Danny, 'welcomed our first chance to tread on the sacred turf, although we were not quite as impressed as some of our officials seemed to be.

'"Great honour, Gerry," one of them had said to Gerry Morgan, our trainer.

'"Great honour, be damned," Gerry answered, "sure the grey-hounds have been running there for twenty years!"'

This was typical of Danny – always ready with a quip or a joke.

Later Ian Wooldridge, the brilliant *Daily Mail* sportswriter, did a brief weekly spot.

The TV studios were out at Wembley which often meant a late dash from Kingsway in the Strand through the traffic on the day I was doing *Cavalcade*. My dressing room was next to Hughie Green's and he was always so enthusiastic and ready with a good quip, though he could get very nervous before a show. His *Double Your Money* had its first showing on 26 September 1955 and was a huge success, though the death of James Dean in a car crash stole a lot of the headlines.

Lloyd Williams was generally in charge of production until he left quite suddenly and there was, I am afraid, not a very relaxed air about the place. People tended to be uptight. A delightful man, Peter Wills, was in charge of Drama. He had been badly wounded in the War and walked with a pronounced limp. He was always cheerful and helpful and did a very good job.

Mary Hill, in charge of Children's Programmes, was another very pleasant person. Caryl Doncaster, very professional and determined, was a tower of strength in programming Light Entertainment; but rumours had a habit of sweeping the place on all kinds of topics. Personalities were regularly assassinated.

I set up a feature on its own called *Solomon's Scrap Book*, which was really a flash-back to a number of old fights on film with Jack in the studio doing the link-up. The 'Televiews' column in the *London Evening News* reported after one of these programmes, 'What a difference the professional touch made to ITV's varied programme. *Hylton's Half Hour* was commonplace until Jack himself took to the piano to accompany Arthur Askey in two saucy songs: then Vera Lynn ended it in glory. *Solomon's Scrap Book* came to life when this second Jack of entertainment showed films of the Louis-Farr and Baksi-Woodcock fights, etc.'

The trouble with getting close to professional sportsmen is that one gets torn between the joy of seeing them doing well and achieving more fame on one hand and one's inner feelings that care for their welfare. I had these mixed emotions about Peter. As we know, he had drawn with Emilio Marconi in Rome in May 1957 and on 28 January of the following year at Harringay he defeated him, thus winning the European Welterweight crown. The referee pulled Marconi out at the end of the penultimate round with a badly cut left eye for by that time Marconi could not have won on points, but at least he had the satisfaction of having put Waterman down twice in the eleventh round in a gruelling contest during which there were far too many warnings for holding.

I will always remember the sheer fun and good humour of a weekend spent at his training camp before his British title fight with Wally Thom, which he won. We were at The Bear in Devizes. There was Peter, of course, and Yolande Pompey, the big Trinidadian heavyweight and 'Snowy' Buckingham – a tough-looking crew to behold wearing their thick sweaters, tracksuits and long scarves; running along the country lanes, doing their shadow boxing, sprints and the like. I remembered an old army pal, Barnes-Gorell, who lived near. I phoned him and later that morning, at his invitation, the unlikely looking 'training camp' descended on their lovely old home with its imposing Tudor front near Marlborough. Here there was the most fascinating confluence of life with the hunting, shooting and fishing hosts entertaining with obvious relish the masters of ducking, weaving and jabbing.

Peter's courage and spirit rose, perhaps, to its height on 24 April 1956 in the vast Earls Court arena when he faced once again the Cuban 'Hawk', Gavilan, the legendary former Welterweight Champion of the World, who was hell bent on reversing the decision Waterman had over him in their first fight. It had been a disastrous night for British boxers by the time Waterman and Gavilan entered the ring. Don Cockell and the then British Champion, Jack Gardner, had both crashed to overwhelming defeats from overseas fighters.

Peter's opening rounds were sensational. He drove Gavilan all over the ring. His courage and endeavour shone like a beacon in the huge gloomy arena; but after a shaky start, the great Cuban champion suddenly found his form and took his revenge on Peter's exuberant but misguided earlier belligerence. This time there was no sensation.

Then came the climax to Peter's career. The fight with Dave Charnley. Mercifully it was over quickly. They refer in the fight game to a condition of a boxer as 'having gone'. That was now unfortunately Peter's condition. Dave Charnley was fighting a ghost. There came that moment of reckoning dreaded by all boxers. Back in the dressing room both his manager and Teddy Waltham, then Secretary of the Boxing Board of Control, insisted that his retirement should be announced there and then. There was much argument and finally he gave way. He broke down and wept.

His friend Peter Jones who, of course had no business connection with him, but guided and helped him at his own expense, pays him this tribute: 'He graced the world of professional boxing with his honesty and courage and his will to win for Britain.'

He had been guided throughout his boxing career by Jarvis Astaire, assisted by Mickey Duff, 'Snowy' Buckingham, Sam Burns and Nobby Wallace.

Peter Waterman married the daughter of a retired police sergeant who was a doorman at Kingsway House, outside our ITV offices. He and his new bride went house-hunting. They bought a large four-bedroomed house in Palace Road, Streatham. They spent large sums on the furnishings and holidays and, no further income materialising, he tried various things: working with his father-in-law, and managing a little fighter, but he seemed very tired and quiet. Following a complete medical check, it was decided he needed a brain operation in the National Hospital for Nervous Diseases in Queens Square to determine the cause of the loss of use of two of his fingers, which he could not control or move. The operation was performed by a great surgeon, Harvey Jackson. They had to open up the whole of the back of his head and did what they could, but no great improvement could be made. I spent a quiet hour with him at the hospital.

Some time after he had a son, Frazer, and married life continued. They sold the house and bought another and Frazer grew up and went to Dulwich College Prep School. The money Peter had retired with was considerable in those days, but today would be looked at with disdain from one championship contest. It was a terrible contrast from the sunny days of being constantly in the public eye, both in the ring and on commercial television, to a tired, baffled, still young man with no particular aim in view. Many fighters take inns or public houses; this provides a small extension and confirmation of fame of a sort, but this was not for him.

They were then moving in a circle whose lifestyle they really couldn't afford any more. Ultimately his wife wanted to end the marriage and in those days, in order to divorce, evidence had to be provided. Peter had never looked at anyone else since he was married, but considered the honourable thing for him to do was to provide the evidence. He went back to ask the young lady to whom he had first become engaged, who, in fact, would have made him a marvellous wife, and after all those years she agreed to sit on the edge of a bed in a hotel room for the people who gathered such evidence to find her. So the marriage ended with access granted to Peter to have his son for some hours on a Saturday and this went on until his former wife, with her family, emigrated to Australia and he never saw his son again.

Following the end of his marriage, which coincided with the end of the money he earned in his boxing career with what there was going to his former wife and son, he drifted from one drab apartment to another and from one unsavoury girlfriend to the next. As each one left, so did some of his few remaining possessions.

One day when attending the consultant, Mr Fricker, he was asked if he did the football pools. 'Yes,' replied Peter. 'Then take this down,' said Mr Fricker. 'You will do the treble chance and three draws.' Then there were other instructions on what to add such as birthday dates and the like. All this Peter attended to faithfully. The following week he won a few thousands of pounds as a result and with a small part of it purchased a coffee stall on Mitcham Common which he kept for a number of years as it brought him some useful income. Then he finally sold it for more than he paid for it.

The benefits arranged for him over the years at least provided him with a second-hand motor car with automatic controls because due to his increasing disability, this was the only type of vehicle he could use.

At last he obtained a flat in a run-down house in a run-down street in Islington. He had a damp basement flat there. In the top floor lived a New Zealand teacher in a business school. A friendship was established between them and she cared and helped him in every way she could. She guided him to golf in an attempt to strengthen his carriage to prevent him from limping in his walking and they went to the theatre together and took holidays touring in France. If anyone can say they made his remaining years reasonably contented, it must be she. Between them they cared for five or six stray cats and these became their family.

During these years, on medical advice, he entered the London Hospital for further surgery in an effort to improve his health. This did not prove to be of any benefit and while he was lying there he began to fret about where his son could be, as no effort had been made by his former wife to contact him and give him any news of his son. All that was known was that they were somewhere in Sydney. Once again the great and good Salvation Army came to the rescue as they traced them in forty-eight hours. Letters were sent, but no joy was received in return. That side of his life was so cruel and sad, it doesn't really bear retelling here. Ultimately his health really started to deteriorate. He was found at the foot of his stairs where he must have fallen and died and so a life full of promise, talent and education, with over half of his brief lifespan spent unhappy and disabled, was over.

His one desire had been to become a professional boxer. No-one approached him to become professional: he approached them, eager for the opportunity to reach the stars. He reached the stars and shone there for all too brief a spell and then he fell to earth with a taste for the better life he had enjoyed and no longer the means to provide it.

He was a fighter's fighter from the very start.

It is all so different in boxing nowadays. A multiplicity of world title divisions only confuses. Once there were eight world champions – all well known to the public. Now there are about twice as many. It remains highly controversial, but there is still a fascination by the public for a big fight.

Two years after Peter's final bout with Dave Charnley, a friend of his also suffered a big set-back in the ring. He was Bobby Neill, son of an Edinburgh fight promoter. Terry Spinks fought him for the British Featherweight Championship at Wembley and for fourteen of the scheduled fifteen rounds Terry was pretty well in control, landing some hard blows. As a result, Bobby collapsed in his dressing room afterwards and was taken to hospital, where he had a blood clot removed.

'By sheer luck,' Bobby recalls, 'the specialist on duty at the hospital that night was a neurosurgeon.' The operation was thankfully successful, but as he says, 'It's afterwards that is the most traumatic of all.'

He took a long time to recover, though his faculties were still there because a year or so afterwards he went into banking and three years after the fight he was back in boxing, this time as a trainer.

'When I retired I wasn't the wealthiest of persons because television wasn't around at the time, so I didn't have an awful lot of money. Having been off for a year afterwards a lot of my money had to go into rehabilitation,' he says. He reflects that there was no move to help him. 'Somebody should really have done something.'

In 1995 Gerald McClennan was carried from the London Arena on a stretcher. He had absorbed a lot of punishment from Nigel Benn, one of the hardest hitters in the game. But the abolitionists would, no doubt, be dismayed to note that Bobby Neill did not turn his back on the game. He was not bitter. 'No, in actual fact, I am a lover of boxing. I love the idea that a young man's got the heart to take it up – and I felt that I should go back and try and help.' So he continued as a well-respected trainer.

There is a unique camaraderie amongst fighting men. Television has brought more money into the sport, though there is less boxing presented these days. There is, too, a lack of lasting compassion for stricken fighters. More should be done to help afterwards.

A footnote to Bobby Neill's experience. Some years ago, hearing that I was off to Holland to visit a monastery, he asked if he could accompany me. The story behind this visit was that Erik, a Dutch scout whom I had met at a pre-war International Boy Scout Jamboree, lived in Hilversum and after the War I had endeavoured to trace him. I discovered that the family home had been used as a hospital. They were apparently one of the richest Roman Catholic families in Holland, but Erik had denounced all wealth and possessions and gone into a monastery. His mother asked him if he would like to see me and he apparently said that he would. I resolved to go and visit him. Bobby heard about this and said that he would like to accompany me, so off we went together.

He is probably the only man in the fight game, certainly in this country, who has ever spent three days in a praying monastery. The monks were, in fact, engaged in almost continuous prayer and never left the monastery. Bobby was a delightful companion and, not to get my syntax mixed, he was a great hit with the monks.

Erik appeared to be very happy and contented. We spent a long weekend and as I left him, he, once one of Holland's richest young men, offered me his one remaining gift – his prayers. It was a moment of great humility.

I began looking for something new. Again the idea of what could be contained most effectively by two participants within the confines of a television screen was uppermost in my mind. I decided to look into wrestling. If this could be well presented without the pantomime stuff of an old lady with an umbrella joining in and so forth, surely this would have a big TV appeal? Accordingly I arranged a meeting in secret in my office with representatives of Joint Promotions.

The meeting went well. After further study of programme content I told them that we would run it as part of *Cavalcade of Sport*. It would have to be cleaned up with good, fast-moving bouts by the top wrestlers. The rate would be £300 a fight (in present money about £2,000).

Later Captain Brownrigg sent for me, far from happy. 'I am putting you on an adverse report to the Chairman,' he told me. 'This is a frivolous contract. It will never be a success. It will be a flop.' He glared at me. In fact it ran for twenty-seven years and made millions in advertising revenue. On one showing alone it would be seen by ten million viewers.

The first contest was to be staged at Lime Grove Baths as part of *Cavalcade of Sport* and as I had to stay in the studio as links-man, I asked Kent Walton to mug up the rules and go down and do the commentating. This he did to such good effect that he continued to do all the wrestling for us, the bouts later being televised from different parts of the country.

35

The wonderful wrestling characters who emerged made great television. Mick McManus became a great favourite. When out of the ring and wearing his big teddy bear coat women found him a real star. If the television ended with Mick in the ring and the winner not yet declared, the switchboard would be jammed by women viewers asking what happened to Mick.

Other names who became nationally known were Jackie Pallo, Tony Mancelli, Musambula, Johnny Peters, Mike Marino, Chick Purvey, Roy La Rue, Milo Popopocopolis, Jack Taylor of Accrington, Tiger 'Joe' Robinson, Wayne Bridges (who now runs The Bridges at Horton Kirby near Furningham in Kent) and 'Billy Two Rivers', who came from Quebec and was an official spokesman for the Mohawk Indians (hence his dreaded 'Tomahawk chop').

Devereux Promotions ran weekly shows at the Wimbledon Palais and these were very popular. On one big night I was introduced from the ring as 'the man who started it all'. Joan Reagan, the blonde star singer, joined me that evening.

It certainly caught on. I remember once when I was on duty at the ITV stand at Olympia where I was interviewing members of the public. The girl on a stand opposite and I had exchanged pleasantries during the day and we met again as the place was closing down. We took a taxi to the flat I had then at Belsize Park and I blush to admit that once we were in the back of the cab she was – shall I say – all over me. When the journey ended and as I staggered out hastily readjusting my clothing, the cab driver turned round with a laugh and the immortal words, 'I've seen you put this bleeding wrestling on TV, mate, but I never thought I'd have you in the back of me cab doing a rehearsal with a lady!'

Wrestling could be absorbing and proved very popular. It was more straightforward without the comedy and drew a most appreciative crowd where quite often well-known faces from the theatre, films and sport could be seen. Of course, the wrestlers became more pantomimic as the appetite for this grew. There was Ricky Starr, for instance, the ballet dancer from the United States who was hilarious in his terphiscorean movements in the ring.

Wrestling boomed as the result of its exposure on *Cavalcade of Sport* and there were few parts of the country where regular programmes were not staged for the public. Even the *Daily*

Telegraph ran a 1,000-word obituary when 'Big Daddy' died. It was dated 3 December 1997. (Note: This was the epitome of the theatrical in the sport.) Part of it read:

Big Daddy

<u>Wrestler who squashed opponents into submission</u>

Big Daddy, the fighting name of Shirley Crabtree, who has died aged 64, was the star attraction of the professional wrestling circuit during its televised heyday in the Seventies and Eighties.

Weighing in at 28 stone and clad in spangled top hat and over-burdened leotard, Big Daddy was a portly avenging angel in a comic-book world of heroes in white trunks and villains in black masks.

At its peak, wrestling drew Saturday afternoon audiences of 10 million, attracted not so much by the finer points of the hammerlock and Boston Crab as by its unvarying rituals.

These began with the commentator Kent Walton's welcome – 'Greetings, grapple fans' – and climaxed with the entry of Big Daddy into the ring, usually to save a small wrestler from the attentions of his *bête noire*, Giant Haystacks.

His arrival was accompanied by chants of 'Ea-sy, ea-sy' from stout matrons in the crowd, in manner the spiritual descendants of the *tricoteuses* who sat by the guillotine.

For Big Daddy's vast belly easily held opponents at bay before he despatched them with his speciality – the 'splashdown'. This was a manoeuvre in which he mounted the ropes, leapt on top of his stupefied opponent, and squashed him flat to the canvas.

These antics brought Big Daddy notable fans, among them the Queen, whose interest in the sport was first recorded in Richard Crossman's diaries, and Margaret Thatcher, who found the wrestler a useful topic of conversation in Africa, where he was a household name.

The persona of Big Daddy was the creation of Shirley Crabtree's brother, Max, and only came relatively late in the wrestler's career. The name was taken from that of the character played by Burl Ives in the film of *Cat On A Hot Tin Roof*.

Crabtree had briefly served in the Coldstream Guards, and would enter the ring wearing a bearskin, to the sound of Joseph Locke singing *The Soldier's Dream*. It was not until 1975 that the Big Daddy character was created, with his first leotard being made from the chintz covers of his wife's sofa.

He was twice married and had six children. [This concludes the Obituary.]

It was the end of TV Wrestling, both the serious and the absurd.

The Milk Marketing Board asked me to make public appearances in connection with their 'Dairy Princess' competition. This usually involved me appearing on stage at a cinema to congratulate the local contestant for the national 'Dairy Princess' contest.

I remember one amusing incident. I was up in the Midlands with some of the cast from the BBC's *The Archers*. We were appearing in a public hall to a large local audience and at the close of the event I was approached by the organisers who said a gentleman was outside ready to drive me to my overnight accommodation. I jumped into the car and he introduced himself briefly with his christian name; as I was pretty tired after having dashed up from London by train and taxi to the place, which was south of Birmingham, we didn't say much, though I remember driving past some gates and up a long drive. We entered the rather ornate doorway and, having arranged for a cup of tea to be brought to me, he excused himself as he had, he said, to make an early start in the morning. We had, in fact, had very little conversation. I was glad to get to bed in what I took to be a rather well-appointed country house hotel.

I slept soundly and in the morning, on hearing a knock on the door, I called out 'Come in', whereupon a butler entered with my morning tea on a silver tray and before he withdrew he said, 'Good morning, sir. His Lordship regrets he had to leave early and said that he hoped you had a comfortable night.'

It then dawned upon me that I was the guest in a private house. Leaping out of bed and drawing the curtains I looked out onto a splendid rose garden and lawns stretching almost out of sight. My host, I discovered, was Viscount Cobham and this was Hagley Hall, a stately Palladian mansion set in 4,000 acres. It was his daughter-in-law, Penelope, who was to go off with David Mellor, the former Conservative Cabinet Minister. His son, the present Viscount Cobham, apparently knew nothing of the affair until Mellor made a public statement.

The present Viscount in 1997 married Lisa Clayton, the round-the-world solo yachtswoman from Birmingham, in what was described as a quiet discreet ceremony attended by Miss Clayton's parents, Dan, a businessman, and Gwen, who live in Bromsgrove. It was the first to be solemnised at Hagley Hall, which had been granted a licence for civil ceremonies and which had been developed as a business centre to face crippling death duties.

I made two or three public appearances with Zoe Spinks, then Miss Great Britain. She was madly attractive and we started going out together. She had a twin sister who was also crowned as a beauty queen. They were from Yorkshire. I must say that dating a beauty queen is a bit of an onerous business as she is obviously in much demand and I was pretty busy myself. Still, we had our moments!

On leafing through old press cuttings, I note in the *Daily Mirror* of Saturday, 15 June 1957 I made the front page. The headline was 'Fire – But the Show Goes On' above a four-columns-across picture of a blazing grandstand as background to a parade of police horses all standing in an orderly line and a crowd facing them. The heading was 'They Thought It Part of the Act!' It was certainly a very striking picture and the story figured in all the radio and TV news bulletins:

Fire swept through the main stand at the Royal Richmond Horse Show – but in the ring the horses stand quiet, the crowds stand quiet ... the show goes on. The police were giving a demonstration of tests which horses have to undergo in training.

The fire, however, reduced the wooden stand to a burning shell within fifty minutes. It was certainly dramatic when it was realised that it was for real.

Just a few minutes before it began Princess Alice, Countess of Athlone, who is the Queen's Great Aunt, had been sitting in the box. There was great anxiety for the horses still in stables and grooms rushed to release them.

An ITV camera next to the stand used to televise the show only a few minutes before the fire started was in danger of being destroyed by the flames.

Camera crews and technicians were caught up in rescue operations and some of them climbed forty feet up the scaffolding to bring down a highly expensive camera to safety.

Commentator Bill Allenby and Associated Rediffusion's sports chief Ken Johnstone helped in the rescue.

I must say, it was all high drama with hot ash blowing hard in every direction, and in particular the need for prompt action to prevent the fire from taking hold – it had already burned a large hole in the top of a 170-yards-long standing marquee housing about 200 horses. No spectators were hurt. The police horses – and their riders – behaved wonderfully well amidst the smoke. Full marks!

There were moments of drama in the office too. On one occasion a visitor from the States endeavouring to sell me a series of 'Famous Fights' on film, on being ushered into my office went straight to the window and whilst keeping to one side, peered nervously down into Kingsway. Gesturing to me to do likewise, he pointed to two men standing in a doorway opposite. 'See these two guys,' he said. 'They're after me, the sons-of-a-bitch. I gotta get out by the back.' He murmured his apologies and dashed out of my office – I never heard from him again!

The press on Tuesday, 3 January 1956. Kendall McDonald writing on 'Sound & TV':

SPORTING CHANCE

The sporting interview on television is very nearly dead, and Mr Ken Johnstone, Head of Sport at Associated-Rediffusion, is one of the first to show awareness of this.

His exact words are: 'We feel that the days of the sporting interview are fast fading, except where someone has something urgent and compelling to say on a sporting topic – and then it should be in the form of a brief news flash.'

At these words many sports fans will jump on to their chairs, wave their rattles and cheer most lustily for Mr Johnstone. Going – from the independent network – then are those inane interviews which start with 'Well, what do you think of your chances, Charlie?' and inevitably get the reply 'Well, I think we will win.'

Substitute for these interviews, where the players are brought into the studio, is 'Sportstour'. This, Ken Johnstone feels, is the possible answer to the much-hackneyed interview. To-night in 'Cavalcade of Sport' you will have your first ration of 'Sportstour'. Nine minutes of it, to be exact. Behind the scenes is the keynote of the tour. Burton, Boston and Bedford as possible 'giantkillers' are the subject.

There was so often an air of anti-climax along the corridors of Kingsway House. Of course there were many different talents housed there, but when the cold wind of 'Financial Control' blew down these same corridors, some were, unfortunately, shown the exit. I lost the services of Peter Bridges and Johnnie Robson, which was unfortunate as they had been part of a great team. Peter went to set up his own very successful theatrical management company and the experience at ITV gave Johnnie a kick-start into his successful career in newspapers.

The somewhat thinned-out department of Outdoor Broadcasts, or 'OBs' as it is known, continued to function manfully, but I had studio items also to develop. It should be appreciated that I was not ex-BBC, nor ex-Navy, nor from the sports desk of a national newspaper, and therefore one of a strange breed and tended to continue to act in the pioneering style as at the outset. This certainly meant that one had to create new ideas and I worked in a kind of pressure-cooker atmosphere, something of a loner. At one point I was desperately in need of a break so I took medical advice and put in for ten days' holiday. I went to stay at Reid's at Madeira. It was a glorious break. The hotel, in its own grounds, has a magnificent setting on the edge of the harbour and is quite splendid in its interior and service. At the end of my week's stay the flying boat on which I was to return could not take off because of a sudden change in the weather. At that time there was no other connection except for the slow boat to Madrid and thence by air to London. We had to wait two days and meantime I wired the office immediately I knew of the delay.

On my return, a rather sardonic remark from Commander Robert Everett, the Head of Outside Broadcasts, about my being two days late and going to places that proved to be difficult to leave, prompted me to reply that I thought with his naval training he would know all about the problems of winds and tides. 'After all,' I told him somewhat crushingly, 'I stayed in the same place as Winston Churchill. He was also held up when his flying boat couldn't get out!'

There was this kind of uneasy atmosphere. Stephen McCormack, ex-BBC, was Programme Controller, but I mostly seemed to work on my own. I missed the meetings we had when Bill Gillette was running the show. Bill had been a great enthusiast. One of the problems was, I think, because I was also the anchorman or front man on my show I had many of the ideas myself, or introduced others so that I was virtually the producer and presenter, but I was too busy to think about personality clashes. I just worked my guts out for the place. There was, I am afraid, quite a lot of jealousy. So many folk thought they could do better. Once you are 'on the box' many seek your scalp!

Another word or two about the fight game. There was another boy called Peter who made a name for himself at the famous Caius Boxing Club. He was Peter Benneyworth. Carefully schooled through his formative years by the club's competition secretary, Alf Hawkes, Peter also went on to sweep the board, but always as an amateur. There were no menacing manipulators at his side. His classic encounter with the Welsh Wizard, Howard Winstone, was a feature of the Empire Games of 1958. Then there was his first championship – the ABA National title in 1961 – and his chess-like battles with the Russian World and Olympic Champion, Grigorjev, became the stuff of legends in the amateur boxing world.

Peter was a bantamweight with not the slightest interest in going professional. He was in the RAF and became Services Champion and boxed at the Commonwealth Games both in Perth, Western Australia and Cardiff. He was just great to meet, always bright and cheerful and when he retired the tributes flooded in from boxing writers, clubs and enthusiasts all over the world. He married a former Mayor of Epsom's daughter, Polly, and had two children. A boy, Dennis, became a jump jockey.

Peter Benneyworth later had a pub in Epsom, together with his parents. Our old friend, Peter Jones, always a great supporter of young Benneyworth through the club, had, I believe, a hand in getting the place for them. Tragically, collapsing whilst painting a room, Peter Benneyworth died on his way to hospital. He had suddenly felt ill and asked the neighbours to call an ambulance. He was only thirty-five. The boxing world grieved at his loss and the press were fulsome in their praise of a really wholesome young guy who became a true champion.

Around this time I began to get visits at the office from a new executive in the company. His name was MacMillan and I think he was an Australian. He asked me if I would introduce him to some leading figures in sports administration, which I thought sounded a bit dodgy. He was not very friendly in his manner and it occurred to me that he might have been setting me up.

There comes a time when the challenge and stimulation becomes diluted by personality clashes and politics and you want out. It is a dilemma of the world of television. It was then that I realised also that I was well nigh exhausted. I have my own personality which is of perhaps an open booming style, but one which I hope and believe to be genuine. Enthusiasm has been my currency, not intrigue. I suppose as a Geordie I am forthright. I cannot abide the ducking and weaving. So Mr MacMillan and I had a set-to and he flushed me out. Perhaps that was what he always intended.

CHAPTER III

Public and Private Relations

SUDDENLY FREEDOM from the atmosphere at Kingsway House was unbelievably refreshing. I resolved to work on my own in the field of Public Relations.

Two old army friends – Ken Millichap and Irving Wilson – unexpectedly got in touch with me. Ken was already a partner in a leading firm of accountants in Manchester and Irving, who had his own business retailing records from a shop in the centre of Manchester, was a client of his. He was also actively producing records under his own label and for the Cetra Record Company of Turin. I set out to get distribution and publicity for them in London and drove over to Turin to visit the Cetra Company. One day Irving asked me to arrange to visit Maria Callas, who was staying at the Savoy, and discuss with her the cover of her latest recording of *La Traviata* for Cetra.

From the moment I met Maria Callas I sensed a kind of empathy between us. Those large luminous eyes were smiling at me and somehow I knew that we were going to get on well together. By repute there were no half measures with her. Either you were acceptable or not and by reports she could be very difficult. But both her husband, Giovanni Meneghini, and she made me so welcome in their suite at the Savoy that they insisted I spend most of the afternoon with them and stay for tea. He was most attentive to her needs – checking for any sign of draughts and obviously devoted to her. Clearly they were in love.

After we had discussed the record cover from Cetra for *La Traviata* she relaxed by telling me an hilarious story concerning some tour official in South America whom she did not like and who had been so rude to her that she punched him in the stomach. Whilst telling me this, they both laughed uproariously. 'Yes, I punch him in the stomach!' she said again dabbing her eyes with a handkerchief. I joined in the laughter and for a few moments she could not continue, but eventually she reminded me that she was, of course, 'A big lady at that time!' This caused more merriment. She had since changed her figure dramatically, having shed as much as 30 kilos.

It was in December 1951 that she had opened the season at La Scala with such acclaim that her fame ran round the world. It was to be the start of a series of huge triumphs. She was to sing *Norma*, *La Traviata* and *Lucia di Lammermoor* in Chicago in what was regarded worldwide as a personal triumph.

She told me how, not many months before, she had worked for the first time with the theatre and film director Luchino Visconti at La Scala and how impressed she had been by his personality and superb skill. Then she leaned towards me.

'A performance is a struggle,' she told me. 'You have to win; you have to dominate your audience and you have to make them yours.' It was as if the stage lights were already upon her as she spoke and gesticulated, then pausing before adding, 'You know, I never, ever missed a lesson! I ate, slept and dreamed only for opera. I lived entirely for it. It was to me a sponge – I absorbed it all!' She lowered her voice, 'To me the stage and the theatre are sacred places.' We held hands for a long moment.

She kissed me very tenderly when we parted and murmured something about my lovely eyes! Even when the lift took me down to the ground floor I was still walking on air!

Naturally, I followed all the news about her avidly and noted that in September 1957 the American hostess, Elsa Maxwell, had introduced her to the Greek shipping magnate Aristotle Onassis. She had sung the previous year for the first time at the Metropolitan in New York and everything seemed to be going well until illness and a disagreement with the Director at La Scala upset her. She was, in fact, fired from La Scala after they had failed to reach agreement on performances for the next season but by December of that year she would make a sensational debut in Paris at a big gala concert.

This was to have a vital effect on her life because Onassis was present and was not only greatly impressed, but he saw to it that they met again. He invited the Meneghinis to join him, together

with several other guests including the Churchills, on his yacht. It was during this cruise that Onassis and she became secret lovers. So began her entry into the international social whirl. Neither Meneghini nor her career now seemed to matter, but in May 1964 she enjoyed a triumphant return to Covent Garden for Franco Zeffirelli in a new production of *Tosca*, which I enjoyed immensely. She followed this in a spectacular production of *Norma* for him in Paris. Sadly, these were to be her last new productions because on medical grounds she was advised not to undertake such heavy programmes.

I saw her give the final operatic performance of her career in a Royal Gala performance of *Tosca* at Covent Garden. Then in 1966 she gave up her American citizenship and took Greek nationality. This technically annulled her marriage to Meneghini, but it proved to be a tragic denouement to her aspirations with Aristotle Onassis. He had other plans and in 1968 he married Jacqueline Kennedy. Maria never recovered her artistic will after this cruel slight. Somehow in 1971 she began to give a series of master classes at the Julliard School of Music in New York, but truth to tell I think her heart was broken.

An old friend, the tenor Guiseppi di Stefano, began to see her again and he persuaded her to join him in a joint recital tour. It was an extensive tour in order to raise funds for his daughter's medical treatment. They quarrelled a lot, but it was a personal triumph and financially a success, although an artistic failure. Their attitude to singing differed. 'She spent her career searching for perfection. He believed he was born with it.'

The final concert held in Japan in November 1974 was to be her last public performance. She was just forty-one.

So the story unfolded. When in March 1975 Aristotle Onassis died, Maria was virtually a recluse living in Paris. Two years later she died alone in her apartment from natural causes.

Since that first rapturous meeting I always followed her career. Tito Gobbi summed it all up: 'She shone for all too brief a while in the world of opera like a vivid flame attracting the attention of

Opposite: Tea at the Savoy with Maria Callas. Photo by Cecil Beaton (Camera Press, London).

the whole world and she had a strange magic which was all her own. I always thought she was immortal – and she is!'

For a time I inhabited the remarkable world of George S. May. With offices in the Strand they were the advance guard, pre-Kinsey, of the business consultants about to descend on Britain's companies.

George S. May were based in Chicago and at first they had a field day in Northern Europe: at least that was the territory in which I had a short but strenuous PR association with them. I remember travelling from London to Helsinki three times in ten days (not as an airline pilot, but on PR work for the May Company). The way they operated was to have a salesman make a cold call on a company and seek to arrange for an analyst, as they called him, to come and spend a few days in order to see if they could be helped. There was no charge for this visit, but if the 'company doctors' were brought in, it was a daily charge. The question was for how many days. There may have been antagonism to George S. May in their somewhat basic and aggressive approach, but the fact was that British business, especially small-to medium-sized organisations, was at that time often old-fashioned, family orientated and slow – and needed such shock treatment. Soon Kinsey and other organisations got into their stride and business consultancy flourished Mr May believed in turnover of staff as well. I remember a cable he sent his son who was then visiting London: 'Just fired a phoney! Regards.'

A bad experience was when, returning from a visit to Russia, I was collected at Heathrow by David, my accountant, in a borrowed car. It was a Saturday afternoon and raining steadily. As we approached Hammersmith Flyover the car appeared to accelerate and swerve. There was an enormous explosion and when I next opened my eyes I was lying on the road in a pool of blood. I was being asked a question and all I could do, apparently, was hold up my passport (for an Englishman on an English road it seemed a strange thing to do, but it seems I was delirious). Then I remember that I felt I was being dragged through a door labelled 'Death' – and I fought – I wanted to live! Strangely aware of what was happening, I vaguely heard someone say, 'He's had it head and legs – take him to the mortuary. The other one's for

Hammersmith General.' I desperately tried to assure myself which one was me. It's very cold when so much blood has run out of you, but like a hunted animal you are acutely aware – you want to live – you fight for life. I learned later that David, the poor driver, had gone through the windscreen. I shot out of the door. It was before safety belts were introduced. Apparently a tyre had burst and we had charged into the railings above the church, bounced back and turned over. The headlamps and other parts of the car had landed down in the churchyard. I was told later that a fur hat I had bought on leaving Moscow, to use up my spare roubles, and which I was wearing at the time of the accident had really saved my head. Though many might contest that fact!

There was later a strange outcome from this accident. It was something that I never discussed with anyone, but as time passed I began to have a disturbing sense of being drawn towards any long vehicle that I might be passing which almost resulted in my spending the whole time in the inside lane. It was something I privately fought against, but found so worrying that I began to have someone drive me whenever possible, especially on long journeys. Shaun, who came from Cornwall, was one who was to fill this role. I helped him to get started on photography and he did some work for me. He came to live in Cheltenham, where I was to have an office later. His good looks were very attractive to women and he lived with a girlfriend. One evening, when he was driving back from Gloucester with another girlfriend, the car went off the road and he was killed instantly. His friend was injured, but recovered. When I went to see him in the mortuary the attendant said, 'Excuse me, sir, was he a film star? I've never seen anyone look like that.' Strange that someone whom I employed primarily for my own safety should kill himself in such a fashion. Later I taught myself by sheer will power to overcome this strange phenomenon.

I had an office next to Fortnum and Mason in Piccadilly – just above the famous clock, in fact. Here I set up my Public Relations business, which had really started with the work for Cetra. I might add that it was a time when most people, if asked, would have described the letters PR as meaning 'Physical Recreation'. Today it is, of course, quite different. We have a government headed by a prime minister who believes in it as a kind of third force. The word 'spin' no longer has merely a cricket connotation.

Yet it was a chairman of the Conservative Party, Lord Woolton, who really started it all when he appointed Toby O'Brien as PR consultant to His Majesty's Opposition. That was in 1946. It was the first time that a professional publicist had been appointed to change the image of a political party, though Sir Stephen Tallents had made PR history in breaking new ground at the General Post Office. Toby may be described as one who was 'well connected'. Even Cecil B de Mille once hired him to help promote his epic *The Ten Commandments*.

At the Conservative Party Headquarters he had his work cut out to get his ideas of PR over – ideas such as attracting the national and international press to the annual Party Conference. On the eve of the Blackpool Conference in 1946, for instance, he was told that there was no separate room for the press and that there were plenty of telephone coin boxes they could use in the Winter Gardens.

When he left the Conservative Party, Toby O'Brien set up his own PR operation, but he worked mostly outside Parliament. He met people in normal business ways and hours, not by hanging around the lobbies of the House. The later development of Members of Parliament, or ex-members, peddling their wares in the political process through pressure groups and 'contacts', which was basically a form of lobbying, and earning fees, was not for him, though they styled themselves as PR companies.

One of his first big accounts was Spanish Tourism. He made a huge success of it and was as much responsible as anyone for putting the Costa Brava on the map. His offices at No. 2 Old Burlington Street became a cockpit of international PR activity – he represented, among others, the Imam of Yemen, Tanganyika Concessions (the giant company with a then £150 million stake in Katanga's Union Miniere) and acted for Cunard in helping to promote the need for the new QE2.

The Labour Party realised the need for professional Public Relations after their defeat in the 1959 elections. Hitherto they had referred scornfully to the Tories as having to employ this professional manner of reaching the public. Now, in 1964, they were at it themselves using skilled PR men – and they won. When Harold Wilson took over from Gaitskell his image was very carefully moulded by busy professional PR men. Suddenly bright young men in trendy suits were at work at Labour's HQ.

The North, too, got in on the Party's PR act. A PR firm in Newcastle upon Tyne, my own home town, got involved. It was run by a Labour Councillor, Dan Smith, Leader of the Council and a master decorator by trade. He became quite 'big time', making frequent visits to London and could, indeed, be impressive. The trouble with Dan was that he was too impressive. He arranged for as many as ten journalists in the key northern marginal seats to 'give advice' on Public Relations to Labour candidates and their agents. His sphere of PR influence appeared to extend rapidly, but unfortunately for him his patronage came to grief in a spectacular court case.

One day I had an appointment to meet a high flyer in the relatively new world of Public Relations consultants in London. He was Michael Rice and he had been asked to meet me by a friend, though I had no knowledge of this until I received a phone call. His fourth floor offices in St James Street, Mayfair were certainly impressive. He would be about thirty years of age, a very natty dresser, very charming and he was extremely polite to me. On the mantelpiece of his elegant office I noticed a splendid piece, described to me as an Egyptian Twelfth Dynasty Statue of a scribe, which was only to be expected as he was also the PR consultant to the United Arab Republic in Britain. He was a very dashing young man and on the day we met he wore a very large signet ring and dark glasses. He was single, lived in a flat in Hyde Park Place and drove an Alvis. His first big political account was to represent the Government of Ghana, which was then moving to republic status and wanted to be well thought of. It was not long before he was repeatedly commuting between London and Accra.

Public Relations was nurtured to some extent in a world of intrigue. On the day we met, one of his executives or contacts – I wasn't sure – had been attacked and wounded in the Middle East. We discussed PR potential for me and he very kindly passed on to me an account which he couldn't handle because they did not pay enough. He would not accept less than £7,000 per annum in fees plus all expenses. (This could be multiplied by ten to reach present-day value for money.) He obtained Jamaica as an account in this country and Lady Huggins, who was married to an ex-governor, became a director of his company. I was to get along famously with her at a later date when we met at a party within the sound of Big Ben.

The company to whom Michael had recommended me were difficult to promote because they insisted that their work was confidential. There was one big service I was able to give them, however, when a confidential report of theirs, of national interest, had been seen inadvertently and through no fault of theirs, or mine I might add, by a reporter on *The Times* newspaper. It was pretty dynamic stuff and on hearing of this I hurried across to *The Times*. It was early evening. There I explained my plight. The Australian who had filed the story refused to help, but Peter Jay, later to be our Ambassador in the States and who was then on the editorial staff offered to assist me and had the whole story scrubbed in the nick of time before printing. It was a splendid gesture on his part. As I have said, I had nothing to do with the report or how it had come into the reporter's hands before the client had seen it.

My work was to be not in the political sphere, but mainly in the world of sport and leisure. Soon after I moved into my Piccadilly office Derek Ibbotson came around to introduce me to Norman Dally. Norman was Sales Director of Edward R. Buck & Sons Ltd of Stockport, Manchester, then Britain's leading sportswear manufacturers. They engaged me as their Public Relations guru and this began a most enjoyable association. The company was privately owned by the Buck family. David Buck was Managing Director and his three cousins, Vivian, Ted and Christopher, formed the Board of Directors, together with John Wilson (Production), Peter Dyas (Merchandising) and Norman Dally.

Ronald Buck started the company in 1880 in London Road, Manchester. The founder of the firm was his father, Edward R. Buck, and there were thirteen children of whom ten were boys, including triplets. Mr and Mrs Ronald Buck, who lived all their married life at Bollin Hill, Wilmslow, had two children: Christopher, a director of Edward R. Buck and Sons, and Robert, who was with Robert R. Buck & Sons Ltd, Carlisle, who made sweaters and other woollen garments.

I want to tell you about this company because it is relevant to the incredible growth in the sportswear trade as we know it today and it is also significant because of the demise of many family-owned firms. At that time there were 36,000 registered football clubs and it was estimated that a million people played organised soccer. At the professional end there were ninety-two clubs and 2,000 registered players. 'We support the retail trade and will never sell direct,' said David Buck. But the company at that time had no proper identity. A four-page article in colour in *The Director*, which I arranged for Peter Hobday to write, featured David Buck saying, 'Forty years ago we were the first company in these parts to employ a lady typist, then the first to use punch cards and now we have just bought the first computer in the trade.'

Soon afterwards I arranged for Ronald Allison to come and commentate for a thirty-minute BBC 2 TV peak-hour film, which was made on the premises, showing many of the 500 operatives at work. The nylon alone used in the course of a year was such that if you started unrolling it at Wick in the North of Scotland you would still be unwinding it on the cliffs of Dover! The company was fully integrated, that is to say, it not only converted and knitted the material, it also made it up. There were as many as 14,000 products in their range. The Board's attitude to industrial relations was a form of benign paternalism. Despite the fact that the then Industrial Relations Act allowed the union – the Garment Makers – to recruit, the workforce in the company's three plants at Stockport, Carlisle and Crewe appeared to be singularly unimpressed at their wooing.

So here was a company with as many as twenty-one of the Football League's top professional clubs on contract and soon to secure the exclusive contract with the Wales Rugby team, the British Olympics and Commonwealth Games teams and several leading Rugby Union and Rugby League clubs, public schools, etc. for their jerseys and shorts. The sports world was at their feet and, talking of feet, I always understood that they had been approached by Mr Addy Dassler, a shoe maker from Austria, to take on the manufacture of his footwear but they had not taken it up, thus letting slip the prospect of becoming the British part of the mighty Adidas empire. I cannot vouch for this.

As it happened Bukta's catalogue had expanded dramatically. Every time a sales representative asked for something different they included it in the sales catalogue! But it was clear that football would always be their top seller. I remember once putting on a display of their clothing on Astroturf in Islington, North London. I had coaches on hand including Terry Venables (then QPR), Paul Went who was captain of Charlton Athletic and Peter Storey of the Arsenal. I seem to recollect that the going rate was a fiver each (makes you think when you consider the modern rates they would command!)

The pull of football was again evident when I arranged for an all-white double-decker bus with an open top to be called 'The Bukta Bus' in which the whole of the Hibernians squad travelled the length of a packed Princes Street dressed in their Bukta playing strip during the Edinburgh Festival.

But there was a huge upsurge in demand on its way for all manner of sportwear and leisurewear. Eagle-eyed entrepreneurs armed with sample designs were catching planes for the Far East and it was not long before immaculate copies were flooding back to a logo-hungry market. 'Made in Britain' was under seige. The long line of machinists at Bukta House were about to be ambushed. It would never be the same again. A famous label was about to be bowled out.

A map in the office of the member of the family dealing with exports still showed areas of the world as part of the Empire when the countries concerned were no longer member countries. Export sales were entirely centred at that time on appearing at the big International Sports Fair held annually, and which I twice attended in Germany.

Less than a decade away lay the beginning of the soaring climb into sales of leisurewear which we know today. The turnover in the Manchester United shop has rocketed in recent seasons. In my home town of Newcastle upon Tyne, United strips sell at £40.00. It is the same at most club shops in the Premiership. The designs are changed quite often thus causing parents headaches as their offspring demand to be ever up to date.

Bukta made as many as 14,000 options of sports clothes in size and colour, but 60 per cent of their then turnover of almost £3 million came from football. (It should be appreciated that I am writing about a time when the pound was worth some sixteen times what it is today, which would make Bukta's turnover on football clothing more like £50m in today's money.)

I arranged for George Best to play for Hibernians. It was part of a deal concerning Hibs wearing Bukta in very clear lettering on their jerseys and obviously there was to be big publicity for George's first appearance for the famous Edinburgh club. This resulted in two nerve-wracking experiences for me. First, ensuring that George was actually on the Friday night plane to Edinburgh; then the reaction of the Scottish Football Association to the size of the lettering of the name of Bukta. This was not very favourable. George's appearance was, of course, big publicity, but on the day the SFA began arguing about the lettering of BUKTA on the jerseys. They created such a fuss when we insisted that it had been agreed that television coverage as a result was in jeopardy. This would have a drastic effect, too, on the Scandinavian TV networks, which took much of their football coverage from Scotland. Only last-minute talking and feverish reduction of the size of the lettering right up to the minutes beforehand saved the situation.

Headaches of the PR man!

When Scotland unveiled their official strip to be made by Bukta for the 1974 Christchurch Commonwealth Games I arranged for two models, Elvina Bennett, 24, and Jack Allan, 31, each dressed in the official top and shorts, to run the length of Princes Street and then go jumping on and off city buses and visiting stores for the whole morning. All this, I am glad to say, attracted excellent press and TV coverage in Scotland.

Bukta always had good connections in Wales. Clive Thomas, who was a well-known First Division Association Football referee, also had a sports equipment business in the Rhondda and was Secretary of the Boys' Clubs Association of Wales. He was a most engaging personality and I was delighted when Norman Dally at Bukta asked me to join a party to visit Clive at the same time that Frankie Vaughan would be there on tour. Frankie did an enormous amount of work for the Boys' Club movement of course. So I went down for a couple of days.

To go with Frankie to one of his performances was great fun. The first thing you noticed was the preponderance of women in the audience – probably over a thousand of them. Then there was the air of anticipation. It was a tremendous atmosphere increasing by the minute as the time for Frankie's appearance got nearer. Then – the opening bars – and – it's Frankie, immaculate in tails and top hat. The crescendo of screams, yells, cheers, claps and sheer wild ecstasy went on and on. It was really something that had to be experienced to understand the wild warmth of it. Later, after a relaxed dinner, Frankie recalled some of his experiences. He had felt that he was being sucked into the Hollywood star machine when he starred there with Marilyn Monroe in *Let's Make Love*. I think that he found Marilyn a bit over-powering and very sexy. His wife, Stella, was none too happy with his set-up out there and in the end Frankie played it safe and returned home. He was, after all, really a home bird.

He always had a soft spot for Bath. 'It was among the first places I ever visited in connection with Boys' Club Week,' he told me.

His string of hits included 'Garden of Eden', which was number one for thirteen weeks in January 1957. His last big hit was 'There Must Be a Way' in 1967, although there were releases of 'So Tired' and 'Nevertheless' after that. He recalled the big crush of well-wishers around his car when he arrived to do concerts at the Pavilion in Bath. 'They were really terrific audiences in the West Country.'

We sat up on one occasion well into the small hours and he told me the story of his life. He was a strongly committed Socialist. His famous song with the 'Give me the moonlight' lyrics had been rewritten by himself and copyrighted. I am not sure, but I seem to remember him saying that it was originally a woman's song, but I may be wrong. His devotion to the Boys' Clubs was partly because he had a rotten time as a kid and really knew what being poor meant.

Another PR effort was the big Bukta travelling sports day for indoor events, where hundreds of schoolchildren were invited to a local sports hall to watch demonstrations and take part themselves in various sports presented by professional players and coaches. Bukta were delighted with all this, but it was a shame that the corporate development of the company was not maintained. It all seemed to lose momentum; Norman Dally suddenly departed; various projects were shelved and it was not long before David Buck arranged to see me privately to explain, insofar as he was able at the time, that they were unexpectedly running down the whole operation which, apart from my own situation, I thought to be rather sad. Yet another fine family company had bitten the dust. Flying fingers in factories in the Far East were at the throat of many old British companies. (Years later, Norman told me that I was so good for Bukta that I could have doubled my fees!)

I was approached by an advertising agency. They had a client company, Perkins, makers of diesel engines and the urgent problem at their Peterborough factory was that they could not get the trained operatives they required. Had I any ideas? My suggestion was to send Henry Cooper up to meet the Works Director to get a little background and then to advertise in the local press that Henry would like to meet any skilled operative, be pictured with him and then have the picture autographed by Henry on the spot. Henry came to see me with his manager, whom we dubbed 'The Bishop', and they appeared to like the idea.

Accordingly the advertisement appeared in the local paper. Henry went up as arranged on the Sunday to await results. The stream of applicants continued for over an hour. All vacancies were filled and a long waiting list was compiled. The local press loved it and Perkins were delighted.

This is what the *Daily Express* wrote in their second leader on the following day:

Done with gusto

Today's best antidote to the pedlars of misery is provided by the news of Henry Cooper recruiting workers for the Perkins diesel engine factory in Peterborough.

Of course it is a gimmick to get the former Empire and European heavy-weight champion to help industry recruit employees. But it is a jaunty one. It shows flair and adds a bit of spice to life.

The troubles of the three-day week companies like Perkins are to be congratulated on their initiative in promoting business. Their gusto and verve symbolises the Spirit of Britain – which is very much alive and kicking.

Another news story in the *Daily Express* of 20 January 1965 concerned my activities in Public Relations. It ran as follows:

When just £300 became £4m ...

by Hilary Doling

A businessman will spot a boom miles away while the others can see only problems. So it was with Ron Harrod who lives in the East Anglian fishing town of Lowestoft.

Years ago, Ron was working for the family scrap metal company. There were lots of profitable deals done with the metal from derelict old trawlers once they had finished their last voyage.

But what on earth was the use of the miles of old herring nets which lay discarded round the quay?

'Once you really start looking, it is surprising the uses you can find for fish-net,' says Ron. 'I had a brainwave and started selling them to local market gardeners to keep the birds off their vegetables,' he recalls.

Twine

That single idea set Ron off on a successful business career of his own. He now runs a business with sales of £4 million a year. The early days were, of course, much more modest.

He began with a single assistant, capital of only £300 and turned over a mere £5,000 in the first 12 months.

Soon Harrod of Lowestoft branched out into Sports netting and in 1957 bought a second-hand net-making machine. Now the loom has been joined by three others which together put five million knots in 360 miles of twine every week.

Nets for football, tennis, badminton and many other sports roll out of the factory and, since Ron has never been slow to grab an opportunity, the posts which go with them are now supplied, too.

You'll find Harrod rugby posts at Murrayfield and their goalposts at Manchester United or Arsenal.

Confident

It took Harrod of Lowestoft 27 years to reach a £1 million-a-year turnover. Now in only five years they have quadrupled it.

'There are a number of reasons for the growth,' says Ron. 'My children have now all joined the firm which gives us more man-power.' Son Chris is production manager, Mark is works manager, daughter Stephanie deals with the computer and wife Margaret does the accounts. Les Saunders, a friend, is Sales Manager.

'We're a real family firm. Our board meetings still take place around the kitchen table.' The new factory, which opened in 1979, uses some of the most up-to-date machinery in the British sports trade.

'The new technology means we can offer an efficient service and 75 per cent of our orders are turned round the same day.'

Harrod also has a thriving export business, with sales in 32 countries mainly in Europe but also to Russia and the Middle East. 'I know it may seem a little like selling coals to Newcastle but we even sell table tennis nets to Hong Kong,' laughs Ron.

But business wouldn't boom at all, he says, if it were not for the co-operation of his workforce. 'You should stay in touch with feelings on the shop floor.'

As he walks around the factory he often stops to chat with workers. 'We have 70 full-time staff and 70 more employed as outworkers and I think I know just about everybody by name.'

As for the future, Ron sees the likelihood of a shorter working week and the increase in leisure time as good news for Harrod. 'People won't necessarily look for more sports equipment, they'll look for quality that will last.'

Cashing in on the fitness craze, the company is already producing a successful range of body building and gym equipment endorsed by the world's strongest man, Geoff Capes. 'We design things then he pulls them to bits and tells us what is wrong.' [It was, in fact, my idea to have Geoff exclusively sponsored by the company. As 'The World's Strongest Man' to be, he was a huge advertisement and had sound ideas on design of equipment.]

Ron doesn't expect turnover to keep increasing at the present rate but, 'I'm confident we'll be pipping the £10 million mark within five years. When this happens the company will seriously think of heading for the Unlisted Securities Market.'

When you think that this story appeared in the *Daily Express* news pages within days of this quite small family firm becoming a PR account of mine, it may serve to indicate both the value of PR, and, spare my blushes, the news sense and awareness of one's work. My objective was to get the name of Harrod into print, but a certain store in Knightsbridge was always a little edgy!

Let me just go off at a tangent here for a moment as I note the following:

A Question of Sport!

Hector Monro, Neil Macfarlane, Dick Tracy, Colin Moynihan, Robert Atkins, Robert Key, Iain Sproat – the foregoing have mostly kept lower profiles than Lord Lucan and yet each has been HM Minister of Sport!

All would doubtless enjoy the Lords Tests, Centre Court seats and the Royal Box on Cup Final Day and I don't for a moment carp about that, but during their time sport was starved of funds and facilities and the nation – and particularly our children – lost out. At least the present government appear to have put together a range of measures which include a ban on all sales of sports fields. This has hitherto been a depressingly lax attitude by previous governments. It remains to be seen how we can counter-act this very short-sighted policy. Our youth must not lose out.

I mention this particularly because I arranged for at least three of these ministers to attend individually, when they were in charge of sport, an open day at Harrod of Lowestoft and I was struck by the fact that sport was merely one of a string of items in their department. Each would arrive with a number of staff in support obviously dealing with what appeared to be a full portfolio. Whilst I appreciated their presence, it was clear from their busy telephoning and timetable demands that sport was only an incidental.

These open days were hugely successful and involved a helicopter ride, a trip on the Norfolk Broads, sky divers, a tour of the works and a splendid lunch. We had about eighty people from the trade

Geoff Capes pauses to try out the new Body Bild Strengthmaster during the 'at home' by Harrod of Lowestoft to officially open their latest factory extensionin 1965.

as guests and, of course, the sports trade press attended, plus local radio and TV. Stephanie Harrod took a leading part in their reception.

I took Geoff Capes to Harrod in order to sponsor their weight training equipment and home gym products. He was indeed the gentlest Strongest Man In The World! When he was a copper, I used to get him a few PR assignments and I regarded him as a good friend.

The *Guardian* newspaper ran a half page company profile on Harrod of Lowestoft and the 'Harrod Herald' became a popular company newspaper.

When Harrod of Lowestoft decided to reorganise, Ron wrote me a letter which included the following:

> We wish to confirm our telephone conversation when it was decided that we would not require your services on a regular basis after the end of this year but to work on an as and when basis.
>
> When you first started out with us our turnover was below 1 million and now it is going on for 6 million and we feel that you have greatly contributed to our success. You have always been so hard working and enthusiastic about us and our products and we thank you whole heartedly for this.
>
> We will undoubtably keep in contact with you and see you at the various Exhibitions and as said previously to work with you on a one off basis.

Today the company flag flies as proudly as ever. Ron has retired and Stephanie's smart new Porsche occupies the Managing Director's space in the car park.

Let me tell you of another client company's success story. Latham made industrial filtration presses and I noticed that their advertisements, though small, had good potential. I made an appointment to go up to Newcastle-under-Lyme, Staffs. There I was welcomed by Kay Latham whose attractive Scots voice and smart appearance seemed slightly out of sync as one of the bosses of an engineering outfit.

Pete Latham met her in 1981 when he set up the company. They married in 1986. They have a wonderful team and Pete is himself a tremendous worker. Kay is very much a working director.

Tim Barber, ex-rugby player, energetic, open faced, is one of the legion of tough-talking salesmen Britain now produces. He is Sales Director. The world is truly his oyster. There is a refreshing sense of a team throughout the workforce.

Now called Latham International, the company has offices in South Africa and Kuala Lumpur and moved to larger premises here in the UK late in 2000. They want me to get Joanna Lumley to do the honours when they open the new factory.

When I arranged for a journalist from the *Guardian* newspaper to lunch with Pete and Kay we were suddenly interrupted on the phone. Pete told the caller, 'Right. I'll be there for lunch tomorrow.'

'Where was that call from?' I asked him.

'Oh. Jo'burg!' he said. That's the Latham get up and go spirit. Overnight they will arrive on a client company's doorstep.

Around the walls of the boardroom are framed articles I have written and had published in newspapers and trade journals charting their progress.

Kay and Pete Latham toast the new factory, December 2000. (Picture by the Sentinel.)

One German competitor was so furious at losing a multi-million pound sterling order to them in Australia that he arranged for a photographer to fly over their admittedly cramped works at New-castle-under-Lyme, Staffs in a balloon and then he sent the picture to Australia, out of pique, saying, 'Look, they're only Fred in a shed!' Some Fred! Some shed!

One morning in London I had a surprise visitor which resulted in taking me into the golf world. He was Paul Millard, Managing Director of Ben Sayers Ltd, one of the oldest established golf club makers in the world.

He invited me up to North Berwick where old Ben Sayers had originally had his relatively small factory. His clubs were virtually hand made and he had gained a great reputation as a teacher of the game and as a player.

Now a large corporation named Grampian had taken over with the result that a modern factory was situated on the outskirts of this very pleasant seaside town.

Their clubs still retained a reputation for almost hand-made attention such as inspecting the 'loft and lie'. The game was beginning to boom and Paul had apparently heard about me and felt that I could really promote their name. Their clubs sold in the professionals' shops on the courses and sports shops world-wide. There thus began a most enjoyable association.

Focus of the trade was the huge trade fair at the scene of the British Open each year. One of the first I attended was at Muirfield, where Ben Sayers had on their exhibition stand the world's most expensive golf bag. This retailed (then) at £350 and was purely a one-off made of elephant hide.

I remember one promotional scheme I set up in conjunction with the House of Seagram, which was that with each of the first 1,000 sets of the new Ben Sayers Centenary Clubs we gave a bottle of 100 Pipers Scotch whisky.

Everywhere colour was becoming the fashion in the game; only the ball remained resolutely white. Players were being signed up for big promotions and in those early days Mark McCormack was busy on the scene as the forerunner of the battalion of agents who would be on the trail of promising pros on the tournament circuit and also would-be sponsoring companies.

A golfing journalist who was close to Billy Casper, the famous American golfer, introduced me to his agent, Ed Barner, who was unmistakably the prototype of the agent with his snappy portfolio, quick handshake and eyes that clicked like an adding machine. Like Billy, he was a member of the Mormon Church.

Our tournament pro, Doug Sanders, was a tremendous character. His wardrobe was extraordinary. Back home in the States he had, I understand, at least 400 pairs of shoes all in the most lurid colours and next to them as many as 200 matching pairs of trousers, to say nothing of the shirts and sweaters. He always regarded himself as an entertainer, though his outfits were not quite as spectacular as the late, much loved, Payne Stewart. Doug's hero was Walter Hagen, the golfing 'bon viveur' of the 1920s, and his aim was to 'out-Walt' the great man. In terms of drinking, womanising and charming everyone in sight he was certainly no slouch himself, as he admitted in his fascinating autobiography *Come Swing With Me*. I remember at one Open in Scotland Doug rented a nice house for the duration of the tournament and he told me he had got the keys and just moved in. Come lunch time on the first day and we returned from a practice round – I hasten to add that he had been playing, not me – to find the house full of ladies who had arrived to meet 'That nice Mr Sanders'. The lady who had rented him the house had gathered her lady friends to meet him, but was told in no uncertain terms that he was not a show-case, that he wanted some peace and it was his house for the God-darned duration. 'Please, ladies, will you get to hell outa here!' Fortunately he said it with a laugh, but I knew he meant it.

Doug never did win a major, though he really lived every golfer's dream: a 30-inch putt to beat Jack Nicklaus and win the Open at St Andrews. Golfers visiting or playing on the Old Course can sometimes be seen standing over this famous putt trying to imagine what it must have been like back in 1970!

'I remember it all,' says Doug, 'Even now at night before I go to sleep I sometimes think of bending down to flick away a speck of grass before hitting the fateful stroke.'

I know what it was like even just standing near to watch and I was, in fact, one of the first to attempt to console him. In all the annals of sport was there ever a moment of such despair? He had only to drop in that short putt to win the Open. He hesitated, removed some real or imaginary piece of grass and then fluffed the putt. In the play-off next day Jack Nicklaus came out on top.

Doug and his wife, Scotty, live on the outskirts of Houston. Pictures of comedians, actors and presidents adorn the walls. He is a great outgoing guy.

When John Player & Sons were interested in setting up a big international golf tournament in this country, I was asked by their agents, Sales Link, to get the world's leading golfers to take part. It had to be in late September. This was a very tricky task because the American Professional Golfers' Association at once moved to try and block any of their members coming over to take part as they did not want to dilute the importance of their circuit, which would still be running coast to coast on the dates planned. The all-important sponsors would not be too pleased if some of the top golfers were missing 'over on this side'.

I resolved to go and see for myself. I was met on arrival in New York by two golfing journalists. Old friends, they entertained me at Sardis, the famous dining room, and broke the news that I was on a tough mission. This became even clearer when next day at the offices of the United States Professional Golfers' Association I had a distinctly frosty reception. The cold attitude was not unexpected. As far as they were concerned I was just a Brit threatening their life-line, the sponsors' coast-to-coast tour, by luring away top names before it was completed.

I resolved to go down to Palm Springs, where the Bob Hope Classic would include some of the pros, and test the water, as it were. But first I wanted to meet the organisers of one of the last tournaments on the US circuit to see if they would co-operate by letting at least a few of the top American golfers miss their date and come over. It was necessary to have our tournament staged by the end of September or, at the latest, very early in October. There might just be time.

The committee of the Greater Hartford Tournament weren't having any. It struck me that they were a group of sharp-nosed descendants of original Scots and Irish immigrants with no intention whatsoever of helping the Brits. They were negative, unhelpful and stony faced, and I flew back to New York empty handed. I was on a tough mission, no doubt, and it looked as though there would be no American pros in the tournament. Players would not be happy and the tournament would suffer.

When I went to get my plane at La Guardia I had a distinct impression that a golfing journalist who had called at my hotel in New York was also travelling, but it was only a fleeting glimpse of him. I may have been wrong. However, on arrival at Palm Springs I distinctly saw him driving off in a hired car. I had the feeling that I was being shadowed. This proved to be correct as newspaper stories began to appear in the States concerning me and my mission. I felt sure that the United States Professional Golfers Association were being stirred up on the issue.

'Don't let our top golfers be lured away – besides, the all-powerful sponsors in the US would not permit it.' So ran the stories. Yet I had been as discreet as possible. Sponsors, however, are God in the States and must not be trifled with.

I was getting worried and needed every minute to try and get round some of the golfers and perhaps win their support. I had got word to Ed Barner that I would be coming to Palm Springs. When I got on the phone on arrival, though, I found that I was speaking to a relative of his. They lived practically adjacent to the course at Indian Wells, but Ed was in LA and unable to attend. Would I go and call on them? I think they were his aunt and uncle. They were quite friendly; probably also Mormons. One lasting impression was of a waterfall cascading through their living room. Well, it was different. I did not stay long; they recommended a hotel. ('Give the porter a good tip, won't you?' was, I thought, a strange request.) It was a top-class hotel made up of a series of very comfortable chalets in Chinese-style grounds. Next morning in the breakfast room Bob Hope, visiting the hotel, called out to me, 'Hi, English! Do you want a lift to the course?' I was, of course, delighted to accept.

Palm Springs is a very wealthy town with a couple of dozen golf courses and about one swimming pool for every six permanent residents. There are stars galore around the place. None more so than Bob Hope and Frank Sinatra. Frank drove a gleaming Rolls

Bob Hope, Frank Sinatra, Doug Sanders and Spiro Agnew (Vice-President of the United States) at Palm Springs (the author took this photograph just before they teed off in their famous foursome).

Royce complete with licence plate, FAS-1, and he had a large place on – guess where – Frank Sinatra Drive. He had a number of what they termed 'bungalows' in the grounds where his guests stayed.

I met Andy Williams in the splendid bar at the Indian Wells Golf Club and he was extremely hospitable. He lived nearby beside a pretty extensive lake that fronted his place.

I met Doug's hosts, Bob and Basie McCullock. He had arranged the stone-by-stone transport of the old London Bridge from England to his land community project in Lake Havasu, Arizona. His own house, Doug told me, was a two-million-dollar 'creative plaything' where push buttons controlled all manner of surprises.

In golfing terms – and in Palm Springs that means most things – the local heroes are Ike, who loved to relax there, and Arnold Palmer, who delighted in winning there. The only thing that can compete with golf, it seemed, was wealth.

On arrival at the La Quinta Country Club, Bob's 12,000-dollar golf cart at once caught my eye. Didn't it just – with its giant caricature of Bob's famous ski-slope nose and its built-in bar, to say nothing of its driver, the Tournament Queen, who happened to be Barbara Eden, dream of America's then popular TV show *I Dream of Jeannie*. I discovered that Bob was playing with US Vice-President Spiro Agnew, Senator Murphy of California and Doug Sanders. This was great news for me because Doug at once came over to me and chatted and then introduced me to the US Vice-President and the senator.

There was someone else standing near him and suddenly I found myself being introduced to him also. He was Frank Sinatra. When suddenly you meet in person the architect of countless magical moments and dreams the world over, a Hollywood star with nearly sixty films to his credit, not merely the greatest of all popular singers, but someone who is a show business phenomenon and he is being utterly charming – yes, and chatting about the weather, and the golf and for God's sake about oneself – well, that alone was worth the trip to the States. He would have been about sixty and looked in good trim.

Of course, the US Vice-President had come to boost the Eisenhower Medical Centre in nearby Palm Desert, the main beneficiary of the tournament, and certainly not to demonstrate his golf swing. Bob had, I understand, talked him into making an appearance, despite the fact that he rarely played. The result was, of course, that the foursome actually became a twelvesome, there were so many Secret Service men around. The ropes were in position to keep the 2,000 or so spectators at bay and I was grateful to be okayed by the security men so that I could step inside them in order to follow the foursome at a respectable distance with the small official party. The Vice-President, playing to an 18 handicap, was accorded some gentle and courteous salutation by the immediate gallery as he stepped up to the first tee. His opening shot was a distinct hook, the ball finishing on a cart path. Senator Murphy, a 16-handicapper at the time, put his tee shot about 150 yards down the right side. Bob, who was a 1 or 2 handicapper, put his straight down the middle for about 200 yards. Doug's shot, also down the right side, finished up about 250 yards away. He stood on the right-hand side of the fairway leaning on Bob's golf cart watching the Vice-President setting himself up for his second shot – the one that would become famous. His ball had finished on a paved buggy-cart path, but he did not move it on to a grass patch as he was entitled to under the rules. He used his three-wood, caught the ball on the toe of the club, angling it right. The ball flew across the fairway and caught Doug on the back of his head on the left side so that he went down on his knee. Several ladies in the vicinity who not long before had been engaged in courtesy bows to the distinguished visitor, were now also on their knees. The Vice-President rushed over to Doug to see if he was all right. The blow had apparently broken the skin and there was a little blood. Meanwhile the gallery were quite non-plussed for a moment or two, but Doug made light of it saying, 'Please don't worry, Mr Vice-President, besides we got you back on the fairway!' The Vice-President apologised profusely to all those near him and was clearly upset, but carried on with the game.

If I may digress for a moment, the 1971 Bob Hope Classic was again to include Vice-President Agnew who misfired once more – at least twice, in fact – sending shots wide into the galleries. Some of the fans, recalling the previous year, apparently carried placards saying, 'He only hits the ones he loves!'

Billy Casper was very hospitable as the gentleman he is, but I could see that it was difficult for him to help me. It would place him in an invidious position. One golfer, Chi Chi Rodriquez, was, however, clearly outspoken on my behalf and there were others who privately told me that they would come over. However, there was this cold fact that the USPGA Sponsors' Tournament would overlap unless we staged the John Player Classic later in October, which would be a problem not only with the weather, but for other considerations. I was on a hiding to nothing in some respects. I felt almost as if I were on a spy mission. Pros were obviously wary of being seen too much in conversation with me. Introductions became guarded. I needed all the time possible. It was good to relax, though, in the evening. There is a terrific star-studded air about Palm Springs. At dinner, at a table quite near, there was suddenly a call, 'Give us a song, Dinah' and minutes later, to great applause, Dinah Shore stood up and after signalling to the band, broke into a number. It's that kind of place; 'My kind of place' as Frank would put it.

Next morning I knew that I needed to get around as quickly as possible as the tournament was almost at an end. However, I got a message at the hotel that Ed Barner had been trying to reach me and would be sending a car to pick me up and take me to a meeting. I presumed, of course, that this would be in Palm Springs. The car duly arrived and I sat back thinking that he would have set something up to help me on my mission.

We had been going for about half an hour when I enquired of the driver where it was we were heading. When he answered 'LA' I suddenly sat bolt upright. We were out on the highway and it was now mid-afternoon. I felt none too happy that precious hours were slipping by. LA is about 80 miles from Palm Springs.

When I at last arrived in Barner's office, which was a room in a vast block, he had with him another guy and they at once began a big sales pitch about marketing Bill Casper in the UK, rather pointedly suggesting results could be better. I had not even been asked if it was convenient and I certainly would not have consented to leaving Palm Springs, where I had little enough time.

I also recollected visits up at St Andrews when I had bumped into Barner leaving a meeting with a famous golf shoemaker, having concluded a deal concerning Casper of which I had not even been aware. This was decidedly unethical. No wonder he had looked embarrassed. So here I was having been more or less hijacked into downtown LA, losing valuable time on my own urgent mission, which was being underwritten by John Player and nothing to do with Barner. Now it would be too late for me to get back to Palm Springs if I was to have any sort of meeting with him. I was livid. This was the kind of big deal American approach that was not the most appealing side of their style. When they began giving me a lecture on how to market Casper, I really went for the jugular, so to speak. Where are the pictures? Where was the sales literature? Barner had often used my office as a base when in London. I told him a few home truths. Defensively he suggested a few names of people back in Palm Springs who might still be around and who might introduce me to certain players if I paid them for the introductions. If I paid them!

The meeting ended with my getting up in disgust. He said that he had to leave for Mexico. I said I hoped the bandits got him. It was now getting late in the evening and he said a car was booked to take me back first thing next morning. He then offered me money for a meal! I spent the night in LA, but I was not in the mood to enjoy it. My hotel bedroom walls must have been paper-thin and I heard a couple arguing like mad for hours. This part of the trip was quite forgettable and so was Ed Barner.

All of which was a pity because Billy is a true gentleman. He had given me a good welcome at Palm Springs, taking me into the clubhouse at Indian Wells. He had won the US Masters Championship that year and was runner-up to Frank Beard in the Tournament of Champions with Tony Jacklin and Gary Player. In 1970 he won altogether 147,472 dollars as second top money winner on the US Tournament circuit. There was an absence of good pictures and glossy promotional material. But Billy was really okay. Ed was ugh!

Incidentally, back home again I received an offer by phone on my return to the UK from a well-known international agent that arrangements could be greatly eased in getting the Americans to come over, but at his price. And what a price – it was all getting too hot. I resolved to get on with my own efforts and I am glad to say that gradually my 'acceptance board' began to fill up as various players or their national organisations confirmed.

One hilarious sidelight to all this: I had got the Foreign Office to help me in dealing with some countries in the Far East where I was trying to track down their golf champions. The day before the opening I got a phone call from a Foreign Office official in Taiwan who said that he had contacted Chang Chung Fa, runner-up in the Hong Kong Open, but that he had not yet got back in touch. At the last minute he told me in another urgent call that he had traced him, but there was only an hour left for him to get a plane if he was to arrive in time. Accordingly the poor fellow was literally hijacked, told to get his clubs and rushed on to the plane. When he got to Heathrow I had an ambulance waiting so that he could rest on the way to Nottingham. On arrival at the course he was rushed into the changing rooms and then to meet the beautiful Miss World Eva Reuber Staier, one of Austria's top models, whom I had arranged to be present for most of the tournament. The sight of a rather bewildered Chang Chung Fa, unable to speak English, perched on a golf buggy being instructed by the photographers to 'Give her a hug', 'Give her a kiss!' was really hilarious. Then he was rushed off to get in some practice holes before he was due to play off in the tournament.

The Notts Golf Club at Hollinwell, near Kirkby-in-Ashfield, proved to be an excellent setting for the John Player Classic and the John Player Trophy, which were held from Monday, 31 August to 6 September 1970.

Golf Monthly reported on the John Player Classic (for £70,000, which was preceded by the £5,000 John Player Trophy):

When John Player & Sons decided to go into golf, they determined that they weren't going to do things by halves. The pre-qualifying rounds for this Tournament were organised as a separate Tournament – the John Player Trophy with a prize fund of £5,000. It was won by Clive Clark with scores of 72 and 69 in a tiresome blustering wind.

The winner of the Classic was Christy O'Connor who collected £25,000. The wind blew up to gale proportions for the third round. For O'Connor, whose game was formed by hours of practice on the windy sands of Bundonun and Dublin Bay, this was perfect! Some of the players formed syndicates with agreements to split the booty if one of them won. Some 10,000 spectators followed the last day, which must have been pleasing to Players as sponsors.

As far as I was concerned it was heavy going. I was not the organiser and my sole responsibility was to find the players, which I achieved as an honest broker, but there was a lukewarm attitude by the press. Harry Carpenter for one appeared less than enthusiastic and I think there were fears that somehow we were attempting to devalue the British Open. No Americans took part.

I first met Paul Trevillion, the brilliant cartoonist, when he came to see me about what he called 'The perfect putting method'. Paul worked from his home, a large Tudor-style house situated between the Bush Hill Park and Enfield golf courses in Middlesex, where he could look out of his studio window and watch golf being played all day and especially note how often putting let down the players. He had perfected what he called the split hand method of putting.

'Most golfers admit,' he told me 'that the number of strokes dropped on the green, if they thought about it, could keep them awake at night. So I have invented the perfect putting method.'

It was his interest in snooker and especially since that day in 1955 when Joe Davis registered his crowning achievement – snooker's maximum break of 147 (15 reds, 15 blacks and all the colours) – that inspired him to develop his 'Perfect Putting Method'. 'When watching Joe Davis play,' he said, 'I always formed the opinion that it was a far tougher proposition to knock a snooker ball into the pocket from ten feet than it is to knock a perfectly straight putt in from four feet. I am sure you will agree,' he told me, 'the mental pressures in all world-class sports are uniform and yet I never once saw Joe Davis attempt to lag up when ten feet from the pocket. This, of course, is why snooker players and the like do not suffer, as do golfers, from the "yips". Every time they line up the ball, and remember, they sometimes have to knock it in off two cushions – every bit as difficult as negotiating a borrow on the green – they have a positive attitude.'

Adam Faith became a great enthusiast for Paul's short putter.

He demonstrated to me that the first stage of his new putting stroke was to split his hands on the club, the same way a snooker player splits his hands on the cue. A right-handed snooker player steadies the cue with his left hand and hits the ball with his right – thinking 'Ball to pocket'.

'I copied this,' he went on. 'I steadied the putter with the left hand, extended my right hand down the shaft and concentrated on just knocking the ball into the hole, using my right hand only. I thought of only one thing – ball to hole! I practised this way with every length of putt from two feet to twenty feet.'

'And?' I broke in.

'And,' he continued with a mischievous smile, 'since that day I never lagged a putt!'

It was all hugely controversial, of course, but Paul is a non-stop 100 per cent enthusiast.

I saw it, however, as a great promotional idea for Ben Sayers. After all, had not Henry Longhurst, the famous golf correspondent, written in the *Sunday Times*, 'The extended right arm is one of the secrets of putting' and Henry Cotton, three times Open Champion, had written, 'Give this Trevillion putting method an extensive trial.' I talked to my friend Tom Scott, the BBC golfing correspondent, about it and he was very keen. 'Paul is the new golf messiah – he certainly gets to the root of things,' he told me with a laugh.

Paul Millard, at Ben Sayers, liked the idea when I put it to him and so the Ben Sayers Short Putter by Paul Trevillion took its bow. One of the earliest enthusiasts was Adam Faith, the pop star, who swore that it had improved his game no end. It ran its course for a time as a fascinating angle on one of golfs great mysteries – The Art of Putting.

One big outcome of all this was that Paul and I got together. I went to Neville Holthan, the Sports Editor of the *Sunday People* with an idea for photo-journalism in which Paul would do a five-column across-strip drawing for each Sunday morning's edition showing a player in action in a movement during a First Division Football game on the previous day. The player, incidentally, would always be Ian Hutchinson of Chelsea for whom I acted. It was a huge success. Paul did a strip of about six drawings illustrating graphically a movement which would have been reported elsewhere in that issue. It has been described as one of the most brilliant ideas in sports photo-journalism.

Ian was better known as Hutch. He had been playing up at Burton before getting his break at Chelsea. He was tall, good looking with a ready smile and soon became a big favourite with the Chelsea fans, especially as he could throw a ball an incredible distance from the touchline. Through him I was to meet some of Chelsea's dream team. It was a time when Stamford Bridge was the trendiest set-up in soccer.

These were the days of Osgood, 'Harmer the Charmer', Cooke, Tambling, 'Baldwin the Sponge', 'Bonetti the Cat', 'Chopper Harris' and Ian Hudson, the quintessential cockney rebel, whose career was marked by clashes, sometimes stern and sometimes hilarious, with the Establishment. The goings on down the King's Road became legendary. A visit I paid to Chelsea Hospital where Ian was temporarily in dock was typical. He was prone to collect a lot of injuries because of his dashing style of play. Here was Ian laid up in a private room, a number of the Chelsea team visiting, when suddenly Dave Sexton, the Manager, was announced. He was on his way up from reception. In a flash all the bottles and glasses were stuffed into a locker just before Dave arrived.

Dave lived in Brighton and his daily journeys to and fro precluded him from venturing out among the trendy crowd in the King's Road I remember during this visit to see Ian I happened to say to him, 'Oh, Dave, I saw so and so in Alexandres the other night.' 'Oh, where's Alexandres?' asked Dave innocently. This was a very trendy joint where the lads hung out. 'Just a chippy down the King's Road, Dave,' one of them replied cheerfully whilst everyone else in the room was squirming with mirth. How Dave contended with this lively bunch always amazed me. They lived in another world.

They were great times, when I went to see 'The Blues' play, waited up in the players' lounge afterwards to be joined by Hutch and others and maybe off to his place for the rest of the weekend after going out to dinner. Chelsea always attracted a fascinating mixture of show business people, all manner of trendies, political leaders and what have you. There was a tremendous atmosphere at a home game – and still is.

Once, having a pre-match lunch at the ground, I asked the well-dressed man next to me – we had not been introduced – for something to say, 'What do you do for a living?' 'Oh,' he said cheerfully, 'I'm a successful professional burglar. What do you do?' I was not sure whether I was having my leg pulled or not, but I knew exactly what the chap on my left side did for a living.

He was Michael Crawford, a great Chelsea supporter and enormous fun to be with. Always a laugh!

I remember once he drove his wife, Hutch's wife and me down to Southampton to see them play. Chelsea supporters, of course, were much in evidence. Southampton at that time were noted for being a bit muscular on the field. Michael got very excited, brandishing a rolled-up newspaper. 'Animals, animals,' he shouted, sounding more like Frank Spencer, his TV character, each time. Soon afterwards there was another incident on the field. A Southampton player was booked by the referee. Michael got very excited, brandishing his rolled-up newspaper again. The man in front had had enough. 'Shut up, you Chelsea spiv,' he roared, 'or I'll bash your face in!' 'It's a very expensive face, mister,' I told him. 'He's just back from Hollywood.' And we roared with laughter.

I must say that Michael is great fun. One can only marvel at his nerve and timing when he does his own incredible stunts on stage and screen but he is very relaxed as a person.

But to return to my old friend, Paul. In the days we did the photo-journalism bit he was always full of ideas about getting more showmanship into football and Don Revie, then Manager of Leeds United, became a willing listener. We both had lots of ideas for promoting the game, such as the players on taking the field kicking dozens of small white footballs into the crowd and running over to salute sections of them. They wore their number visibly beneath their garter tags. I introduced white football boots on behalf of a manufacturer and got some players to wear them.

The England jersey was revered as white with a red rose insignia made by Bukta. It was hugely controversial when Don became the Manager of the national team and set about getting the strip changed. This led to some healthy espionage which ended up with a question in the House about the price being charged for the youngsters' replica shirts. Bukta no longer had the contract. There was a fair amount of argy-bargy about the whole idea, but it took root and thus began the seemingly endless series of strip changes that must cause some heartache in households having to cough up the at present astronomical prices for replica shirts of both club and country.

At Ben Sayers I had the idea of a Professionals' Senior Tournament. It was an instant success and became an annual event. In the first of these I had five British Open Champions taking part at North Berwick. They were Bobby Locke (1949, 1950 and 1952), Max Faulkner (1951), Kel Nagle (1960), Roberto de Vicenzo (1967) and Tony Jacklin (1969).

Bobby Locke always amazed me with his relaxed air when playing. It appeared to him to be more like a day at the office – and the way he could make the ball bend in the wind! Years later his Open Championship-winning medals were to be sold by auction in London for £82,800.

One year when the British Open Golf Championship was held at Muirfield I had large self-supporting signs like billboards about the countryside with the following wording drawn tastefully on them:

'YOU ARE NOW IN BEN SAYERS COUNTRY.'

A visitor, a friend of Paul Millard, enquired whose idea it was and as a result arranged an introduction to me. He was Ken Evans, Marketing Director of North British Steel Group. He asked me if I might be interested in acting for his company. The company was at Bathgate, about fifteen miles from Edinburgh – halfway to Glasgow. They made mostly heavy steel castings at their Bathgate and Armadale Works; there were about 500 employees in the two works. The Menzies family had the major shares in the business which was well established. Again, I was a new kind of bird in this heavy industrial world, but I set about it and felt that with the introduction of the *North British News* newspaper and a few innovative ideas in their excellent welfare hall, I had soon made my mark.

Bathgate's sporting hero was Bernard Gallacher, who captained the European Ryder Cup team in an epic victory against the Americans in 1995.

An annual event that I helped bring about for the town was for it to stage the gathering of pipe bands from all over the UK with the North British Steel Group as sponsors. This was a two-day affair and I don't mind saying one needed nerves of iron at the outset when hundreds of pipers were hard at it tuning up, followed by the seemingly endless stream of marching bands. It was a very keenly fought competition. I used to sit on the dais next to Mr Menzies the Chairman of the NBSG, for the march past. There was a great move for me to wear a kilt!

There developed a difficult management period when inter-departmental attitudes appeared to be strained and morale had dropped. 'Right!' I told members of the Board, 'I'll bring Denis Law up for the day.' I was at lunch at that moment in the Directors' Room and those within hearing froze, food halfway to their mouths. 'Denis Law? You mean the footballer. THE Denis Law – what on earth has he got to do with it?'

'Wait and see,' I replied. 'I think you will be agreeably surprised.'

To give these hard-headed Scots their due, I think that they had got a little used by now to this man, Ken Johnstone, and some of his ideas. As I explained soon afterwards to a board meeting, 'Denis Law is a footballing hero and a great personality. I'll bring him up for the day, he'll tour the works and just watch how the mood will change.'

They fell in with the idea, though cautiously, and I set it up. Having phoned Denis, it was arranged for a mid-week visit three weeks hence. Accordingly, I duly flew to Manchester on an early morning plane from London, collected Denis and we flew together to Edinburgh. Here Alex McMurdo, Managing Director, waited to greet him. There was also a fleet of Ford cars I had arranged, each with a banner which read 'DENIS LAW JOINS NORTH BRITISH STEEL'. This tie-up with the local Ford agent proved hugely popular. Denis had, in fact, joined NBSG – but only for the day. The procession of cars created much interest and on entering Bathgate, with all the media build-up working, there was a great turnout of people. And what a day it proved to be. The media loved it. The works people loved it. Denis was tickled pink. And the directors were aghast, but happy.

He is a great Danny Kaye-like personality, of course, full of charm and in Scotland he is a hero. Not only that – he rose to the whole idea of the occasion. He talked to the apprentices about their team being North British Steel Group. 'Work hard for it,' he said. With about forty people following him, he toured both works, trying his hand at various tasks, meeting everyone with great cordiality and signing autographs. He was pictured using an electric drill, plate laying and a dozen other tasks and at lunch break played an impromptu match in the yard with a number of apprentices. The directors were over the moon, entertained him to a late lunch and the media were delighted with the visit. People were talking to one another again. The whole mood of the place changed and valuable publicity was achieved. It only needs one idea, often enough, to spark a solution to a problem if the right professional attitude to public relations is employed. The story made all the TV news programmes in Scotland and all the press on their front pages.

As I write this I note that it is a week in which Denis Law and Jimmy Greaves both reach the age of sixty. The press hazard a guess that today's managers would have to fork out some £30 million each for these two legends from the 1960s. Arguably the two finest goal scorers in British footballing history, they were arch rivals with club and country and they were both good friends.

At Huddersfield, where Denis was signed by Andy Beattie as a fifteen-year-old, Beattie's successor, the fanatical Bill Shankly, used to yell at him, 'Remember you have two feet <u>and</u> a head.' Law became lethal with all three.

Just to get things in their true perspective, when Denis travelled to the Huddersfield ground to hear of his £55,000 move to Main Road at twenty, he went by trolley bus. When I once or twice took Jimmy out to lunch in the West End, it was obviously a delight for him as an apprentice. 'Have you seen, Johnny Haynes has got himself a car?' he would say. 'I would love to have one of my own.' Johnny was then the first £100-a-week footballer. When 'Greavsie' scored 22 League goals for Chelsea he was still only seventeen and he was earning £17 per week and living in a one-room flat. But he had got himself a car – a dilapidated Standard 8.

'Help the lad if you can,' Ted Drake would tell me, 'but remember – no beer adverts!'

Football today needs to be taken by the scruff of its neck. It is, indeed, the beautiful game. The supporters are now of all income groups, but, coming from the North-East, I know what it means to the ordinary man in the street; yet there is a flaccid lack of guidance and far too much tolerance of bad behaviour by players on and off the field. I remember when, with Ian, I was at Manchester United's training ground and saw George Best come out of the showers, his legs below the knees covered in old bruises and marks. He took enormous punishment with his fantastic dribbling style, but he was always a brave player. He never took a dive.

One morning, back in my office in London, I received a call to say that the BBC had a couple of people at NBSG. 'What are they doing?' I enquired. 'Oh, it's about exports,' came the reply.

The author talks over old times with Jimmy Greaves.

'Find out what their names are,' I asked and on being told I phoned through to BBC Edinburgh to ask what programmes they were on. Clearly they were nothing to do with exports. I found out in fact they worked on a programme called *There's Something In The Air* so I caught the first plane to Edinburgh.

The background to it was that apparently the worst hit area for lung and chest complaints was in that part of Scotland and interest was centred by these investigative reporters on the NBSG Works at Bathgate where there happened to be a very tall chimney stack. From inside 'tip-offs' they apparently already had a camera on a hillside to catch the worst blow-outs. They were also checking on washing hanging on clothes lines and on the surfaces of parked cars to look for films of dust. The programme concerned had caused huge worry and damage in the asbestos industry when they reviewed it. Now I saw the dangers to NBSG in environmental problems, apart from industrial troubles with the unions. I arranged to give the Managing Director training in TV interviewing and plan our side of the story. There were only two weeks to go. Already they had found a widow of an employee who had died from lung cancer and paid her to be pictured next to his grave. They had also been interviewing extensively. I returned to London, went to the producers of the programme and began to vet some of their intentions. Three of the directors travelled down to join me in my last-minute efforts at editing it and when the programme went out, I am glad to say, a lot of the most damaging items had been removed. The directors were so pleased that they sent me a cheque for £800 and asked me to buy something for myself. I decided on a lovely second-hand walnut wardrobe which I have still.

In my NBSG News for Christmas 1978 the headline from the Managing Director, Alex McMurdo, was '1978 Was a Big Challenge – Now For 1979!' I had written and produced a colour brochure and brought out a bumper issue of the 'NBSG News'. Some of Scotland's football team had signed photos in it. Enthusiasm and confidence – that was ever the message.

Another client company was the Canterbury Mortgage Centre. My usual ploy being the printed word in the form of a lively house journal, 'Money Matters' soon took a bow. In the first issue I featured Rick Shortle. 'Exciting Plans for Canterbury Mortgage for 1988 – On the Grid.'

A very likeable personality, Rick became our sponsored driver at Brand's Hatch. On the day we made this announcement I was at Brand's Hatch with Mike Otley and Shaun Allinson, the two young go-ahead partners in the firm. On a previous visit to the track, I had undergone a driving test merely for the fun of it and had chalked up the requisite points enabling me to actually drive at Brand's Hatch. This was regarded as a fun thing – a laugh. Imagine my horror when on this visit to the track the public address system announcer suddenly called my name and said would I please go to the pits to prepare for my practice circuit! The announcer really enjoyed himself. All the folk in our hospitality suite seemed to be in on the joke. I almost panicked. I am not a motoring enthusiast, let alone a car racing buff. Now I knew why they had persuaded me the day before to take a driving test. Like a lamb to the slaughter I was led to the pits, there to be issued with all the gear including overalls and helmet. In no time at all I was 'shoe-horned' into the narrow driver's seat and the car was being pushed on to the track. To say that at that point a form of terror began to seize me would be putting it mildly indeed. I started it up and the engine roared far too heartily for my liking. Willing hands gave me another shove and I was off, a hurried prayer on my lips.

Then began a strange interlude in which the track came rushing at me at what seemed well over 100 m.p.h. I had been told to accelerate into bends. These came tearing towards me, swooped upwards and away at an angle – they were surprisingly steep and I had been advised that on one of them at the top of the gradient I was to look for the 'E' in a big advert on top of a building and point the car at it before swooping down on the other side. Ahead of me another car suddenly span off the track and stopped. I at once braked and made to get out to see if the driver was all right. Stewards rushed over to me and said, 'You never stop on the side of the track like this!' The gears were so low I had to have a push start. The tiny mirror on the side appeared to me useless and the waving flags every time I rushed past the pits were very confusing.

What did they mean? Were they waving at me? There was no time to wave back. I began to go faster and faster and secretly enjoyed it as a form of madness began to take over, but third time round I got the feeling that some of this flag waving might really be directed at me. I took my foot off the pedal and coasted into the pits. Yes, it was me they were flagging down. My average speed – 94.5 m.p.h.

When visiting Canterbury I stayed in a small hotel near the Cathedral. I used to manage to slip away from my business meetings to attend Evensong. How fortunate we are in this country to have such magnificent churches and cathedrals. The atmosphere in glorious Canterbury was such that one left feeling refreshed and uplifted. As for Mike and Shaun, they were really hard grafters. They had a very good radio advert running and their business appeared to prosper. They paid me my fees all right and everything seemed to be going well when I observed something of a rift growing between these two young go-getters. So often when two young guys go hard at it in a very competitive and demanding business there is a personality clash and so it was unfortunately here. Thus a very enjoyable association was lost as their partnership ended.

How I introduced golf buggies is quite a story. It came to my attention that Harbilt, a company in Wolverhampton making, among other items, milk delivery vehicles, were interested in developing into the sports world. As a result of a meeting with them the possibility of making a golf cart developed and I undertook to investigate this through my golf connections. There was then, of course, a decided antipathy towards the use of golf carts or buggies in this country. Indeed, they were not permitted. Today in the USA golf carts are mandatory, largely because the courses make money on them and, of course, over here they are now also in general use. But at the time I am referring to there was distinct opposition to them.

I tried to get Peter Aliss interested and Ferndale Golf Club were, if I remember, very helpful, but the breakthrough came when I succeeded in getting a fleet of eight 'buggies' installed for the Senior Service Scorecar Park at Royal Birkdale for use in the 1966 Ryder Cup. Thereafter the idea, of course, quickly developed, but

this, I believe, was the start of golf buggies in this country (see illustrations).

One amusing incident in my PR activities was with a company who were about to market a new style of life jacket for yachting enthusiasts. It was designed by Uffa Fox and we had the press launch at his home on the Isle of Wight. This was, of course, for the chaps writing in the yachting journals. We had a slap-up meal and Uffa was in tremendous form with his charming wife in attendance.

In order to avoid the high cost of having demonstration videos made professionally in preparation for a forthcoming exhibition, I decided to do a low-cost job myself. I had recently been on a business trip to Poitou Charentes, the beautiful region in the West of France, where I had been attempting to interest the Tourist Board in having me do PR work for them in the UK. I didn't come to any agreement, but I was certainly well entertained to what could only be called superb epicurean delights at La Rochelle, Ré, Aix and Olerou. My local liaison representative was Francois Voyer, who later asked if he could come and work for me for experience, to which I agreed. We now had opportunities in the Common Market and all that.

Thus, having to make a video for the life-saving jacket, I engaged a model in London and with Francois we three travelled to the Rock Hotel, Gibraltar, where I met a local cameraman I had engaged for the purpose. Off we went next day in a small boat and when we were well out at sea I instructed the model, who wore a swimsuit, to don the Uffa Fox jacket and prepare to go overboard. With the cameraman ready in position, we waited for her to plunge into the ocean. Suddenly she burst into tears and trying to comfort her I enquired what was the matter.

'I cannot swim,' she sobbed.

'But the agency said ...' I began. Actually nothing could be better for testing the jacket than to see her floundering in the ocean, but she began to get somewhat hysterical.

At this point Francois, ever the ladies' man, took over. He sat with her in the prow of the boat, which was bouncing up and down halfway to the Moroccan coast in what was a decidedly freshening breeze. Suddenly the girl jumped to her feet, put on the jacket and stood swaying about holding on to Francois, who signalled to the cameraman to be ready; whereupon she jumped overboard, disappeared from view and came up again, giving us excellent mid-ocean filming.

'What happened – what did you say?' I asked Francois eagerly afterwards.

'Ah,' he said, the worldly Frenchman pulling on his Gaulois, 'that is my secret!'

Marje Proops, the *Daily Mirror*'s long-serving columnist or 'Agony Aunt' was great fun. I remember on one occasion dancing with her when my braces suddenly gave way. 'You must be the only man I've ever helped keep his trousers up,' she said, almost helpless with laughter.

Her editor at one time, Hugh Cudlipp, had years before insisted that she never used three syllables where two would do. Her 'Dear Marje' page was, of course, read by millions. At a Foyles literary luncheon in her honour on the publication of *Marje Proops – The Guilt and the Gingerbread* written by Angela Patmore, she was surrounded at the top table by some of her old friends – Lord and Lady Cudlipp, Baroness Castle, Michael Foot and Michael Grade among them. She said, 'The book has caused me quite a lot of pain and suffering. Gradually it gets to be worse and worse – more and more painful, peeling off years of your life like an onion!'

Michael Grade, then Head of Channel 4, said that he had read in his local newspaper, the *Hampstead and Highgate Express*, an agony column which began, 'I make no apology for returning to the subject of premature ejaculation because my post bag is full of it!'

I suppose that many of us keep in mind the memory of some enchanted place that is forever a joy to recall. Whether or not one returns to it the dream remains.

When in East Africa to write an article for a magazine, I was accorded splendid hospitality by the Kenya Tourist Board who placed a small aircraft at my disposal. One day we flew from Mombasa to Malindi and on to Lamu. It is Lamu that will forever remain in the windmills of my mind. We came in low over the small town of Kipini where the waters of the Tana River tumble into the Indian Ocean after rising far away in the foothills of Mount Kenya, dropping lower still over Shella, a small fishing village, with its picturesque mosque, minaret and sand dunes, we literally skimmed over the roofs of the brilliantly white Peponi Hotel until in a matter of only a few minutes we were bumping gently to rest on the airfield at Lamu.

Lamu is one of the oldest towns on the East African coast; the streets are narrow enough in places for only two camels to pass; most doors are carved and gateways are ornamental. Conversations are quiet and to hurry would be unforgivable. Much of the conversation, I was told, was about sex. Maybe I was having my leg pulled gently. At the time of my visit there was no shortage of labour and everything was spotless. I discovered that this was because many ex-Mau Mau prisoners were located there at the time.

The triangular-sailed dhows that sail between Oman and this coast have varied little since the days of Vasco da Gama. As far back as the seventh century the Omani Arabs came on expeditions down the East African coast trading silks, beads and porcelain as they went, all the time the hot breath of the khaskazi monsoon at their back, until it was time to head back to Arabia and home again laden with ebony, ivory and spices. Not forgetting slaves.

The hotel name of 'Peponi' where I stayed is a Swahili word meaning a kind of 'Paradise' – a place of coolness, rest and relief from trouble. It is situated at the entrance to Lamu Harbour and I was fascinated to learn – if my informant was correct – that Rider Haggard had stayed here with his brother, whose residence it was as the Consul, whilst he wrote *King Solomon's Mines*.

Not long ago I was watching one of those interminable travel shows on TV when I suddenly shot bolt upright, as they say. They were actually filming in Lamu. My Lamu! Still, I suppose the world no longer has any secrets. The long arm of tourism sees to that. The hotel steps still reach down to the beach from the long-pillared verandah overlooking Manda Island and the spring tides will still send the sea washing the hotel walls. Anyway, Lamu, thanks for the memory.

On that same trip to Lamu I stayed en route in Nairobi. There I was overjoyed to find the hotel featured Leslie Hutchinson, better known as Hutch. What an unexpected thrill to sit back and be entertained after dinner by the man who in his heyday was likened to Noel Coward. Hutch took London by storm in the 1920s and 1930s. He was the leading cabaret performer in the country, so it was a total surprise to find him there. His rich baritone voice was almost as when he used to top the bill at the Cafe de Paris – I say almost, because there was, of course, less of the fire as age and alcohol had begun to take its toll. But chatting to him afterwards one could find in his impeccable upper-class accent still something of the charm and fire that brought him lovers such as Lady Mountbatten, Ivor Novello, Princess Marina of Greece, Tallulah Bankhead and Cole Pole. Hearing *A Nightingale Sang In Berkeley Square* in downtown Nairobi by the master himself was certainly a bonus.

A day or two before we had spent the night at Treetops. Here one had the remarkable experience of watching whilst some of the big game of the forest came by in the night. The hotel was virtually in the tree tops with walkways to connect the rooms high above an area about the size of a football pitch which was illuminated. The approach to Treetops was with an armed guard and one reached the hotel-in-the-trees by stout rope ladders.

It was here – or if not on this actual site, in one identical to and immediately next to it as the original was, I think, destroyed by an accidental fire – that Princess Elizabeth was told by her husband, the Duke of Edinburgh, that she had become Queen. A journalist in the royal press party had heard by telephone from London that King George VI had died in his sleep. The Queen took it calmly, though it was little over a week since she had said goodbye to her father at London Airport. The new Queen's immediate concern was to let the people in Australia and New Zealand know that she would not be able to continue the royal tour which it had originally been intended that her father should make. Meanwhile, in London the Accession Council was doing its job without the presence of the new monarch. It was already dusk when the Queen arrived back at London Airport She came down the steps a slim, pale figure in mourning black. The Prime Minister, Winston Churchill, and the Opposition Leader, Clement Attlee, both greeted her on arrival.

I am staying in a hotel beloved of Winston Churchill, in a city whose walls were built in the twelfth century from the red mud of the plains around it. It is Marrakesh, the 'Pink City', and my abiding memory is of Djemaa el Fna, the main square in the heart of the old city. Just what it is like today I cannot say. Maybe the rough red earth has been replaced by black tarmac, but the enchantment surely remains. Here there will be jugglers, acrobats, snake charmers, drummers and quite possibly there is still a man dressed as a woman with a tea tray on his head: and, of course, the monkeys and the watermen calling out 'Lunaa'. Veiled women dangle jewellery, guides try and entice one to accompany them to the souk and amidst the growing sense of mystery there is the reality that other women want only to sell bread – round loaves in brown and white and black. By night the square is lit by the surrounding cafes and the mystery deepens into the shadows where can be heard the cries of the men with magic potions and some who have religious stories to tell. You can sit on a top terrace of one of the cafes whilst the sun goes down and you look out on to the food stalls with their long metal benches and catch the faint smell of kebabs, fried fish, pigs' trotters and the rest.

I once wrote a story entitled 'Murder In Morocco'. I am afraid, as one publisher said, it was too Boys' Own stuff whereas today it needed to be more Indiana Jones! But the writing of it drew me several times to Morocco with its sounds and smells and colours; to the Atlas Mountains and the coast, though not to Agadir, for I knew it soon after its earthquake. Now it is too cosmopolitan, brassy and touristy from what I hear. But there was, of course, the old Tangier and parties where Barbara Hutton, the Woolworth heiress, would appear with her latest young escort and a bar where many famous faces were sometimes to be seen.

The power of good PR is such that it behoves the consultant to be wary of what he or she is really helping to promote and, without wanting to appear smug, I have turned down assignments for that reason – companies with 'get rich' schemes, West End establishments that were really fronting luxury massage parlours and the rest. There was certainly nothing shady about the lady who ran Property Packs in North London. She appeared to have a good business idea. It was that your house purchase would be handled in its entirety from A to Z, including carrying out inspections, finding a mortgage, and so on. She was, I think, Czechoslovakian. Her manner was one of supreme confidence.

I began to place some quite good success stories for her in the London evenings and North London weeklies. We had arranged a fair and equitable fee for my services. One day she invited me to have breakfast with a friend, Anthony Dobson, in his flat at Prince's Gate, overlooking Hyde Park. I did not stay long, but understood that Anthony Dobson was reorganising the business, Property Packs, to be part of a much larger enterprise.

'We are going to make a lot of money,' the lady told me, meaning herself, of course, not me. I said that I was not impressed by Mr Dobson.

Events moved very quickly after that and I was invited to offices on the edge of the City. Now the company was to be known as Homes Assured and new desks and equipment were being hurriedly moved into at least two floors; people were being interviewed for jobs and the lady was over-spilling with confidence. Would I arrange a press coverage for the launch in their new offices? I did not feel easy with what appeared to be their new business plan. At this time it had just become possible for tenants in council flats to buy them. The pressure was on at Home Assured to obtain lists of tenants likely to want to purchase. They would call upon them, endeavour to arrange a mortgage and at the same time press to arrange an extension for a larger bathroom than that which existed. The hunt was on to somehow obtain lists of tenants from councils. The particular kind of tough, wannabe salesmen I saw coming in for interview for jobs told its own story. There would, I felt, be some pressure on these unsuspecting tenants.

Accordingly, I did not give this opening my full treatment and attention. I was careful who I asked from the media as I was uneasy at what lay behind the hurried preparations at Homes Assured. I felt that it was not deserving of big coverage. I wanted to know more about what they were up to.

Sir Edward du Cann suddenly appeared at the offices and, on meeting me and hearing that I was once a prospective Conservative candidate, greeted me in such a manner as to suggest that we were old friends. He occupied an important position in the Conservative Party as a former minister and was the £400,000 per annum Chairman of Lonrho. I had in fact never met him before and wondered how he fitted into this company.

Various shareholders began to arrive and I got the impression that some were resident in the Isle of Man. There was an air of investors moving in on a good thing. I began to wonder at such enthusiasm. Obviously there were to be some rich pickings.

As the shareholders assembled that day I decided I did not like the set-up at all. The poor unsuspecting council house tenants appeared to be easy meat. Accordingly, when Dobson said that they wanted to have a big launch party at the Royal Garden Hotel in Knightsbridge and he wanted me to handle it, on returning to my office in Bath I wrote and posted my resignation. After a tussle I got my account settled.

On 16 September 1989 the *Daily Telegraph* reported, 'Failed mortgage broker, Homes Assured Corporation has an estimated deficiency of £9.6 million – 50 per cent higher than expected – an angry creditors' meeting heard yesterday.' (This had been incurred in about twenty months.) Homes Assured and four subsidiaries, also in liquidation, had fifty company cars, including top-of-the-range BMWs, many being described as 'less than utilitarian'. It was disclosed that Homes Assured received money from up to 15,000 council tenants seeking to buy their own homes.

The *Daily Telegraph*, Saturday, 28 August 1993 reported, 'Anthony Dobson, the founder of Homes Assured, was convicted yesterday of two charges of deception by an Old Bailey jury.'

I did promotional work for two footballers, Colin Todd and Roy McFarland, two fine players. This brought me into contact with Brian Clough, Manager of Derby County. Never a dull moment, would best sum up my dealings with him. 'Cloughie' came over big and strong. You either loved him or hated him. I loved him! He and his sidekick, Peter Taylor, always treated me like a gentleman. But neither treated fools gladly and were not slow to express their feelings.

Together they fashioned teams of footballers whose eloquence was in their boots – honest players who gave of their very best because they were inspired particularly by a man whom they knew to be special and who knew how to coach players.

He loved to tell the story of how one afternoon in his office he picked up the telephone to the dressing room and ordered one of Forest's apprentices to brew some tea. (He was then Manager of Nottingham Forest.) 'Hey, young man,' said Cloughie, using his favourite term of address, 'you do know who I am?' 'Yes, Mr Clough,' came the answer, 'but do you know who I am?' 'Course not!' he roared. 'Then make your own bloody tea,' said the boy. 'I'm busy cleaning the boots!'

He made it his business to find out the identity of that quick-witted young lad – and promptly gave him a rise.

Cloughie either took to you or he didn't; no half measures. I am glad to say that we got along famously. He could put the fear of God into his players, though. He carried a small notebook in which he jotted down reminders. For instance, he would go striding into a hotel reception room where the lads would be sitting around relaxing the day before a game.

'You,' he would address one of them, whom he caught sitting with his feet up on a chair, 'I've told you before about that. You're down for a tenner!' And so he would jot it down in his little book as a fine to be paid up within seven days and to go to a charity. Cloughie frowned on the lads swearing and insisted on good conduct on the field. What an example Derby County and Nottingham Forest were in those days compared with some of our football teams now.

I was with Toddy in his house one day when the phone rang. 'Yes, Boss, no I didn't do it yet ... right, for sure tomorrow.' 'What's that about?' I asked. 'Oh – I haven't put my name down in the haircutting book – and he's fined me £10!'

It was a pity that Peter Taylor and he later parted company. They had played together in the North-East and in management they were a formidable team. Peter had a huge knack of spotting talent and Brian could inspire them and mould them into a team. Before a game he would have them all together while he put a ball on a towel in the middle of the changing room – and almost make it talk. 'That's yours,' he would say. 'Now get after it.'

If a player had a bad game he didn't tear into him after the final whistle as some managers might do. He would, in fact, say very little except, 'My office, ten o'clock Monday!' That would ensure that the rest of the player's weekend would be one of considerable discomfort. Cloughie was perhaps one of the greatest of all football managers.

Barbara, Cloughie's wife, was delightful and understanding. I remember sitting next to her at Roy McFarland's wedding reception. Suddenly Cloughie disappeared. After about a quarter of an hour I enquired of her if she thought he was all right. 'Oh, don't

Opposite: *A happy picture of Brian Clough acknowledging the terrific welcome he received at the ground of Nottingham Forest when he arrived on the day a stand was named after him and a bronze bust unveiled in his honour.* (Picture by PA.)

worry, Ken,' she said laughing. 'He's always up to something!'
Sure enough, Brian was soon back whispering his apologies. He
had in fact gone off to present a trophy and make a speech. He
just didn't want to let anyone down. You never knew with
Cloughie what was going to happen next.

There was the time when Ian Storey-Moore, the Nottingham
Forest forward, and I had become good friends and I was promoting him. The following is an example of the excitement that
Cloughie could create. It was when he was still managing Derby
County. Ian was under a good deal of scrutiny by Manchester
United and he phoned me to ask me to join him as Frank O'Ferral,
the Manager of Manchester United, wanted to interview him. It
was arranged for them to meet privately – away from the media
– at a hotel in the Midlands. I joined him there.

Frank O'Ferral duly arrived and Ian and he met privately. It
should be appreciated that I was not then and never have been
an agent. I helped promote a player commercially, but had no
dealings whatsoever with his money for playing. I was therefore
not present at discussions about money on that day. Their meeting
together did not take long and Ian was suitably impressed. However, no sooner had Frank left on his way to London, presumably
confident that a deal was in the offing, than we had a phone call
to say that Cloughie was on his way. At this, the Nottingham
Forest directors, who had been in the background, took to their
cars and disappeared in a cloud of dust. Cloughie duly arrived,
greeted me and Ian and at once went into a private discussion
with him. Afterwards Ian was ecstatic. The moment that Cloughie
departed he told me, 'He is fantastic – he's gone over tactics with
me. I know exactly what is expected of me – and the money is
good!'

It all happened quickly after that. Derby County always stayed
at the Midland Hotel, Derby prior to a home match. It was already
Friday and Ian and I were invited to stay at the Midland that
evening. Amazingly, Cloughie had everything moving ahead. Ian
met the Derby County players that evening and to my surprise
next afternoon Ian, who was not on duty with Forest due to a
slight injury, was asked suddenly by Cloughie to join him out on
the pitch before the match, whereupon be introduced him through

the loudspeaker system to the crowd as Derby's latest capture. Brian Clough had this amazing ability to make things happen, but even this seemed a miracle.

I wrote and filed a 1,000-word story on it all for Frank Butler and it appeared in the *News of the World* the next morning. They paid me handsomely.

A sequel to this was some time later. Cloughie had to answer for some irregularities at the office of the Football League, which was situated at St Anne's in Cumberland. Hearing of this I at once interrupted my visit to the Open at Muirfield and drove down to offer evidence on his behalf if required, though this did not happen.

J.L. Manning, the famous columnist, ran a half-page story in the *London Evening Standard* on 9 March 1972 as follows:

Manchester City's cheque-napping of Rodney Marsh was a public relations flop compared with Manchester United's capture of Ian Storey-Moore.

But then, my old pal Splashy Johnstone wasn't in the middle of it.

Johnstone was working with me on one of Lord Kemsley's newspapers when Manchester City's chairman of the early 50's wrote to his Lordship demanding my instant dismissal, instead of the more usual slow one.

His was the extraordinary view that I had criticised Manchester City for not releasing Roy Paul and Ray Clarke to play for Wales against England merely to enhance my prospect of winning Pontypridd for the Tories in 1951.

Extraordinary, because there was only a 23,000 majority against me.

Splashy and I roared with laughter at Lord Kemsley's reply to Manchester City.

It said: 'Dear Mr Smith, thank you for your letter about our Mr Manning. It was very interesting to me personally. I am President of the Welsh FA. Yours sincerely, Kemsley.'

My nickname for the sole owner of Kenneth Johnstone Associates came from his habit of splashing fantastic ideas all over the place, but only soaking the right people.

He is an oddly exciting Graham Greene character who has

organised El Alamein nights; introduced all-in wrestling to TV, and nearly got fired by Associated Rediffusion for having such crazy ideas; insured Winifred Atwell against hijacking; floated life-jackets off the North African coast for Uffa Fox; tried to import snow-flakes for a ski-run on Hampstead Heath and said he got the idea while learning marketing with Procter and Gamble.

Storey-Moore was a PR man's dream. 'I didn't think of it,' said Johnstone, 'because although I'm good, I'm not that good.'

'All I did was to work the PR at a nice pace so it didn't get gobbled up all in one killing, and tell him that Manchester was a better selling area than Derby.'

'So you didn't arrange the transfer?'

Lovely Story

'Good Lord, no. It was a lovely story, but all I did was to offer advice. I don't deal with transfers and club contracts. I'm not a 10 per center hanging around dressing rooms.

'You see, these players are for the most part quite helpless when it comes to business, and off-field, there's a huge business building up for them, as there is in the whole field of sport and leisure, but it will take time for all this to happen. A decade from now we will be talking astronomical sums about the transfer of players and about their wages in the game.'

Johnstone thinks there is an almost certainty of agents being used to buy and sell footballers for clubs.

'Its not for me, but it's obvious that when the fees get up to £500,000 specialist businessmen will be needed. The League can look askance at the whole thing. But it's their system, and they will need experts to run it properly.'

In the Storey-Moore case things just happened.

'The clubs did not come out of it very well, but let's face it, the muddle was marvellous PR.'

Splashy says he has discovered that the way to sell the Concorde is the way to sell soup and fish fingers.

'I've proved it with North Sea gas, as well as aircraft,' he said. 'Football is just another marketing job. Pity Rodney Marsh wasn't one of mine. What a double that would have been, with Storey-Moore.

Lovely stuff to lap up, and all very pleasant and harmless. I had lunch with Rodney once. Just before the sweet he said that he wanted to go and check his car. He didn't come back. Nor did he ever thank me for the lunch!'

Yes, I like Johnstone.

He will PR all that's good in life except cricket.

'Sponsors can't quicken the dead,' he says.

Pity that. Because I thought one day he would make a splendid job of my obituary.

I always made it clear that I had nothing to do with players' pay and indeed at that time the kind of agent we know today as representing players did not exist. I was not, in fact, an agent.

I was with Winifred Atwell when Belita, the famous skater, who was starring in 'Champagne on Ice' at the Hippodrome, gave a novel 'stunt' birthday party. Frankie Howard, Sally Anne Howes and her father Bobby, Pat Kirkwood, Frances Day, Shani Wallis, Bernard Braden and dozens of other stars turned up.

The Hippodrome stage had been turned into an ice rink and as the guests arrived each was handed a pair of skating boots. Winifred, among several others, had never skated in her life, but in no time she had joined in slipping and sliding about in hilarious fashion.

Belita cut her twenty-ninth birthday cake – even the table itself was on ice – and we drank champagne – obviously on ice – to toast her as the clock struck midnight. Then she gave a fantastic skating display just to show us how easy it was!

Frankie Howard invented a game in which he scrabbled around on the ice whilst he held an apple on his head and in no time was leading a bizarre kind of hokey-cokey. 'Musical Chairs on Ice' was another favourite, but gradually the constant connection with the ice started to tell and I know that Winny, for one, began to feel the cold. She had drawn the attention of many of the press cameramen, who were requesting her to 'Do it again' when she made some spectacular falls. She had to leave early. 'I long to get to bed with some hot water bottles,' she told me. She had grown used to winter since leaving Trinidad, but this, she said, was 'Too much!' Actually she got quite a chill through it all.

I was to include her later as a client, looking after her promotion. To appreciate what Winifred Atwell came to mean to the British public, one has to think back, of course, to pre-television days; to the times when variety was really the spice of entertainment. The great days of the music hall. She arrived from Trinidad ostensibly to complete her studies at the Royal Academy of Music with the intention of establishing herself on the concert platform. Nothing was further from her mind than that she should become a music hall and radio entertainer.

Her mother, back home in Trinidad, was intent on her daughter pursuing her undoubted musical talents, but when Winny appeared in a full-length picture in the London *Tatler* she began to approve of what she called 'the lighter stage' – what she really meant was the music hall.

Early on in London Winny met Lou Leversohn who was to guide her as a husband and friend. He helped her get her first disc cut. It was 'Gipsy Samba'. Jack Jackson, who had a popular radio show, helped to boost her recording of 'Jezebel' and she got a weekly Sunday spot on Radio's *Starlight Hour*. She became so busy that she found herself taking over Pat Kirkwood's spot in *Fancy Free* at the Prince of Wales and doing her own act across at the Brixton Empire on the same evening. She at one time lived around the corner from the theatre in a tatty little flat in Brixton: her wildest extravagance was then a ticket for the gallery to see the stars, never dreaming that she would become one of them.

Her own arrangement of 'Swanee River Boogie' suddenly became top favourite with juke box enthusiasts in the United States. She recorded Litoeff's *Piano Concerto Symphonique* with Mantovani and his 120-piece orchestra. 'Nothing can ever beat that,' she told Lou. That was in 1951. Little did she realise what lay ahead.

She had made a recording, 'Cross Hands Boogie' and the record company had a conference about a backing number. Frank Lee, the recording manager, suggested an old tune, 'The Black and White Rag', but neither he nor anyone else could find a copy. In desperation he put on overalls and searched in the cellars of the music publishers, Frances Day and Hunter. There, after several hours, he found a pile of 800 copies of an old dance album and in it 'Black and White Rag' was one of the numbers. This was great news, but when they heard the playback of Winny's recording of the number, they were not impressed. Then Lou hit it. 'Winnie – we should do this on an old honky-tonk pianner!' he said. They dashed out at once to start looking for one. It was a gimmick that was to make Winifred Atwell world famous.

She composed 'Coronation Rag' which sold 23,000 advance copies by Phillips. In three weeks Frances Day and Hunter had sales of 70,000 copies of its sheet music. In June of Coronation Year 'Latin Quarter', with Max Bygraves and Winny starring, opened in Blackpool and every seat was sold a month before opening night.

Then the BBC televised what they called a mammoth 'Stars at Blackpool' show from the Opera House. It featured Eve Boswell, then appearing at the Opera House; Morecambe and Wise from the Winter Gardens; the Three Monarchs from North Pier and from the Hippodrome Max Bygraves and Winny; and, of course, Reginald Dixon, the Tower organist, played his world famous signature tune 'I Do Like to Be Beside the Seaside'.

Winny appeared in the film *Shoulder Arms* with Diana Dors and Frank Randle. Diana was a gem and to have any dealings with her was just great fun. Another film she made was *Pardon My French* with Frankie Howard. In one scene in which she was dressed by St John Roper, Winny played a huge grand piano backed by fifty girls each wearing only ostrich feathers.

She had reduced her waistline considerably by the time we were up in Blackpool again to do a season at the Queen's Theatre where we had a lot of fun with other show people who were appearing in the town. Hylda Baker, the comedienne, for instance. She had a Rolls with 'HB' monogrammed on the doors. The great joke was that Hylda had a pet monkey always travel with her and nobody liked to 'follow her in' as they say because of the smell in the dressing room.

Winifred was a very big star in Australia, where she was the first Trinidadian to be given the accolade of 'Freedom of the Country' as an honorary Australian citizen. I was so sorry when they told me of their plans to return. Winny always spoke enthusiastically about the country and obviously adored it. 'Australians have the right idea about life. They work a five-day week and at the weekends flock to the beaches. I've never seen so many wonderful beaches as there are around Sydney. You would love it!' Lou and she had a beach house at Bilgold, twenty miles out of Sydney and after the Saturday night performance would motor there. 'It is sheer heaven,' she told me. A joke between us, incidentally, was that it was terrific to be a housewife who cannot wash dishes because of her high priced hands! (Insurance policies stipulated that she was not to wash up.) I used to tease her because of this and refer to her as Lady Winifred following her accolade by the Australian Government. But there was no doubt that she was a sensation when she first did a show in Sydney and this is how she described it to me.

'I shall never forget that fabulous, glamorous opening night at the Tivoli, Sydney.

'When David Martin came round to wish me luck before the show began he said it was probably the most distinguished audience the Tivoli had ever seen. The Lord Mayor had brought a party, and there was another from Government House.

'My opening gown was a dazzling white velvet nylon embroidered in a tracery design in silver, with deep bands of silver-grey and rose pink round the hem, another St John Roper triumph. I wore a new set of diamond costume jewellery, and I scintillated and shimmered and glittered ... literally. For I was shaking with fright. My teeth were chattering. My hands had the jitters.

'Were they going to like me out there in that packed house? Had Lou's tremendous press build-up been overdone? Were they expecting too much? Maybe it was better to creep in quietly and make your impact with an unexpected whang!

'It was my first experience of Australian audiences, and I had heard they were warm-hearted and responsive – IF they liked you.

'But I had also heard they could be pretty tough if they didn't.

'Well, they liked me, thank the Lord!

'I am accustomed to excited audiences, but I have never known anything like the non-stop roar that shook the Tivoli to its foundations when I took my calls! Again and again I gave them the encores they shouted for, but at last I had to stop, and then I just stood there with bowed head, the lump in my throat almost choking me, afraid to move lest I broke the spell of this out-of-this-world reception. Bouquets kept being pushed on me, I held as many as I could, they started piling up on the floor all around.

'The other artists sent me a lovely bunch of red roses. I had a hard job not to start crying, I was in such a state of emotion.

'I couldn't speak when they cried speech, I was too choked. A man in the circle yelled out, "England can keep The Ashes, if we can keep you, Winnie."

'And that just about finished me, but I bit my lip and took a deep breath, and kept grinning.

'Eighteen curtain calls later they finally dropped the tabs and David Martin said, "You can stay here for ten years if you like, Winnie, you'd fill every house to capacity, I'm certain."

'What a welcome!

'People crowded into the dressing-room to congratulate me but the one I remember most is an old-timer, Frank Bridgewater, a fan who had made the 1,500-mile journey alone and unaided from Broken Hill, New South Wales, for the opening performance.

'Frank was blind, that's what made it such an achievement. His wife ran a dancing school and he had wanted to meet me ever since he had heard "Black and White Rag". "It makes me feel happy," Frank told me, and I remembered how Poppa had said the same thing when I played it over to him in Trinidad. Things like that make you glad you're a star.'

The *Sydney Press* ran big stories with pictures. The *Sun-Herald* was the nicest report:

The Tivoli rocked and rumbled last night – not only to the piano rhythm of Winifred Atwell but to uninhibited hand and hoof applause of a wildly enthusiastic audience. She came on late in the programme and did not stay long, just long enough to survey in a few short pieces the entire history of jazz, boogie, swing and jive, and even present a tidy interpretation of Grieg. She is more than a pianist, she is a personality, and she can convey across the footlights her own, sensuous feeling of music, her own delight in both classical and modern rhythm.

Back to their decision to return to Australia. When they left London Airport I arranged a farewell PR stunt that really pleased Lou, the old showman that he was. There had been a spate of hijackings of well-known people, so I put out a press release that before leaving Winny had been insured for a record sum. The amount of £250,000 or even £1 million was bandied about. Come departure time, I had a huge turnout of press and cameramen gather at the airport; a record number for any star, according to the airline.

'Show us the insurance policy, Winny!' they called out. Anticipating this, I had already given her an important-looking document. She waved it over her head. The cameras whirred. (It was, incidentally, my old laundry list folded to look impressive.)

'Come on over, Ken,' she wrote to me later. 'We can easily fix you up with the big theatre corporation doing PR work or taking a show out on the road, or doing some television.'

Winny was so persuasive that I decided to join her. She had played the Mandarin at Hong Kong on the way over and she now offered to arrange for me to break my journey for a couple of days and stay there as she knew the management well. This was typical of her thoughtfulness. Besides we had become very good friends.

I was beginning to seriously formulate plans for going out to Australia and take her up on the invitation, when one morning I had a phone call from *The Times* in London. It was the Obituaries Editor. Winny, he told me, had died suddenly. Could I help him with copy for the next morning's paper?

Cubby Broccoli could not have been more helpful when he received me in his office at Pinewood. I already knew some of the executives working on the Bond films. As the gag about the Broccolis goes – they may sound like a vegetable, but they're not green!

Cubby started the Bonds with Sean Connery in *Dr No* in 1962. His delightful daughter, Barbara, and stepson, Wilson, now carry on with great success. Harry Saltzman, his co-producer, stocky and slightly plump, never had time for 'small talk'.

'Superman', 'Batman', 'Rocky', 'Die Hard', 'Lethal Weapon' and 'Star Wars' all have dozens of stars, but the Bond films – all nineteen of them – are centred on Bond himself. Sean Connery, Roger Moore and Pierce Brosnan – a Scot, an Englishman and an Irishman – are, of course, the three big-time Bonds, whilst George

Lazenby and Timothy Dalton were never really convincing. I went up in the same lift as George Lazenby at the Hilton on our way to the press conference for *On His Majesty's Secret Service*. He appeared to be sweating with nerves. He was, I suppose, an unexpected choice. I think it was a chocolate commercial in which he had been appearing that gave him a little bit of publicity, but he had already been spotted and given the break. At that press conference Diana Rigg was in terrific form. The film was to be set partly in Switzerland. 'How will you manage when, I understand, you can't ski?' she was asked. 'Same as he will have to manage and he can't act!' was her laughing reply indicating Lazenby.

David Middlemas, the charming and highly competent Production Manager for the Bond films, was a good friend and through him I was able to visit the set at Pinewood quite often. Art work, direction and casting were all superbly carried out.

The typical American all-action hero has never got near Bond, who is all style and no sweat. He is marketable throughout the world with about 25 per cent to 30 per cent of the gross takings coming from the USA. (Most big films take between 50 per cent and 75 per cent from the States.) The Bond films are seen by about 500 million people in their first five years.

Sex, violence and the stiff upper lip proved to be a captivating cocktail, though with Lazenby I think they tried to make Bond too caring and he was certainly not the easiest of stars to deal with, from all accounts.

Cubby knew the dangers and temptation of what is known as 'star loading'. 'We go for very competent actors, not for stars,' he said. That's what sunk Batman. They have the best action technicians in the world at the brilliant Pinewood studios, plus a solid supporting cast, including three or four babes, one of whom must die, a director and a studio willing to act as little more than a banker. Publicity and promotion are mostly and unusually done in-house.

Pierce Brosnan is probably the best of all the Bonds. He grew up in Putney in South London, having been born in Ireland. He is extremely popular on the set. Of Connery he says, 'He WAS Bond. He is the one I grew up with. He was the whole era of Bond. Connery had a style about him that I can neither emulate nor would I want to.' What is a fact is that whichever Bond you fancy, he is a very very ruthless man.

Ian Fleming, as I write elsewhere, was my idol. Noel Coward once said of him, 'I think James Bond was Ian's dream of what he would like to have been.' Ian had worked at the Admiralty during the War and had, in fact, been in contact with genuine spies and the MI Chief in Paris. I went to his house in Victoria several times and met his wife, Anne.

In December 1985 he had completed a second novel to follow upon his *Casino Royale* of two years earlier. This tale was entitled *Moonraker* and introduced a well-drawn villain, Hugo Drax, and a climactic card game. I believe that earlier when the germ of the James Bond idea was growing in his mind and he was hatching the plot for *Casino Royale* whilst at their modest but idyllically located cliff-top place in Jamaica, Anne protested about him always scribbling away in notebooks. Incidentally, he got the name James Bond from reading a local travel guide which was under the name of James Bond.

Perhaps the most thrilling of all fights in which James Bond was engaged was that epic struggle in a railway compartment in *From Russia With Love*. The other man was Robert Shaw. He was a great guy and in real life married to lovely Mary Ure. I remember once I was with him and Stanley Baker and others in Cardiff for a big open-air fight. After dinner at the Angel we drove back to London in the early hours with Stan at the wheel of his Jaguar more like Kay Don. It was almost as gripping as watching any James Bond movie, and was one of those hilarious and joyous occasions that stick firmly in one's mind. When we arrived back Bob Shaw took me to his place, got out his beautiful yellow Rolls Royce and we sped off to Spitalfields to get an early breakfast with the meat porters.

Incidentally, Stan – or Sir Stanley Baker to be precise – had the splendid penthouse on the Thames opposite the Houses of Parliament later occupied by Jeffrey Archer, and he used to delight in showing his amazing array of golf putting practice devices.

An afterthought about the Bond and other British film successes: how badly Margaret Thatcher let down the film industry in this country. You only have to see the latest Bond film to realise the brilliance of our production capabilities. For instance, those stunt men, whether they are rolling the boat in the Thames 360° in mid-air – no rehearsals, they only need to do it once – or at full throttle over the top of another launch with a double turn in mid-air, are terrific – and British! John Major was no better than Margaret Thatcher in this ill-advised attitude to the film industry.

Through thick and thin, danger and triumph, James Bond has had an unfailing ally. Sitting at her desk, going about her normal secretarial duties, or on the phone, we always knew that she would be there to soothe him, to encourage him with a knowing nod – an oasis of calm and understanding amidst high-level talk, top secret plans and the odd bit of sexual innuendo. She is, of course, Miss Moneypenny. Over the course of fourteen films she was on screen in total for less than an hour, but she became an integral part of the James Bond epics.

At twenty she was a Hollywood starlet, playing opposite Ronald Reagan and was once photographed in *Life* as one of a group of promising actresses which included Marilyn Monroe. She is an erstwhile columnist for the *Toronto Sun*. Her real name is Lois Maxwell, a Canadian, tall and lean with a very tough cosmopolitan air, who at twenty-four married an English TV executive, Peter Marriott. Peter was 6 foot 6 inches tall with good looks and was, in fact, screen tested for the James Bond part, without success. Three weeks after her screen test for the first Bond film, Peter had his first heart attack. She was thirty-three with a daughter of four and a boy of two. She became the breadwinner. She tried for one part in the film, got it, and then asked for the role of Miss Moneypenny and got it. Her pay was around £100 a day, with each film rarely more than a day's work. So life has been tough and became tougher still when Peter had his second and fatal attack.

I first met her at a health farm where I can tell you she was huge fun. At that time Peter had begun to find his ill-health a worry and I remember she tried hard to get him work. There was some small property in Canada, which helped out, but she had a difficult time.

Now after all these years she is sitting opposite me in my lounge and we are laughing our heads off. Tall, lean, worldly looking and of infinite charm, she has a great personality. We are talking about that old adage, 'You are as young as you feel!'

She lives in Frome, Somerset, near her daughter, who is married to a graphic designer. Miss Moneypenny in Frome! Surely James Bond himself cannot be far away. She told me that kids sometimes ring her doorbell with the obvious excitement of seeing Miss Moneypenny from the James Bond films. If she answers the door, they usually stand and just gape in disbelief.

Her son, Christian, is an exploration geologist in Australia. She has visited him there and in Mexico, the Yukon and Botswana, including accompanying him into gold mines and the jungle.

I have enjoyed some great James Bond post-production parties hosted by David Middlemass. An excellent cook, he used to put on some marvellous get-togethers at his place. At one of these I became friendly with Jessie Matthews and this resulted in many a long telephone chat afterwards.

Thora Hird was another regular at these parties. Everyone's idea of a 'real trouper' she was always turned out in lively colours. From her well-coiffured domed head with the aureole of burnished curls rising like fine wire to her dainty shoes, she was bright in appearance and in manner. What a star! All the parts we've seen her play – the battle-axe, mothers-in-law, the thorny wives and the rest, and, of course, her magnificent performance as Doris in Alan Bennett's monologue *A Cream Cracker Under the Settee*. Thora loves to talk and she was always so proud of her daughter, Janette Scott, who married the singer Mel Tormé. Thora then lived in the tiny mews flat in Bayswater that she shared with her husband, Jimmy Scott. They met in her home town of Morecambe when he was a drummer in a sixteen-piece orchestra and she was in rep, making her stage debut in 1912 at the age of eight weeks as the illegitimate child of the wronged village maiden. Since when she has never stopped working.

But the biggest surprise was when I was ready to leave hospital after having a length of steel taken from my leg following my bad road accident. The unit had just returned from Japan, where they had made *You Only Live Twice*. I was asked to their party where a certain lady wanted to meet me. Nobody would reveal her identity beforehand. Imagine my anticipation when, a trifle weak, the taxi conveyed me to the party. I was to discover whom they had arranged to look after me. Why, it was none other than Ava Gardner! 'Come sit with me, Ken, I'll make you feel better,' she told me. Make me feel better? I began to go weak at the knees. After all, had she not once been described as the most beautiful woman in the world? Mickey Rooney said she was 'A woman of strong passions.' He ought to know: he was her first husband. A boy star, everything came to him far too quickly. The marriage collapsed after a year due to his drinking and outlandish behaviour.

She was to become perhaps the most sumptuous Hollywood demi-goddess of the post-war era and there she was prepared to give me her full attention! I could see why so many men had fallen helplessly for her.

Band leader Artie Shaw was husband Number Two. In 1950 she became the love of Frank Sinatra, but their two years of marriage degenerated into rows that became so public even Hollywood raised its eyebrows.

Her great success a few years before we met had been Joseph L. Mankiewicz's *The Barefoot Contessa* (1954), which was all about Maria Vargas, a lively Spanish cabaret dancer who was attracted to Hollywood, only to be destroyed by its double standards. Ava went very near to enacting the plot in reverse in real life when she left MGM and settled in Madrid, where she became the lover of the great matador, Luis Miguel Dominguin. She also became a close friend of Ernest Hemingway, she told me. She then moved to London and when we met she was living in Chelsea. Later she was to move to Ennismore Gardens near Knightsbridge.

'Did you learn to dance flamenco?' I asked her.

'Of course – and frequently, but without knickers, darling,' she rocked with laughter.

This was Ava. Deliciously irreverent, sexy glossy lips and big expressive eyes. In company with many American film stars she loved England. When she moved here it was to escape what at that time London managed to do without – the harassment of celebrities, except for some pop stars. That was before *Hello!* magazine began their expensive intrusion into other people's lives. It's remarkable how some people, irrespective of who they are, will barter their privacy. She told me that she loved to walk across Hyde Park, unrecognisable in a sweatsuit and scarf, with her little black corgi named Cara.

Sitting next to her, one felt immediately at home – she was so

worldly, so knowing; the sort of woman to whom you would suddenly find yourself telling your secrets. Hollywood was at that time closer to London than it is now and the major film studios had full production facilities. Her pet hate was Margaret Thatcher and she certainly came over to me as a confirmed left-winger.

Ava was born on Christmas Eve 1922 in Grabtown, North Carolina, the seventh child of a poor sharecropper. A talent scout saw her picture, taken aged twenty-one years, in the window of a New York photographer's studio and as a result she was signed up by Louis B. Mayer.

Of Sinatra she told me, 'Frank was one of those compulsive womanisers who also enjoyed "a night out with the boys". You know, he was also nearly always in pursuit of women.' She listed them for me, 'Anita Ekberg, Lauren Bacall, Marilyn Monroe, Kim Novak, Natalie Wood – and many not so well known – but, believe me, he could go off them just as suddenly.' With Ava, though, he encountered a woman whose allure was as powerful and careless as his own. Their relations were tempestuous and after they married in 1951 she treated him with a contempt that only inflamed his passion. Although they did not divorce until 1957, she had pretty well sent him on his way.

I got the impression that Ava had a high regard for Gregory Peck, with whom she had starred in *The Snows of Kilimanjaro* for 20th Century Fox. She regarded him, I think, as a true friend.

When we talked about her film, *The Little Hut*, she had obviously enjoyed working with Errol Flynn and the two English-born stars, David Niven and Stewart Grainger. I told her that I had met the latter's mother, Mrs Stewart, in Bournemouth where he used to be a motor car salesman.

I was sorry when the evening ended. I suppose that we had never stopped talking. Ava liked to be escorted sometimes by handsome young black men and on this occasion she had with her Freddie Davis. He gave me a 45 record he had just made in Spain to his own lyrics 'He's very good, Ken,' she told me. 'Try and get him some work!'

* * *

Opposite: *An evening with Ava. (Picture by* Camera Press, *London.)*

I lived in Pimlico in Dolphin Square on the north bank of the Thames between Vauxhall and Chelsea bridges, probably the best known block of flats in London and according to the *Guinness Book of Records* containing the largest number of flats or apartments under one roof in Europe. Guides on the river pleasure boats point to it and describe it as containing luxury flats in which live, and have lived, the famous, the infamous and the wealthy. One American travel writer, in fact, described it as a 'minicity'.

There are 1,200 flats around a 3½-acre garden, with an indoor swimming pool, squash courts, a tennis court, croquet lawn, saunas and steam rooms, conference and entertaining rooms, a gymnasium, underground garages, a mooring on the river Thames; plus, of course, a large dining room, club rooms, an arcade of shops – and more. It is owned and managed by a non-profit making Housing Association formed by Westminster City Council in 1964. The builders, the Costain Brothers, created Dolphin Square a hundred years after Thomas Cubitt, master builder, created Pimlico, which is the area bordered by Vauxhall Bridge Road, Buckingham Palace Road, Ebury Bridge Road and the Thames.

All these facts do little to convey the extraordinary atmosphere of the place whose various wings were named after Admirals of the Fleet. I lived in Beatty House – number 507. The level of personal service was extraordinary. There were uniformed porters, wearing pill box hats and white gloves, who saluted tenants. The garage staff would bring cars round to the house entrances. Tenants and their guests in evening dress could dine and dance to a resident band. Drinks were served at tables around the swimming pool – and so forth.

Going out shopping within the arcade one would often mingle with many well-known people who lived their. Rod Laver, Ken Rosewall and Fred Stolle were there during Wimbledon. Most of the Crazy Gang had flats and also Charles Laughton, Stewart Grainger, Diana Dors, Shirley Bassey, Tony Hancock, Tommy Trinder, Katie Boyle and many others in show business and the media; plus a host of politicians as it was so handy for Westminster. Sir Oswald and Lady Mosley left their flat there to go into internment. Vassal, the spy, once lived there.

There is a lovely story told by Ken Morris, General Manager from 1974 to 1983, in his excellent book, *A History of Dolphin Square*. Bud Flanagan's widow, Curlie, decided to return to Raleigh House and was shown over a flat which Lady Bowes was leaving. There was a light bracket over an oil painting and she asked Lady Bowes if she would be leaving it. Lady Bowes said that she would and asked was there some special picture Curlie wanted to put up beneath the bracket?

'Yes, it's a picture of Bud,' she replied.

'Oh, is it an oil painting and who is it by?' asked Lady Bowes.

'Oh,' said Curlie, 'it's one of those Rembrandt things – but we've cut the head out and put in Bud's.'

My favourite of all fellow residents was Sarah Churchill. I can honestly say that I fell for her. Surely Winston's favourite daughter, she was said to be the light of his eye. She told me how her parents looked upon Chartwell Manor, their home near Westerham in Kent, as a dream place. They had moved there in April 1924 and everyone worked hard to get it into shape. Winston liked to try his hand as a 'brickie', helping to built a garden wall. It became their Christmas rendezvous. She also told me of a letter that her mother, Clementine, had written to Winston dated 26 or 27 July 1921, extolling the beauties of Chartwell Manor, which she hoped that he would buy, and adding, 'Sarah's school report has just arrived and it is excellent; she is said, however, to talk too much in class.'

I got the impression, though, that a few years later the Churchills had found the place very expensive to run and that Winston tried to make various rules on how to keep costs down. Always so bright and clearly interested in what I was saying or doing, Sarah was a warm, lovely person. She certainly knew the high and low notes of life. A highly talented actress, she danced with Fred Astaire in the film *Royal Wedding* and played opposite Dirk Bogarde in *Serious Charge*. Her marriage to Vic Oliver, the comedian, sadly broke up with a divorce and there was a tragic ending, too, to her second marriage to Anthony Beauchamp, with whom she lived mostly in New York, where he took his life. Back in London, she obviously tried hard to cope with these set-backs. I remember once when she was recuperating in a nursing home she thoughtfully invited a small

party of friends to come to her flat at Dolphin Square, where she had arranged for Harrods to deliver all manner of good things to eat and drink and then, having entertained us all liberally, but as far as she alone was concerned, abstemiously, she kissed everyone, bade us all 'night, night' and returned to her hospital bed.

When she married again, it was to Lord Audley in Spain and this drew considerable press attention, of course. Whilst the 'rat pack' were descending on the scene, some of them stumbled on the hitherto secret affair between Arthur Corbett, eldest son of Lord Rowallan, and April Ashley. Arthur had a club in Spain and April had gained some notoriety as a sex change. It was strongly rumoured that Arthur and she wanted to get married. The result of all this was that I received a desperate telephone call from Arthur in the very early hours one morning. He urgently appealed for my help and explained that the press over in Spain for Sarah's wedding had become so intrusive about him and April that he had told April to make a dash to London and come straight to me at Dolphin Square to seek my advice and protection.

It wasn't long before my next telephone call. It was from April herself. She told me that she was, in fact, already at Heathrow and had travelled with 'Toots' Lockwood, daughter of Margaret Lockwood, the actress, who also lived in Dolphin Square. They had thus far dodged the press, but were by now becoming frantic. I told them to cover their faces, get a taxi and come to me at once. I gave explicit instructions which entrance to make for on arrival. It was by then about three o'clock in the morning. The rat pack would soon be gathering, though thankfully it was slipping past last edition time for the dailies. It seemed a long-drawn-out interval before the door bell buzzed and a rather dazed April arrived. Toots had gone straight to her mother's flat. One of the windows of my flat was above a street entrance to Beatty House and it wasn't long after April's arrival that press men could be seen tumbling out of taxis or their own cars, whose headlights they then fixed onto the street entrance. Soon the door bell went.

Opposite: *My erstwhile neighbour, Sarah Churchill, second daughter of Sir Winston and Lady Churchill.*

It remained unanswered, of course. April got on the phone to Arthur in Spain, who then spoke to me again. He was a very courteous man and really appreciative of my help. The press had now left him in peace as he had refused any interviews. He thanked me profusely and asked me to do whatever I thought best to help April in any way and to play down the news of their affair. The ball, it seemed, was now firmly in my court!

My door bell continued to ring intermittently and now my phone also began ringing again. It was all about letting in press men to take pictures of, and interview, April. I would have none of it. Money was offered. I refused. More phone calls. More money was offered and refused. The TV and radio at that time were not so intrusive. I decided to contact Peter Earle, then chief crime reporter of the *News of The World*, as someone I knew and trusted. By this means, once the rat pack knew that the story had gone exclusively to one paper, they would hopefully back off: and this is what happened. The seige of Number 507 Beatty House was over. Arthur was in agreement when I phoned him and, to say the least, very relieved. Now I had to try and get some control on their behalf. Lord Rowallan was away in Tasmania where he was the Governor, and thankfully off the scene, but I made it clear that there was to be no follow-up to him nor with the Australian Press and no syndication of the story. It was, I insisted, to be about April Ashley and not the Rowallan family, though, of course, Arthur's intentions had been made clear publicly and all I could do was try and control news stories. It was very delicate.

I must say that April, who was twenty-seven, looked stunning and as her story became known, she attracted much attention. In fact, she appeared at the Astor Club in London's West End. I was there one evening watching her act, which included a song with lyrics by a friend, Mark Pollard, about 'There's been a change around here', when the phone on my table rang. It was the Chairman of the *News of The World*. They were about to start running the story in weekly instalments. She had become a minor sensation and was in demand as a model, being absolutely stunning in appearance. 'Tell me, Johnstone, there's just one thing I want to know about April Ashley. Er! Is – er – everything above board about her story?'

'Oh yes,' I was able to assure him, 'all above board.'

I have a cutting from the *Scottish Daily Express* of Tuesday, 1 May 1962:

When I Was A Cabin Boy – by April Ashley
By Ann Kenny

Glamorous model April Ashley went to a Mayfair hairdressing salon yesterday and talked about the days when she was a cabin boy. April, who is 27, is to marry Lord Rowallan's heir, Arthur Corbett, now living in Spain.

Wearing a frilly pink blouse and cream suit, April chatted about the days when she was a cabin boy on the *Pacific Fortune.*

'It was a marvellous ship. I loved being in the Merchant Navy – adored every minute of it. It's a good life.'

Heads turned in the salon to watch April's long brown hair being combed out and then brushed up high on her head – 'very feminine' style, said the stylist.

'I adore London. I don't want to settle in Spain when I marry Arthur. It's terribly gossipy. The great thing about London is that you can get lost. The only thing about this fuss over my engagement is that it may be news to my mother up North. I don't want her to be upset,' said April, peering at herself in the mirror.

She studied her chin and said: 'I must go on a diet. I'm getting too fat.'

Too Gossipy

As she left the salon she said huskily: 'I'd love a drink, but the pubs aren't open yet.'

She linked arms with model Nina Parker. 'Nina and I are going twisting tonight,' said April.

'April's simply marvellous at the Twist,' said Nina.

So much for the Arthur Corbett and April Ashley saga. Arthur remained in Spain to run his club and April, who was I think in some demand as a model, opened a restaurant in Kensington. It was all an example of how one's credulity can suddenly be tested in the world of Public Relations: a world which often becomes more private than public.

But let me tell you about two of my PR accounts. Gewiss, the Italian company, makers of industrial lighting, retained me to carry out PR for them in the UK until setting up their own department at their headquaters in Milan. Two quite challenging action picture stories I planned and carried out for them may be of interest. One concerned the Channel Tunnel, then under construction. Photographers were not allowed in the tunnel at that time, but I particularly wanted to get a shot of a tunneller working right on the rock face with the aid of Gewiss lighting. Poor lighting and shadows would be extremely dangerous for such work and I wanted to demonstrate my client's product. However, I got inside the tunnel with a photographer. It was eerie walking in the darkness, but after about three miles we reached the work face and were able to get some marvellous close-ups of a tunneller aided by his Gewiss lights. It made a splendid picture story.

Another quite exciting story I arranged was when Gewiss lighting was in place in part of the London Underground and I wanted, in the form of pictures, to show the difference it made. Accordingly, down in the Underground at a point where the rails divided before us into two seperate tunnels, one of which had the old lighting and the other the new Gewiss lighting, I took up station with a photographer to get the shots. We were both accutely aware that we had to be alert for any approaching trains, apart from the other quite significant fact that we were within three feet of a live rail.

Both these stories gained due prominence. I was sorry when Gewiss elected to run their entire European operation from their office and factory in Milan.

To some extent I was back in the world I knew with Bukta when I was asked by Spall Sportswear to give them a PR boost. They were, of course, very much smaller, but they had a marvellous spirit down at their factory and offices in Shenfield, Essex which I am sure are still retained. The highlight at that time was their connection with Wimbledon FC and I began to see quite a bit of refreshingly unusual Wimbledon who wore Spall Football clothing. Bobby Gould was the Manager. Before him, Dave Bassett used to give the lads commando-like training. 'You couldn't hit a cow's backside with a banjo,' was his oft-used derisory remark – though not put quite as politely as that!

It was 1988 and they were in the Cup Final – a year which brought the drama of the Cup more than ever to light. There was this wonderful Crazy Gang atmosphere down at the club ground, then in Plough Lane – Vinny Jones with the press photographers. 'Do another one showing your studs, Vinny,' they would call out during a spell after training. 'That'll cost you!' demanded his agent, the irrepressible Eric Hall. Vinny was the lovable 'Bad boy', always larking about. What a character, and now what a success in his own right in Hollywood as an actor, complete with villa and pool and all the trappings. Good on you, Vinny.

Lawrie Sanchez, now manager of ambitious Wycombe Wanderers in the Isthmian League, got the only goal of the match in that Cup Final. Dave Beasant in goal kept a clean sheet. That's the true romance of football. Wimbledon 1: Liverpool 0.

The fascination with PR has not faded. Currently I am involved with a city for a multi-million pound project by a world-famous company in North Wales and the likelihood of being Director of Public Relations for a proposed new international airport in the UK!

CHAPTER IV

Jesmond Days

(In which I first go back to my boyhood)

IT WAS THE SHOES THAT UPSET ME. Highly polished, size ten, I would suddenly see them in the corner as I entered the living room. The sight of them dismayed me. I wanted to hurl them out of the open window. They were not often there. They were my father's shoes.

We lived in a flat, 138 Bayswater Road, West Jesmond, a suburb of Newcastle upon Tyne. It was an upstairs apartment with an outside loo, the door of which represented, with its chalked stumps, the setting for many a 'Test Match'. Hitting the ball over the wall into Mrs Tronn's back yard meant not only that you were out, but you had to go and get the ball from her. It was a tennis ball, of course.

I lived with my half-sister, Doreen, who was ten years older and my brother, Gordon, who was five years older.

My father had ended the War as a Captain stationed at the prisoner-of-war camp at Catterick. He was a handsome guy, I suppose, and as I grew up, on meeting men who discovered I was his son, I had to listen to them roaring with laughter amongst themselves as they recounted his exploits with women, even though he was then married to my mother. I always found this distasteful.

I suppose the 1920s were a time of a certain madness. Men wore voluminous, tent-like trousers called 'Oxford Bags'; everyone appeared to smoke, cigarette holders got longer and longer and there were stunts like 'marathon dancing'. In the States the craze for marathon dancing featured a girl in Cleveland who wore out five male partners in winning a title, though her ankles were swollen to five times the normal size. At the seaside women were not considered properly dressed without a matching hat to their swimsuits. Skirts became shorter and controversial. As well as endangering women's moral welfare, some doctors claimed that current fashions for shorter skirts may be bad for physical health, causing puffiness and chafing of the legs. In Paris, Josephine Baker, the sensational nineteen-year-old dancer at 'Le Revue Negre' was the talk of the town. Her dance, slapping her buttocks in tempo to 'Yes, sir, that's my baby!' and her bare-breasted mating dance, wearing nothing but strategic circles of coloured feathers, raised audiences to a frenzy. People went to Paris to see her rather than the capital. But one of the biggest innovations in Britain was the dance that scandalised America, the Charleston. It took its name from the South Carolina town where it was born and was almost as much detested by their mothers as the 'flappers' or young women who loved it. The dance, performed at frenetic tempo by turning in your toes and kicking out your legs while syncopating your arm movements, took the States by storm and then swept the country over here around 1925. It could get a whole room bouncing. Somehow it was the true expression of the time – 'I don't care what I look like, but I am darned well going to have fun!' It was all part of the post-war escapism. There was a lot of drinking and house parties.

My father was at the centre of various outrageous stunts, as I learned later. There was the night when, together with two friends, one who was the director of a large retail furniture store in the town centre and another who had well-known photography studios – all three being in evening dress – they ended up in a somewhat inebriated condition asleep in a bed in the store. Unfortunately it happened to be in the main window, which was fully lighted up. The early morning crowds were entranced. The police had to be called.

Another story about my father, whose forename, by the way, was Corrie, concerned the comedian Jimmy James. The way I heard it was that Jimmy's car was parked outside the Turk's Head Hotel in Newcastle upon Tyne and whilst he was inside having a drink with his pals, the wheels were taken off, the car lifted on to wood blocks and when Jimmy decided to leave, a number of his friends in the know – my father apparently was one of the ringleaders – came out to see him off. Jimmy got in the car, lots of shouts of 'All the best, Jimmy,' and of course you can imagine the rest of the story!

Then there was the fun and games up at Holy Island when the local vicar went swimming only to find afterwards that his clothes had disappeared.

Once or twice we were promised a spin down to the seaside, about fifteen miles away, on a Sunday. Picnic basket prepared, we would sit around awaiting my father's return from the pub. Then he would appear, bundle us all into the car and off we would go, racing down to the sea, the afternoon almost spent.

He had a good business, I believe, importing glassware from Belgium, and his customers were mostly hotels and restaurants, but there is no doubt he had so many women in tow we saw little of the proceeds. My brother Gordon, though, went to a boarding school in Yorkshire. I heard in later years that on the annual sports day there was great interest in who the Mrs Johnstone would be this year. Even bets on whether she would be blonde or brunette. Afterwards my brother went to the Royal Grammar School, Newcastle upon Tyne, an excellent establishment.

My father began to disappear for longer periods. Maintenance money was supposed to be paid, but seldom arrived. There was, however, a dogged cheerfulness on the part of my mother. She began to go out selling sweaters from a large suitcase and I used to help her. One large tenement building in the town called Suttons Dwellings had a stone stairway and this was quite steep so that I vividly remember struggling with this heavy suitcase, praying that we would sell the contents as soon as possible. I had to wear my school cap inside out so that only the lining showed in case they thought I went to a posh school and they needn't help my mother. But we were a cheerful household. My mother did her morning exercises to music on the gramophone. She joined the Women's League of Health and Beauty, adored Prunella Stack and once carried a banner at their parade at Wembley.

To go back to my school cap. It was that of a private school in Gosforth – just about fifteen minutes walk away from where we lived – and there was a stretch of open ground known as 'The Little Moor' between. It was a very large private house known as

Coxlodge Hall standing in its own grounds. This had been converted into a mixed day school by Rev. T. Wilson who also had a commercial training establishment for typing, book-keeping and shorthand named Smart's College down in the town. So, after early days in Miss Kelsey's junior school in West Jesmond, off I went to Gosforth, aged about eleven or twelve.

I cannot say that I greatly enjoyed school. I was best at essay writing, literature and history, tolerated geography and hated maths. Sport was a little unsatisfactory. There were several good tennis courts and a gymnasium of sorts, but cricket and football were on grounds some distance from the school and semi-public and there was little or no coaching. There was also a big snag. My mother, worried at the looming bill for fees, had to explain our predicament to the Headmaster. There seemed little chance of me remaining. The only alternative was West Jesmond Council School and I was quite prepared to settle for that. But my mother would not permit it. Rough lot! And the rest of it. However, Rev. and Mrs Wilson wouldn't hear of me leaving. So it was arranged that I would hand in a sum of money in an envelope each Monday morning. That worked quite well, but inevitably there were times when I had to stay behind after Assembly in order to give my apologies or hand in my mother's note. The fact that I often used to stay behind after morning Assembly caused some comment or 'mickey taking' as they called it. I gained quite a dashing, if undeserved, reputation for having to see the Head after prayers.

What I really wanted to do was to get a reporter's job on the *Newcastle Chronicle*, but age and the need for the School Leaving Certificate were barriers. One possible way would be to get employed as a 'copy' boy, though it was, I believe, pretty rare for them to make it as a reporter. Many a time I stood at the rear of the *Chronicle* building outside the big steel doors which when opened brought the sudden roar of the presses and a blast of hot air. The copy boys were certainly tough and rough, but that didn't put me off. When the call 'Copy' came in those days from the editorial desk, one of the boys had to dash off smartly distributing the contents to other desks. But they were at least 'On the *Chronicle*' and could get to know people. Besides, I always liked writing and perhaps I could learn the dreaded shorthand at night classes.

Admittedly, the copy boys were probably a tougher lot than at West Jesmond Council School, which incidentally produced some splendid young men and women. But on the other hand, can you blame my mother desperately trying to do her best for me despite the trials and tribulations of having the gas cut off for non-payment, and a Christmas dinner with rabbit as the star attraction?

But being poor can greatly sharpen one's appreciation and must never blunt one's sense of humour. On the contrary, we were a happy little household. Without meaning to preach, I do, however, feel strongly about the one-parent family. It has become a very weak link in today's society. All very well to moan about the youth of today. It's the parental side of life's contract that so often lets society down.

One evening, aged about twelve and a half, I was introduced to a scout troop in Gosforth. They had a large hut on the edge of a moor. The scoutmaster was Dugald Paulin, and it was about a mile and a half out of the town; to me an exciting new world. The place buzzed with activity. It was to become like an enrolment into the university of life.

I remember soon after I joined the troop they put on a concert in a church hall in Gosforth. The lights failed in the middle of the show. Somehow I got pushed on stage. I already had a large electric torch in my hand which I had been using to help back stage. Quite impromptu, I began to spot members of the audience in its powerful beam and got them to sing part of a song or do some cross-talk with me. When the fuse was mended and the lights went on again I was the hero of the troop and the audience thought it was all part of the show!

Soon Easter camp came round and we were off to the Cheviots. This was a new world – breaking the ice in the mornings, getting the wood fire lighted, the smell of bacon frying and desperately trying not to be the tenderfoot who burned the porridge.

You can walk all day in the Cheviots and never see another soul. We would strike out, packs on our backs, climbing out of the upper Coquet Valley on to the lumpy heather moorlands with only sheep for company. It is more rhythmic to hike here than in mountainous areas. The central crags and dales have wide views and a varied terrain where the warlike past has left more castles, fortalices, peles, bastles and barmikins. The Romans, of course, built camps here before retreating behind Hadrian's famous Wall and William the Conqueror marched back down the Coquet after giving the Scots a sharp dig as a prelude to three centuries of raiding and skirmishing.

I am constantly surprised at the number of people who have no idea about the Northumbrian coast where you can walk for miles along beaches and dunes with the wonderful sea air filling your lungs. The breakers roll and roll again up the shelving red-golden sand.

And who can forget the first sight of the spectacular hilltop ruined fortress of Dunstanborough, nine miles south of Bamburgh which has a castle now converted into flats. It's three miles from the little fishing village of Craster.

As a kid I used to love visiting Holy Island which lies about two miles off the Northumberland coast. It could be quite exciting crossing by car on the ebb tide with a high curtain of spray rising behind us.

There were and probably still are, huge wicker baskets attached to sturdy posts with the idea that if the tide came in and caught some daring motorist making the crossing, the baskets could become a haven for the beleagured occupants. We were never caught but my father loved a challenge of this sort and we had one or two scary crossings, I can tell you!

We used to stay in one of the fishermen's cottages and everyone was so hospitable. Some of our friends stayed at the Iron Rails, which, I remember, had a wonderful atmosphere of friendliness and there would be late-night singing and the sound of laughter long after I had, supposedly, gone off to my own 'Blanket Bay'.

The castle which dominated the skyline added a touch of romance and, of course, the fishermen had plenty of stirring tales to tell, and sometimes took us out in their cobles, the traditional inshore fishing boats, each about 27 feet long in which ten of us would be wedged into seats along the side.

Greatest of all treats, was the visit to nearby Farne Islands, famed for the story of Grace Darling and the Longstone Light-house. She had accompanied her father who was the lighthouse keeper in a daring rescue in an open boat when the *Forfarshire* was wrecked nearby on a terrible night in 1840.

The islands are home to an amazing collection of puffins, seagulls, cormorants, eider ducks and the like. They certainly make a huge chorus of discord when they are in song!

St Cuthbert's Way leads from Melrose on the borders, where the seventh-century saint began his ministry, to Holy Island where he was buried and his followers later produced the Lindisfarne Gospels.

Scouting aided my confidence. One morning I walked into the offices of Thomas Hedley & Co Ltd, the soap manufacturers. They were in the centre of the town not far from St Nicholas Cathedral. I asked if they had any vacancies, but I didn't tell them that I was aged thirteen. 'Come back next week,' they told me. Accordingly I kept the appointment and got the job as office boy. When I got home I told my mother, who had, of course, no inkling of all this, 'I've got the rent!' My pay was 12/6d a week.

Next morning when I went to collect the mail at the General Post Office I was glad I had someone with me 'to show me the ropes'. Hedleys ran coupon schemes for Fairy Soap. The mail consisted of three huge bags each nearly as tall as me. Jean Blackburn, a very hard-working and attractive blonde, was my boss. The salesmen, or travellers, as they were known, all had dockets where their mail was stored in the corner of a large office and at the end of the day this was put into extra large envelopes which, once they were franked or stamped, were piled up for me to get off to the Post Office. Sometimes these salesmen visited Head Office. To me they were like minor gods. Now I could see what they looked like, these denizens of the field, for Thomas Hedley had become part of the great Proctor and Gamble Corporation of Cincinnati, USA and we were locked in battle with mighty Lever Brothers. It was Fairy Soap fighting Sunlight!

The company had a house journal called 'Moonbeams'. I read avidly about the experiences of the salesmen. I think the name Kenneth Huggins comes back to me. A Yorkshireman, his number of calls a day became a record. I realised later that all this was part of the new Americanism – the high-powered approach then beginning to hit the UK.

Jack Caygill was the Sales Manager. To me he was 'King Jack'. Later our scout troop moved out of the hut into what was known as 'The Lodge', a spacious old cottage that stood near some gates at what had once been the drive to a large house. It was in Oakfield Road, Gosforth. Jack Caygill lived in the private road quite near and I would loiter on the way to the scout lodge in the hope that this tall, flaxen-haired Englishman, who seemed to be always chewing gum and who wore large horn-rimmed spectacles, might see me. But I was, I am afraid, too young to be a salesman.

I hated trying to keep my stationery cupboards neat and tidy, but it had to be done. One day, however, I had the chance of a move. The salesmen had to change the coupons collected by the shopkeeper and often carried cash so that they had to be bonded and be at least twenty-one years old. There were no junior salesmen, but one day I was asked if I would like to be what was known as a junior displayman. Of course, though I had reached the grand old age of fifteen, they just assumed I was well over sixteen, if not seventeen. The team I was to join consisted of eight girl canvassers – the Fairy Soap girls. I was to go ahead and put up window bills that were transparencies of the cherubic looking baby in nappies – it's still a familiar advertisement – with 'Fairy Soap is coming' bills. The canvassers went door to door giving out coupons. It was a tie-up with the firm's soap powder, Oxydol. I also had to hammer in plates advertising Fairy Soap outside the shop and put up display stands made of cardboard inside.

Arriving at the shop, I had to introduce myself, read out word for word from my presentation manual and get the shopkeeper to let me put up my display. The salesman had either already called or was to call to sell in the stocks. That was all very well, but Ardath and Craven A, not to mention other commodities, were also at it and the smaller shops had their counters festooned with free gifts connected with gift merchandise. There were teapots, coffee jugs, clocks, all on display. I also found that on my calls, which numbered at least twenty-one in the day, I sometimes had a smart-looking guy come and stand behind me to ensure that I went word for word through my spiel. Invariably he was an American and the shop-keepers sometimes got irate at this high-powered invasion, especially when he corrected me if I got it wrong.

My instructions were to go by rail to Bath and on arrival I walked across the bridge from the station to the Royal Hotel. That was when I first fell in love with the city. At least I could see the famed Bath rugby team play and savour the atmosphere across on the Rec and walk freely along the riverside. After about a month we moved to Exeter and I began to enjoy the work, though hammering in cleats to hold up the plates outside the shop was tricky in the winter. Also Thomas' Puritan Soaps were strong in the West and once or twice a fiery shopkeeper would take umbrage at all 'this American pressure' and show me the door in a less gentle manner than I had come to expect of West Countrymen. This particular campaign came to an end and I was now surplus.

Walter Goodenough, the Assistant Buyer at Thomas Hedley, introduced me to a friend R.P. Spinks, Area Manager for H.J. Heinz. It seems that they employed junior salesmen. I went along to see him and he at once offered me a job. Again the age factor was suitably camouflaged. I had achieved my dream to be out selling.

I was given training about their famous '57 Varieties' and in no time I was turned out in a natty business suit – specially chosen by my delighted mother – and even, at times, wore a bowler! I am bound to say that all went off superbly. I called on smaller retailers and in my smart bag I had an array of tasty samples. Needless to say, our menus at home began to be augmented with Heinz macaroni, beans and soups from my liberal allowance of samples.

About this time I was also helping to run a scout troop and was able to restart another at St George's Church, Jesmond, where we had our investiture ceremony on the attractive green in front of the church. I won a prize at HJ Heinz and the award was a week at their head office at Park Royal in North London.

Back home again there was a big drive on Heinz Olive Oil. I decided to go for nursing and maternity homes for orders. Coming out of one after a sales interview wearing my bowler hat and dark suit and carrying the special HJ Heinz black sample case I encountered a doctor. 'Morning,' he said. 'First case, I presume?'

I sometimes arranged demonstrations of some of the famous Heinz soups in stores. From my display point, where I had flasks of hot soups ready waiting, I approached unsuspecting shoppers and invited them to sample one of the soups. This was invariably on a Saturday morning and as the time got past midday I began nervously consulting my watch. Then at about half past the hour I closed the demonstration, packed and rushed off madly, complete with my rugger kit in a holdall slung over my shoulder. If it was an away game we met outside the Crow's Nest at Barras Bridge by 1.15 p.m. at the latest. Not playing rugby at school – Newcastle upon Tyne was a soccer-mad city – I learned it at Gosforth and fell in love with the game playing at what was then known as 'wing forward'. It was great fun. Sometimes we changed at the back of a hedge at some away fixture in the country, using tap water for a wash-down.

I suppose the West Jesmond Picture House was our window on the world. Opposite the station, which was on the excellent electric railway, this was our Mecca, particularly on a Saturday night.

This was where young heroes met after playing or watching football or rugby, or dashed from an afternoon's work. Some perhaps after a game of billiards – the girls had just had time to put on a bit of glamour – and there were families, too, but it was the back seats in the stalls on a Saturday night where the young elite gathered and the ice-cream girls moved with a dexterity born of experience in avoiding 'pinched bums'. This was our own world of 'pre-television'. 'Going to the pictures' had its special magic as Hollywood came to West Jesmond. Marlene Deitrich and Gary Cooper in *Morocco* made by Paramount; the huge chorus lines from *The King of Jazz*; Douglas Fairbanks Jnr and Richard Barthelmess in *The Dawn Patrol*; Greta Garbo and John Barrymore in *The Grand Hotel*; Mae West in *She Done Him Wrong*; Greta Garbo in the arms of Clark Gable; Leslie Howard and Bette Davis in *Of Human Bondage*; Harpo, Zeppo, Chico and Groucho Marx in *Monkey Business*; Pola Negri in her first talking picture *A Woman Commands*; Joan Crawford; Clara Bow; Katherine Hepburn; Cary Grant; Bing Crosby – such was the pageant of stars captivating us week after week. All quite unforgettable. And there was always the travelogue to bring us back to earth, ending with the familiar voice of James A. Fitzpatrick: 'And some say farewell to ...'

Then there was Jimmy, who pasted up the posters and did odd

jobs, and paraded outside the cinema in the evenings for big attractions. He would always be suitably garbed on these occasions. I remember once for *The Sheik of Araby* he was so taken with himself in the outfit that he insisted on wearing it all day to impress his neighbours. The Manager wore a tuxedo on Saturday nights, rushing outside at intervals to count the numbers in the queue – 'Circle on the right, Stalls on the left' – 6d and 9d, and a scramble for the back seats. Then for a big attraction, a pianist was engaged to add to the atmosphere.

Of course, there were the bigger cinemas such as the Queen's in town, where a feature was the organ – an instrument which could, it seemed, reflect a whole range of audience moods. The organist, who appeared before and after the 'Big Picture', became part of the show. The local picture house, though, usually made do with a pianist. If it was a big enough feature film, that is.

How carefree we were. There was no hooliganism. Nobody got beaten up, shouted abuse or threw up on the pavement. No drugs. If a policeman was to be seen in the vicinity, it was rare and a cause for concern. There was a better sense of values.

Another attraction was speedway racing. The smell of burning oil, the screech of tyres on cinder on the tight bends as the riders bent over their machines, revving them up noisily as they jockeyed for position. The track was round the County Ground at Gosforth.

In the music halls the acts toured regularly for there was no television to blanket the nation in one performance. I loved the Newcastle Hippodrome. It was 10d for the side circle. All the acts came round – Afrique, Clapham and Dwyer, Billy Bennett, Wilson, Kepple and Betty, Ella Retford, Max Miller, Teddy Brown and the rest. I often stood at the stage door for autographs. Seymour Hicks described me as 'a very nice little boy'. Jackie Coogan's parents were so taken with me they had me round to where they were staying to meet him. Talullah Bankhead gave me a kiss!

I would like to reprint a piece I wrote for the *Newcastle Journal*, who highlighted it as one of their main features. It was entitled 'The Newt Gives Lie to Faint-Hearts'.

Troop Leader Newton Shipley, of The High Gate, Kenton,

Newcastle, is today awarded the Boy Scouts' VC – the Cornwell Badge. Below is told the reason why.

By Ken Johnstone

This is the story of a boy and a bomb. It begins on a December night when the stars looked down uncertainly on a darkened, hushed Tyneside.

It is four days after a strange Christmas, when the world seems to have forgotten its message. It is 1941.

The boy – quick, tousle-headed and friendly – is eight years old.

But even as he sits and plays in the warmth of his home in Matthew Bank, Newcastle, his fate becomes inextricably linked with an anonymous hand gripping a lever high in the heavens above.

One moment the grip tightens. The next the boy is catapulted into a nightmare of falling rubble and debris.

I'm a Wolf Cub

Two hours later, an air-raid warden, loath to give up the young body for dead, stands, holding him in his arms. The boy suddenly opens his eyes and smiles.

'You're a very brave lad, aren't you?' says the warden. 'Of course, don't you know I'm a Wolf Cub?' is the wounded boy's whispered reply.

And here is the sequel to a story whose high drama was the accepted pattern of our daily lives ... Near-six-footer 17-year-old Troop Leader Newton Shipley, of The High Gate, Kenton, Newcastle, is today awarded the Boy Scouts' VC, the Cornwell Badge. He joins the select company of some 300 Scouts whose 'exceptional courage' has won this simple bronze badge, which commemorates the supreme valour of Jack Cornwell, the Jutland boy VC – a London Boy Scout who died a national hero.

Newton – or 'The Newt', as all his pals call him – fought his battle against pain in the Ministry of Pensions Hospital at Dunston. Both his legs were badly crushed and one had to be re-set several times. The other – his left leg – was amputated below the knee.

But this Cub off the old British Lion was the master of his circumstances. He shed no tears. 'Do your best' is the Wolf Cub's motto. And he did.

Chief Scout wrote

Lord Somers, the then Chief Scout, wrote and commended him for his amazing cheerfulness. 'The Cub Spirit is a grand thing, so hang on to it,' he wrote.

Sir Ralph Mortimer, County Scout Commissioner for Northumberland, was a frequent visitor to this bright-eyed model patient who propelled himself fearlessly in his bath chair.

Good wishes came from all over the country. A well-wisher in Sheffield enclosed a one-pound note 'towards a new leg'. A Boy Scout of the same age wrote from Michigan, USA, and remains a close correspondent. One day they will meet.

Knitting, stamp collecting and handicrafts filled his hospital days. He improvised in every possible way to keep up his Cub proficiency tests, and as soon as he could talk his way into it, he was down with his pals of the 33rd Newcastle (Oaklands) Wolf Cub Pack - crutches and all.

Spoke for four

Now, I want to bring this story up to an evening two years ago when a deputation of four eager youngsters called upon me. Their spokesman was a fast-speaking, sturdy 15-year-old, sporting a natty pair of flannels and suede shoes.

It was 'The Newt', then a Scout in the 3rd Gosforth Troop, and he asked me to start a new Boy Scout troop. 'Because,' he explained, 'there's no troop in Kenton, and very little social life for chaps like us.'

'Go and get me six more names,' I countered. They did.

We started meeting the good old-fashioned way that 'BP' knew so well. Underneath a lamp post. Then around Kenton Quarry, until a good samaritan, Mr William Younger, local farmer, gave the use of a fine spacious building, which is now a headquarters abounding in arty crafty log fireplaces, patrol meeting dens, and all the gadgets that boys love.

Thus the 88th (Kenton) Newcastle Group Boy Scouts became a thriving, living contribution to the community, engaging the spirited and loyal support of some 60 youngsters. And 'The Newt', instigator-in-chief, is its first troop leader.

Commando-like

Characteristic British phlegm has taken this boy right through from early Tenderfoot tests to his First Class and King's Scout Badges. Some of these tests are tricky and Commando-like. They involve Morse-signalling, ambulance training, crossing rivers, bivouacking, tracking, sport, map reading, night compass marching, and a host of varied activities. Newton just won't hear of anything but the real thing.

A man I know, who is a chauffeur, said to me, 'I saw a couple of your lads hiking out near Milbourne, Ponteland. One of them wasn't half limping!'

It was 'The Newt', nearing the end of a 16-mile high pressure mapping journey. And small wonder he was limping. The stump of his amputated limb was raw from the friction of his artificial leg.

But it's all in the game. Like playing goalie for the troop footer team, running the touch-line for a Dame Allan's School rugger XV, or merely getting ticked off from a strange Scouter (Scout officer to you!) for wearing corduroy longs with uniform.

Mountaineer

One final mental snapshot. I remember the silent tribute paid this resolute lad when, clean on the summit of a 3,000-ft mountain, I turned to find him behind me, framed against the Lakeland August sky. He had accompanied us without fuss from the bottom to the top.

Well, there it is. I get so tired of the folk who bleat about degenerate youth, and something being wrong with England. There are more ordinary honest-to-God heroes to the square mile here than in any other country. And up here – famed as workers and fighters – we have our full share.

There are so many who bravely and without fuss battle against all sorts of personal odds, like war wounds and other disabilities, and, in a way, I have tried to represent them all by telling this simple story of a Tyneside lad who beat the bomb that sought to destroy him.

'The Newt' was one of a trio of youngsters who knocked on my door one evening and asked to see me. Their quest was to ask me to start a Scout Troop. They were Newton Shipley, Johnnie Robson and Allan MacLaren. I agreed to do something about it and it wasn't long before we were excitedly inspecting an old air-raid shelter nearby as a possible headquarters.

So the 88th (Kenton) Newcastle upon Tyne Troop came to life and in no time at all it seemed we had graduated to meeting weekly in an old hut at the foot of Kenton Lane. This was then rebuilt into a splendid headquarters entirely through the efforts of the parents as much as anyone, I might add.

'The Newt' has only just retired. This completed his successful career as Area Manager of a large motor insurance company – and he still lives in Ponteland opposite to where my late sister, Doreen, lived and not far from Ponteland Golf Course. I mention this because he has always been a good golfer and was Captain of Ponteland Golf Club. Now he derives much pleasure from actively promoting the British Amputee Open Golf Championship last held at Staverton Park, Daventry, Northamptonshire on 24–28 August 1999. I have a good idea how hard Newton and his wife, Chris, worked to make this event a great success. They and their family have always been such a great team. In the programme Mark James, European Team Captain, wrote, 'If the team I am taking to Boston in September shows the same amount of courage and determination as all of you, holding on to the Ryder Cup should not present too insurmountable a task.' Unfortunately we lost it!

Gary, their son, is a very successful professional golfer attached to the Whitley Bay Club, Northumberland.

Newton and Chris have visited the States for their Amputees Golf Association Tournaments. The wonderful sporting opportunities provided there and in this country for its members in archery, athletics, badminton, bowls, cycling, football, powerlifting, shooting, table tennis and volleyball, in addition to golf, are highly commendable. I remember having my clients, Canterbury Mortgage Company, sponsor a young man named Matthews, a truly remarkable blind runner, who took part in international events for disabled athletes.

Johnnie Robson, who figures elsewhere in this story, was another of the gang who hijacked me. He was, like the others, an enthusiastic scout. Once when I gave him a little talk on the facts of life, as I have done with one or two of the older boys, I asked if there was anything that he would like to ask me. There was a long silence until he looked up and said, 'Well, there is one thing I would like to ask you.' Slightly tensed up at the prospect of having to answer some difficult question of a personal nature I said, 'What is it, Johnnie?' There was another long pause before he answered. 'Well, I was wondering, could you get me two tickets for United's match on Saturday?'

Johnnie got a job as a reporter on the *North Shields Evening News* and, as you may have noted elsewhere in my story, he came to work for me in London. He later went to Great Ancoats, the newspaper centre in Manchester, on the *Daily Express* and ended up as Editor of the *Scottish Sunday Express* working directly under Sir John Junor before taking early retirement.

A good friend of both Newton and Johnnie was Dixon Barker who, whilst not a member of the Scouts, was always ready to join in and help. Dixon, who is now a millionaire, is based at Hartlepool and we last met when I was up there with Bath Rugby Club when we played West Hartlepool.

Johnnie had shown great fortitude when sadly he lost his wife Heather. It was a great test of character. He was devoted to the children and even when working a long week in the grind of newspaper life in Manchester, he never failed to drive to Newcastle upon Tyne to be with them for what was left of each weekend. It was wonderful to hear him on the phone saying that he would be 'seeing in' the millennium with his five grandchildren – Emma has two and Mark has three – in a holiday home Mark had taken over in the Lake District.

Another milestone in my early days in Newcastle upon Tyne were the Ralph Reader Scout Gang Shows. They were a big success in London and we decided to stage our own version. There were four of us who originally embarked on this adventure. They were Ted Potts, Doug Gibb, Denis Dodds and myself.

We descended by appointment upon an old variety theatre – the Grand – which stood rather unimpressively at Byker on some waste ground, allegedly an old pit heap. When we first went to see him the house manager, Tommy Moat, heard us out with growing excitement. We proposed to take the theatre for a week, put on our own show, have a big opening night with the Duke of Northumberland and other distinguished guests and Ralph and some of the London Gang would fly up and appear on stage on the Saturday night. This was almost too much for Tommy, who was ecstatic. He couldn't have been more excited if we'd said that the Queen would attend. Suddenly the curtain was to be pulled on the sword swallowers, jugglers, trick cyclists, sweating girl choruses, knockabout comics, wannabee Sinatras and dedicated instrumentalists. Anyway for at least one week. He had a trick of turning back a corner of the lace curtain at his office window and peering out, which he did periodically without offering any explanation. As our plans developed Tommy got more and more excited and dashed to and from the window – what he was peering at remained a mystery, but it appeared to rekindle his enthusiasm. He got so excited that he went off and got himself a new evening dress suit.

Opening night duly arrived after ten weeks, during which we rehearsed most evenings. Nellie Potts, who ran a dancing school in Jesmond, worked tirelessly – she had no option, for Ted, the producer, was her brother and very persuasive.

The week of the show was a storming success. The Duke of Northumberland and civic party duly attended. Tommy Moat, as proud as Punch, wore his new evening dress and Ralph, with a couple of the London Gang Show, flew up to Hampden Park for the international in the afternoon then down to Newcastle upon Tyne to arrive just in time for the Saturday evening show.

Our Gang were ecstatic. The week's performances went over with a bang and the Saturday night was pure magic. The Byker Grand had never seen anything like it. I was the compere, to be pushed on if the scenery stuck! My appearances on stage became less frequent following the opening night as everything began to run smoothly. Thus began my love of the theatre and was to give me a fascinating extra field of activity in my army life.

The Newcastle Gang Shows became highly successful annual events, moving to the Empire Theatre in Newgate Street – now a hotel – and the Theatre Royal in Grey Street. Even after the long interlude of wartime we were back again and the annual shows continued with the indefatigable Ted Potts at the helm.

Group Captain Ken Angus as our Scout Commissioner, was a huge asset to the movement. He was always anxious for me to curtail my booming laugh when later I was visiting the show as a member of the audience. It always seemed to send some of the audience into convulsions.

Ted Potts, who did a marvellous job as producer of our Gang Shows, was the Secretary for the Boy Scout Association for the city, which was a very successful movement in our part of the world.

I remember, after the War, when I was Assistant County Commissioner for Senior Scouts, I was so imbued with the idea of tough training that I put on a weekend-long exercise in which about 200 senior scouts (aged 16 to 18½) were dropped off the back of lorries out in the country. They had to make their way to a number of checkpoints. The only snag was these had to be found by map reference and were on remote moors, or in some feature like the grounds of a castle or behind the tower of a village church.

I had a friend, Keith Millican, who loaded his light aircraft with dead rabbits and then flew over the points where senior scouts would be due to arrive in the evening, unloading the rabbits over the side of the plane as he flew. They had to find them, skin them and then cook them.

CHAPTER V

Army Days

BACK AT THE 11th BN DLI, the TA unit I joined just before the War, I was given command of the Carrier Platoon – a fleet of light-armoured tracked vehicles equipped with Ford V8 engines, each armed with a mounted Bren gun. Down in Devon, following Dunkirk – at which, incidentally, I was left fuming in charge of a platoon of reinforcements – we were now guarding the coast of England from Start Point to Dawlish. As a young subaltern I was in charge of a detachment at Stanborough House, a fine country house about twelve miles from Slapton Sands. It was taken over completely by the Army. We were able to impress vehicles if required and so my mobile force comprised a bus and a large saloon car more like a wedding car, in addition to my three motorcycles, one 15-cwt truck, two jeeps and three Bren-gun carriers. That little lot could convey as many as fifty soldiers all told.

Lieutenant Colonel Richard Ware, our CO, was suddenly whipped off to form an Area Command and Major Freddy Taylor, an old Regular, who had been a lieutenant quartermaster, was in charge. I remember he was a master of army regulations. He would spend hours working out his allowances. Our Adjutant was my friend, Denis Hamilton, who had been promoted captain and had celebrated by growing a moustache which he was never to shave off.

At the centre of our defensive area lay Slapton Sands where it would be possible to bring a destroyer almost into the shore itself. We had our first call-out, which was either due to a rather jittery admiral or as a test run, it was never quite clear. It was a bit of a nightmare, really. The code word 'Cromwell' came suddenly around midnight on the telephone. I pulled on the bell rope above the vast four-poster bed I occupied in the master bedroom and it came away in my hand. That was to be the alarm! So I rushed out on to the landing yelling for everyone to get up and get dressed. Soon men were tumbling out of hay lofts and barns amidst squawking hens and ducks, the old wedding car coughed and spluttered into life, the Bren-gun carriers revved up their engines and the bus rammed the gateway. Somehow we got straightened up and made for Slapton Sands. That was our first practice run and we certainly improved on our turn-out time later, so that when next in the middle of the night we got the code word 'Cromwell' we were good and ready. Our turn-out time from the moment of the alarm to arrival on the beach twelve miles away was, I think, about thirty minutes, which was pretty good for the middle of the night when we had to get up and dressed. As we thundered down those country lanes and through the village of Halwell, rifles and guns being primed on the way, I fervently hoped we would frighten Jerry, for by God it put the wind up me!

Apart from all these night-time rehearsals, our first defensive task was to demolish some small bridges across marshy land, the idea being that it would thus be impassable to the invading Germans, particularly if they came at night. One small bridge was left for communication purposes.

Suddenly one day hundreds of civilians arrived with shovels and spades and began digging long trenches from the sea back to the road. Apparently the District Council Engineer had decided that the sands were a perfect place for enemy parachutists to land and therefore the beach had to be dug up. Denis, our Adjutant, protested that this would simply provide ideal slit-trench positions for the Germans to sit in and fire at us. The local invasion was chased away.

Next we laid about twenty boxes of mines along the beach and around the Royal Sands Hotel, a small but once attractive-looking hotel which had stood in the centre. I say 'once' because only the bare outlines of the building remained since a poor unfortunate dog named Pincher, belonging to a local farmer, had earlier set off a mine, killing itself and demolishing most of the hotel. I should imagine every regiment along the South Coast stood to as a result in the belief that the invasion had started.

Then there was the business of the gas piping. Hundreds of feet of this arrived and we were urged to fill them with petrol. If the Germans invaded the idea was to set the lot on fire by remote control.

The Home Guard arrived dashing around changing all the road direction signs so as to confuse the enemy. Captain Mainwaring in command! Dear old Cyril Maude, the actor, was one of those who observed through his glasses should there be any enemy action in the sky. He had a cord attached to a bell downstairs which would give a warning ring. There was also the pioneer version of the Molotov cocktail, using a beer bottle with rags dipped in an acid solution. When a German tank got near enough, this was to be hurled through the observation slit or lobbed into the tank commander's position.

We stood to about half an hour before daylight each morning, straining our eyes towards and across the Channel, but Brigade was informed that Intelligence did not consider that the Germans would invade that winter. We had, in fact, stood to day and night for four months along a vital stretch of our beaches. Now we were withdrawn to the Totnes area before embarking for Iceland.

A sad postscript to all this was that Slapton Sands was to figure later in one of the most extraordinary and tragic events of the War – an event which unfortunately can only be described as a complete 'cock-up' or fiasco, but which was officially known as Exercise Tiger. It involved some 30,000 men of the US Army and the US Navy, plus small contingents of the Royal Navy, in what was to amount almost to a full-scale rehearsal for D-Day. It took place in April 1944 – long after our departure from the area. The exercise was based on and around Slapton Sands because of its likeness to Utah Beach. There had been an evacuation of many local people in the South Hams because it was to be used for practice for assault landings before a Second Front opened.

The breakdown in communications and the resulting confusion caused on this exercise, which involved the use in part of live ammunition, was almost unbelievable. It is a fact that whilst some 200 were killed during the actual landing at Utah, almost 1,000 men lost their lives at Slapton whilst members of the US High Command watched.

Although there were a number of British ships stationed off the

South Coast, including those facing Cherbourg, only two vessels were assigned to accompany the follow-up convoy – a corvette, HMS *Azalea*, and a First World War destroyer, HMS *Scimitar*; but after being damaged in a minor collision, the destroyer put into port and a replacement vessel arrived at the scene too late.

It was on 27 April that the first landings were made following the 'bombardment' part of the exercise, and unloading followed for the next two days. It was then that the follow-up convoy of another eight LSTs – Landing Ships Tank – was expected, but it was this convoy which would meet death and destruction beyond all contemplation. Soon after midnight some German torpedo boats – E-Boats – got into the act with tragic results.

Today a Sherman tank stands on Slapton Sands. It was put in position through the efforts of Ken Small of Torcross and his friends and is now the memorial to nearly 1,000 American soldiers and sailors who lost their lives in this chaotic and unbelievably mismanaged exercise. Ken has written a book about it called *The Forgotten Dead* and I have used this for my information. He ran a boarding house near Torcross and due to his beachcombing hobby, he gradually found items that bore very important relevance to the tragic exercise: most especially he discovered a submerged Sherman tank which he got back on shore. His perseverance gradually enabled him to piece together the astonishing story, though the UK and American governments had shown little or no interest. However, an official memorial now stands on Slapton Sands, erected by the American military in thanks for the people of South Hams having evacuated their homes in the Second World War. There is no mention of the men who lost their lives there, but Ken has rescued the Sherman tank and it now stands as a memorial to those who were the victims.

To pick up my story again – the whole of our brigade travelled on the one ship, a Cunarder. It took us three days to reach Reykjavik harbour. On board was an RTO (Railway Transport Officer) and sergeant, complete with supplies of railway warrants – the fact that Iceland does not have a railway seemed to have escaped the notice of the War Office!

The ship returned to England with officers and men of the

Toronto Scottish on board. We took over their barracks, which comprised a group of huts built around a large parade ground made of lava dust and crushed stone. These Canadian-built huts were fitted out with huge stoves and were agreeably warm. When the bad weather turned in May and June 1941 to a delightful, if short, summer the troops began to forget the stories of inhospitable climate. Only the arrival of millions of mosquitoes from the inland lakes formed or swelled by the melting snow caused some aggravation. It was a luxury much appreciated by the men to be able to slip down to a stream of hot water gurgling only yards from their sleeping huts for their morning shave. Later we were able to read a newspaper out in the open at near midnight. Then there was the reversal of long hours of darkness.

Our battalion, the 11th Durham Light Infantry, part of 70th Brigade, now joined the 49th Division, our new divisional sign being a polar bear shown on four legs, pawing the ground.

It always appeared to me that Iceland had as much in common with Germany as the Scandinavian countries, though historically, of course, the Danes were closer to them. Denmark had granted Iceland independence on 1 December 1918. Traffic policemen – in fact all their police force was, I understand trained in Hamburg – seemed rather disdainful in directing our vehicles, while some shopkeepers appeared to be less than enthusiastic at serving us. The girls, the stulkas, were not, however, lacking in enthusiasm in their welcome.

It was not long before I was involved with the local radio station, running a weekly forces programme in addition to my duties with the Battalion. One day an actor serving in the Royal Navy and who had come ashore wounded on HMS *Prince of Wales*, came to see me at the radio station. It was only when he arrived that I discovered he had lost his sight in the action with the *Bismarck*. He was Esmond Knight. He was so cheerful and so obviously a real pro that in no time, with the use of a strong hanging mike that he could not knock over, he was reciting Shakespeare and making other splendid contributions on the radio. I like to feel that in a very small way I helped to restore his confidence in continuing his distinguished career as an actor which was to include, of course, his brilliant appearance as Bernardo in the 1948 film of *Hamlet* produced by Laurence Olivier who starred in it with Jean Simmons as Ophelia.

We soon had regular forces broadcasts of our own, though this was entirely in one's own free time as I was busy with my Bren-gun carriers and discovering how lava-strewn fields were no respecter of tracked vehicles. Long after an exercise with troops had ended somewhere out in the countryside my lads would continue hammering home the pinions after repairs to the tracks which had been broken by constant strain on the uneven rocky surfaces. The trick was to endeavour to get the right tension on the tracks, but the armoured carriers had a more than ever useful part to play as much of the terrain excluded the use of motorised vehicles.

I was given leave of absence from the Battalion in order to take a concert party I had organised on a tour of detachments and some ack-ack (anti-aircraft) sites. We were away for three weeks. We had the use of a small trawler, complete with skipper and two deck hands and off we went. Our stages were extremely makeshift and our audiences sometimes only about two or three dozen. Once we played to only ten men, but the object was to let these servicemen feel they were not forgotten. Some of the detachments were perched on really desolate cliffs from which they maintained watch for enemy aircraft. Of course it was all impromptu knockabout stuff with the signature tune – and what else? – of 'Ama Polar', a popular song of the time, one item being a chorus of what appeared to be polar bears.

So with all my duties as Carrier Officer with the rank of Captain and this tour, plus staging a revue for two nights at the Fish Theatre, Reykjavik, and my weekly broadcasts, I had no free time. But that was by far the best way to be in a land that could be inhospitable. There was also a need to keep up morale in one's own detachment, apart from my voluntary efforts to help entertain the Brigade. I remember how when Vera Lynn's voice came over on the radio, all the lads stopped and listened.

I began to write to my soldiers' families where I heard that they had illnesses or some other worries, to say nothing of the dangers of their being bombed. Our huts had semi-circular tin roofs which I thought made them look inside like tube trains, so I had them painted with London Underground signs and advertisements. We soon began to experience the shortened hours of the day which could be depressing.

It was a strange, muted kind of life. We lived within a community yet without too many ties. But one day all that changed. The Americans arrived. Standing beneath a statue of Lief Ericson in the main harbour at Reykjavik – he is the man Icelanders claim discovered America – I watched as the first of a convoy of white-painted ships anchored outside the entrance. I think it was Senator Wheeler who had let the secret out of the bag in Washington. Anyway, the news was out, the Yanks were coming. Yet America was not yet in the War. That didn't bother the stulkas. The Yanks got a hero's reception. They always did. We got on well enough with them. Many of them appeared to be quite bewildered. It's a long way from Arkansas. We soon traded jeeps for trucks.

Icelanders tend to be physically large with slow smiles and seemingly a rather serious view on life. They were caught up in a situation that was obviously not at all to their liking, but as the second-largest European island after Britain it was impossible for them not to be involved. I am sure they meant to be friendly, though detached in their manner.

Almost treeless, hedgeless and without any fields to speak of, the only cultivation is on the flooded coastal plains and elsewhere the predominant colour is black, mostly from lava crust. Thousands of tough little ponies roam the rough terrain. The fact that it has much of the world's best salmon fishing in some sixty superb rivers – one of them runs through the capital itself and yields some 1,800 fish a year – was not much more than a statistic to an occupying military force, though fish was at first a welcome item on the menu. We were able to see the tremendous two-step waterfall of Gull Foss and I for one gawped at the geysers at Geysir: white steam jets, tiny blue puddles, rotten egg pongs. The population is only six to the square mile and most of them live in Reykjavik, which as a place made Milton Keynes look smart. From what I hear it has not greatly improved.

The airstrip at Kaldarnes was of immense strategic value and everyone in the military personnel based in or near Reykjavik was obliged to take part in its building. Regardless of rank, each did several hours stint a week labouring work. This included General Curtice himself. This airfield was, of course, vital to the Battle of the Atlantic. It was from here, for instance, that the successful attack on the *Bismarck* was launched.

One day at fairly short notice we paraded for the visit of 'A Very Important Person'. Mr Churchill inspected us on his way back to Britain, having met President Roosevelt in Newfoundland. Walking down the lines he came face to face with several companies of Norwegian soldiers, obviously experts in arctic warfare. This must have prompted him to talk about reinvading Norway, for there was this sudden interest in glaciers, how to cross them and how to climb icy cliffs, though that did not, at first, extend further than an exploratory group of about thirty officers who were despatched for training to the centre of Iceland. Later the Mountain and Snow Warfare Centre was established at Akureyri in the north. And who should be sent on the course? Why, yours truly – a month of living out in the open, virtually in the sub-Arctic, building and living in igloos, or in snow holes, or in two-man tents. There was a strict drill. First man lay full length in the tent whilst second man took the first man's boots off. These were, of course, caked in snow which had to be kept out of the tent for obvious reasons. Second man puts his feet in doorway of tent whilst first man, who is inside, cleans the boots free of snow. Movement of two heavily garbed men inside the small tent was done by warning the other man that you were about to turn, or whatever.

The instructors included Norwegian Army personnel. We wore all-white overalls over our uniforms and mittens. Underwear consisted of string vests and long johns. Laundry was seldom. It was a pretty dedicated sort of existence. My only worry was trying to achieve the skiing standard required for military purposes – which was difficult – involving skiing with and using a rifle (all white), wearing a pack (all white), moving at speed and being able to take rapid evasic action. Also, to achieve sudden firing positions much target practice was required. Snow shoes were, I decided, easier to use, if slower.

The main diet was pemmican and hot drinks. The best description of pemmican is that it is a kind of concentrated form of meatballs which has the effect of clogging up the interior works!

My presence on this grinding course was probably due retribution for having inconvenienced a number of people a few weeks previously. Let me explain. There was to have been a big brigade exercise across some of the country's least inviting terrain. I knew that, as the senior carrier officer in the Brigade, I would be actively involved for at least the two days and nights of its duration, which I found very worrying. The terrain, being across a vast lava field, was really abominable for tracked vehicles and I was most unhappy about it. I tried to register my discomfort to no avail, and was therefore anxious to do a reconnaissance on my own. Two days before the exercise was due to take place I took a 15-cwt truck with four of my carrier drivers on board for some miles along a road parallel to some of the worst lava fields. Leaving the Sergeant in charge of the truck to carry along the road that ran along the side of the Hvalafjord, I took my driver, Corporal Billy Percival, to try and 'walk the course' as it were. It would be three to four miles across to where I expected to hit the road again and I instructed the truck to keep patrolling the road to pick us up. Map references on this kind of wild territory are impracticable.

That seemed a reasonable enough operation and Percival and I on foot made quite good progress at first. It was, as I had feared, a very bad section for carriers. Part of the lava bed in that area was made up of boulders the size of a carrier itself, which would make their use impossible. Also, a number of fast-flowing streams were strewn with jagged rocks. They were themselves like anti-tank traps. A strong wind sprang up and veered round almost all the points of the compass. Dark clouds rolled close overhead and in a matter of minutes we were lashed by heavy rain. It should be appreciated that due to the presence of lodestone, the use of a compass in Iceland is impossible. Often the pointer just swings erratically. We tried to keep in the right direction, bending into the wind, but the compass needle kept swinging. Then came the sleet. In a matter of minutes we were at the centre of what can only be described as a blizzard.

I thought if we could find running water that might lead us to a valley, so, painfully slowly, we edged down a fall in the terrain. Suddenly my foothold slipped on a rock that gave way and I was upended so that I shot down an incline and at the bottom my head sustained a sharp blow. It's true – one really does see stars. I must have been out for the count for several minutes until, rain sodden and with a now painful shoulder, I got going again. All this time Corporal Billy Percival kept up his spirits like a true Durham lad.

Now with the blizzard rapidly increasing it became much colder. 'We must keep going,' I told him. 'It will be fatal to stop.'

But we made very slow progress having to bend into the wind now raging all about us. It becomes very tiring being bent almost double like this the whole time. The wind had the trick of suddenly dropping, enabling one to stand upright and begin to make better progress, until with a sudden squall spiked with icy daggers it came roaring in again, bringing all movement to a standstill. Then it took some time to get upright and get started again, but it was essential to keep going.

I don't know how long we kept battling on – probably another four hours – when suddenly the boulder-strewn lava bed beneath us began to flatten out in places and there was sudden relief to our trudging, ankle-bending progress. There was now spiky grass underfoot and incredibly we began to walk freely. In less than an hour we had reached a track along which we stumbled eagerly and were knocking on a farmhouse door. We were at once admitted and, believe me, it was a wonderful feeling. The farmer told us later that a rough track ran on for about half a mile to the road where we had intended to rejoin the others. We had arrived as planned – almost. By that time Carrier Sergeant Dabner MM had returned to camp and quite rightly given the alarm.

The farmer's wife fussed around us and I will always be grateful to her and her family. We were fed and our sodden clothing was exchanged for long john combinations made of delightfully soft sheep's wool. We had even more hot soup and went to bed, while the farmer undertook to inform the military.

Denis Hamilton, our Adjutant, arrived in due course and we were transferred to hospital in Reykjavik to be treated for suspected minor frostbite. Conditions were so bad, in fact, that the whole exercise was cancelled. Some press men who had arrived from London to cover it instead filed stories about our adventure. Apparently I had been trying to shoot ptarmigan for food! Now there's a good twist to a story.

Once out of hospital, a month in sub-Arctic conditions certainly hardened me up physically and created a strong self-confidence which, added to a natural interest in others and an ability to communicate, was to lead me into a particular sphere of army life.

After Akureyri I caught up with my battalion, which was now based at Pontypool in Wales. It wasn't so much the arrival of a north country mining battalion that had caused a stir amongst the locals, as the Indian mule teams complete with Indian grooms. These splendid animals were kept next to Pontypool greyhound track and all officers had apparently been told to report there by 7.00 a.m. the next day so that the commanding officer, Lieutenant Colonel 'Jumbo' Sanders, could give a demonstration on how to handle a horse. Of course, I missed all this, but I understand that the sight of most of our Infantry officers trying to cope with these highly bred animals was wonderful to behold.

Soon we moved to North Wales to a delightful spot in the Black Mountains where further horse trials took place. Transforming a Durham Light Infantry unit into mountain troops certainly had its funny side. Each battalion had something like fifty to a hundred mules attached to it and the troops were shown by Indian NCOs how to load them with ammunition, machine guns and mortars. No doubt Mr Churchill had his eye on us once again for warfare in the mountains.

I enjoyed the day-long marches and bivouacking, but this was not to be for long for there was now an urgent push on tough training and the Army's own 'assault and battery' course, officially known as the Advanced Handling and Fieldcraft Centre, was set up at Llanberis based on the Dolbardan Hotel. My name, it seems, was already with them. Jumbo Sanders moved on as he was now forty-five years old, and our new CO was a real corker, Lieutenant Colonel Nigel Poett. He was destined to finish his service as a full General. He was very tall, extremely good looking and forthright and I liked him immensely. He was not to be with us long, however, and he was later promoted to command an airborne brigade which was to gain immortal fame on D-Day when capturing the vital Pegasus Bridge.

Anyway, off I went to report to Llanberis. We were based in basic rooms in the hotel and in tents in the grounds. It was a little distressing to note on arrival that the Explosives Sergeant had two fingers missing and somewhat alarming that the CO, Ivor Evans, a dynamic Colonel in the Royal Welsh Fusiliers, seemed always to carry a shotgun over his shoulder. Also, on my first day I noted that signals to the Mess staff that we were on our way back after a reconnaissance of the area were done by exploding hand grenades.

We were told that sick parades would not be tolerated. Rations were to be minimal. Full kit would be carried at all times. Anyone reporting late would be at once returned to their units.

We worked on and around Pont Pen y Cenglog (946) and Gylder Jack (994) reached via the Pass of Llanberis and over to Pont Cyfyng above Capel Curig and areas around Mount Snowdon itself, including the Watkins Pass, named after 'Gino' Watkins the explorer. Unfortunately I gradually developed a badly swollen foot which went septic. I got hold of a civilian doctor whose surgery I had spotted near the hotel. I asked him if he would privately and secretly slip in at night to deal with my foot and give me sleeping tablets and injections against pain. I also arranged with a sentry to wake me each morning around 4.00 a.m. in order that I could plunge my foot into a bucket of cold water in order to get the swelling down and thus get my boot on. I made no indication to the Directing Staff whatsoever that anything was amiss. Unknown to me, however, they had become aware of all this. Anyway, I got a 'D' for the course – that is a 'Distinction' pass. On return I was on Brigadier's Orders so that he could have me up and congratulate me.

Back at the unit I had my beloved Carrier Platoon once again. The Bren-gun carriers were tracked vehicles, lightly armoured and with Ford V8 engines, usually carrying, in addition to the driver, the Sergeant or Corporal in charge of the vehicle sitting next to him and at the rear four others, two abreast, facing one another, all armed. A section comprised three carriers, each with a Bren gun and mounting, commanded by an officer in a jeep. There would normally be three sections making a total of nine Bren-gun carriers.

The next highly prized promotion was to command 'A Company' which comprised a platoon of thirty soldiers (transportable in two

15-cwt trucks), a section of three Bren-gun carriers with their crews, numbering nine men, and about a dozen motorcyclists. With mechanics it made about sixty-five all told. This is what I wanted and got – that is until the War Office started playing their games.

After Dunkirk, it had demanded that a firm emphasis be put on physical fitness. Also it would not permit any officer of forty-five or over to command a battalion. The War Office started what was then termed a battle school. This was at Barnard Castle, County Durham and the idea of battle schools was soon to be duplicated at divisional level in various parts of the country, but Barnard Castle was the official War Office School of Infantry. There was widespread urgency to increase personal awareness, get toughened up and employ new basic tactics for the Infantry, and yours truly was selected to attend. It was an amazing sight. There were stuffed models of German soldiers bobbing up across open ground where there were all manner of awkward obstacles to be negotiated under real overhead fire – the description 'overhead' had been taken too literally for a number of tracer bullets started getting very close indeed and there were, I am afraid, casualties and, I believe, a question was asked in the House of Commons as a result. Buckets of pigs' blood were available and the models of German soldiers were liberally douched in this mixture and then bayoneted – 'in, out' – to the accompaniment of raucous yells from the instructors of 'Could you kill a German?' Live hand grenades, booby traps and smoke screens – it was military mayhem!

'Down, crawl, observe, sights, fire' was to be the automatic reaction drill on being held up and the Infantry Section Commander would clearly indicate 'Bren gun there!' to the man carrying the Bren gun, who would at once fling himself to the ground and get ready to fire.

This new kind of tactic, simple as it was, swept through the Army dispensing with the old training manuals, and I must say I could not help but notice, for instance, how incongruous it seemed when Major General Neil Ritchie, Commander of the famous 51st Division and just back from the tanks hiatus at Knightsbridge in the Western Desert could be seen attending a lecture on this given by a TA Lieutenant Colonel who had never himself been in action. Still, this was the spirit of the new and now urgent drive for toughness and improved basic tactics in the field after our severe setbacks in France.

Afterwards I got back to my unit again and took over my carriers. My report followed showing a 'Pass with Distinction'. One day soon afterwards I was out on a reconnaissance with one of the companies when a despatch rider arrived and approached me. Would I follow him to the scene of an accident involving one of my carriers? I immediately followed him in my jeep. I was, of course, desperately concerned and I was then told that one of my carriers, under the orders of one of the Infantry companies on an exercise, had turned over. I raced to the scene. It was highly improbable that a carrier should turn over unless it were driven along an extremely steep side of a hill. Apparently it had happened less than fifteen minutes before. On arrival I could see a body lying face downwards. It was Corporal Billy Percival, my driver. On inspection I could see that his lower back and abdomen had burst open under the weight of the upturned carrier. It was a desperately sad loss of a popular, hard-working and loyal young man who had never let me down. He was a true example of these splendid Durham lads.

I have to include when referring to the unit's general high standard of discipline and morale, the fact that due to the high mortality rate of pitmen in action it was decided by the Government that battalions drawn on mining personnel should be helped out by Royal Scots Fusiliers and others who mixed in very well and were excellent lads.

Back home for a week's leave, one of those demanding War Office telegrams reached me. It read, 'You have been posted as Instructor to the School of Infantry – stop – to report by 18th February at latest – to return here by Tuesday night in order to hand over before departure – 11th Durhams.'

'There we go again!' I thought. 'No sooner back with my own mob than it's handover time again.' Back at the School of Infantry I was soon in the thick of it, but this time as an instructor and I concentrated on the work of the Carrier Platoon. Later I was informed in writing by the Commandant that I would make a good Chief Instructor of the Carrier Wing and that my appointment was imminent. I was really chuffed about this, but whilst eagerly awaiting confirmation, yet another of those tiresome telegrams arrived. This time it was an obscure message about reporting to the War Office.

Quite in the dark as to what it was all about, but somewhat frustrated, I went up to London to an address in Whitehall where I was duly shown into a small office. At a desk sat a Lieutenant Colonel whose lower face was partly obscured by an enormous moustache. My first reaction was to be on my guard – my thoughts were 'Blimey, what have we got here? Seems to be part of a Victorian melodrama!' The thoughts raced through my mind. 'What's this all about? Is it about being parachuted to join Tito's men in Jugoslavia, or what?'

I had mixed feelings, ranging from obvious curiosity as to what it was leading up to, some excitement, but especially frustration at any interference with my imminent appointment as Chief Instructor, Carrier Wing at the War Office School of Infantry.

He introduced himself as Lord Rowallan and then told me how the Adjutant General, Sir Ronald Forbes Adam, on being appointed in 1941, had discovered considerable weaknesses in the method of selecting men for commissions and the posting of officers to the various arms of the service. The failure rate had risen as high as 50 per cent in some instances, which was alarming. This was interesting enough, although it still did not make much sense to me and particularly as to where I came in, but the enthusiasm of the speaker began to dispel the feeling that I had landed in some sort of bizarre situation, especially when in a light-hearted touch he said that he had vowed not to shave off his moustachios until we had defeated Hitler.

The outcome of it was that he explained how he had been given the job of setting up a centre where potential young officers could get a programme of such a tough and challenging nature that they would be able to greatly develop their own powers of leadership. They would have to undergo considerable physical endurance. The centre would be in either the Mountains of Mourne, or in the West of Scotland. He had apparently visited both Llanberis and the School of Infantry, said that he had followed up my reports and thought that I would be admirable as a member of his staff. He was very persuasive.

As to myself? I was not so sure. Of course, I loved the idea of the out-of-doors challenge and all that, plus one's interest in the character development of others, but I realised that I would be tucked away in a remote part, far from my cherished War Office connections and, of course, my beloved Battalion. Taking part in some nutty War Office experiment wasn't going to help me get into action, either, and I began to think up ways of avoiding my selection. I would go to my Battalion CO and appeal. I was, in fact, given no choice as yet another telegram speedily arrived instructing me to go to Kingussie.

Thus, early on a bright day in late May 1943, the town of Kingussie in Invernesshire saw the arrival of twelve officers, of which I was one, and twenty-four sergeants. Rumour spread quickly, after our disappearance in a convoy of trucks up the track to Glenfeshie, that the military had further designs on the area. The War had thus far thankfully kept its distance from this quiet and pleasant community, though, of course, some of its men and women had departed on War Service and there were ack-ack posts in the locality.

In the glen itself there were Newfoundlanders cutting and storing timber, and a small army establishment which was the old Mountain and Snow Warfare Centre I had known in Iceland, now greatly reduced in numbers and activity, almost down to a mere holding company. Their presence, however, had given rise to some romantic tales in the district for they had a number of huskies which local people had seen being exercised in the hills. They were, in fact, kept in large kennels behind Glenfeshie Lodge, a spacious house at the head of the glen, which was to become our officers' headquarters and Mess. The sound of some fifty huskies howling to the moon was quite eerie.

When the time came for the use of the huskies to be ended, the dogs were distributed elsewhere and the late Gerard Jordan, one of the HFTC (Highland Fieldcraft Training Centre) Directing Staff, 'adopted' one of the Icelandic husky puppies, which he eventually had sent to his home at Malvern. Some time later contact was made with a member of the Eskdale Outward Bound

School who had a Siberian husky puppy named Sister, which had also been brought back from the expedition. Provisional arrangements were made for a mating and this resulted in surely one of the strangest telegrams ever handled by the Post Office. It read 'Regret Sister not on heat, am writing.'

A handsome labrador puppy was presented to me by the Snow Warfare Centre before they left. I called him 'Brinjie' which was the name of the Norwegian-made string vests we wore. Brinjie became a most wonderful companion and was to travel with me on land, sea and in the air. He revelled in the exercises – what we called 'Bashing on across the hills'. Sometimes when we were out overnight sleeping in a bivouac or out in the open, I would use him as a pillow, but often around 4 or 5 a.m. he would creep away on the prowl, causing me a jolt and rude awakening. He was to retire to my home in Kenton, Newcastle upon Tyne, thence to London and finally ended his days with my sister Doreen in Ponteland near Newcastle upon Tyne.

Seconded to us were four of their officers. Major Bill Williamson, who was to become our Chief Instructor, Major Tom Peacock (Climbing Instructor), Major Tony Tunnard (Ski Instructor) and Captain 'Sandy' Wilson (Small Arms Expert). Except for Bill Williamson and Tom Peacock, the above named were soon transferred elsewhere and, in fact, I took over command of No. 1 Company from Tom Peacock after a few weeks. The announcement of my elevation in rank came when Billy Rowallan said jocularly, 'Ken – you are improperly dressed,' meaning that I should be wearing a crown, which was the correct badge of rank, on my epaulettes – we usually wore thick army sweaters and no jackets – whereupon Duncan Chisholm, a Staff Sergeant who came from the Lovat Scouts and was, I believe, Lord Lovat's Head Gamekeeper and attached to us, went out to shoot a stag in celebration. His shot happened to ricochet with the result that he got two stags with the one shot. I was able to grab three days leave and take home a sackful of venison, which greatly pleased the neighbours.

Our programme aimed at inculcating the independence and self-reliance characteristic of pioneers and included daily muster parade and arms drill, care of arms, weapon training, woodcraft, observation training, botany, map reading, compass work, astronomy, make and mend of clothing and equipment, pioneering, signalling, improvised methods of crossing rivers, swimming, bayonet and unarmed combat, rock climbing and the use of explosives. Also the study of 'man management' – very important. There was quickly a strong sense of teamwork and esprit de corps in what became one of the toughest training schools any army has ever devised.

The transition from the first day of the students' arrival to as early as ten days hence was truly remarkable. Like Topsy, they just grew and grew in character. The old story about the Gurkha soldiers who were taken for parachute training comes to mind. As the plane flew over the dropping zone, so the story went, the Gurkhas mildly asked if for the first jump the plane could fly at a lower height. The officer in charge pointed out that this would not give enough time for the parachute to open. Great smiles came to their faces. 'Oh! You are giving us parachutes, then!'

The cadets were periodically shuffled then reshuffled into new groups or platoons within the company. This encouraged adaptability to new companions. When this was done, for instance, every fortnight, the cream, as it were, could be regrouped with the cream. Hidden talent emerged. One man is not necessarily the best leader in all circumstances. Sometimes in a tricky situation in the middle of an exercise – perhaps on reaching the peak of a mountain trek – we would whisk away the leader and either suddenly leave the second in command to cope, or take him away as well and thus see who then emerged as the leader out there in rather alien conditions. Afterwards reporting privately in writing on their opinions of how the others had coped may have seemed a bit un-British, but it was very revealing. The guy who thought he was 'the cat's whiskers' could have wilted had he read some of the other opinions thus expressed. These reports were always destroyed immediately on being read by the instructor.

When the cadets, on arrival at the railway station at Kingussie, were put into trucks for the journey up the valley, they must have wondered a lot, but then no doubt were encouraged to see about an hour later at the end of the track some rows of quite superb wooden huts which had been left by the departing Canadians.

Paraded outside with their kits they were later given an introductory talk. They were instructed to look up to the treeline on the nearby hills. 'That is where you sleep tonight. You will proceed there once you have been given a hot meal here. You will be allowed one blanket each, some rations and cooking utensils. That will be where you will spend the next twenty-four hours.' (Or words to that effect; I am not sure at this lapse of time.) The effect was stunning.

This, then, was the setting. All around were the rolling tree-lined mountains and through the camp ran the river – about thirty yards wide and to be the scene of much frantic bridge building and exhausting obstacle courses, to say nothing of the assault course which crossed and recrossed it, to be negotiated in full kit with rifle – plus all manner of divertissements. I vaguely remember doing it six times in one day, in full kit, cajoling and yelling at the poor fellows who were either wallowing in mud, splashing in the river or tearing along its bank screaming blue murder while bayonetting wretched dummies.

Lord Rowallan gripped the imagination of all and often referred to the exploits of his friend, Brigadier Bernard Fergusson (Lord Ballantree) with the Chindits.

We were in a landscape that, barring some afforestation, had remained unchanged for a thousand years. Here in the glen was reputedly the place of Landseer's sentimental evocation 'The Monarch of the Glen'. The Highlands of Scotland are utterly intoxicating, causing the imagination to work at times feverishly as the beauty around one lifts one's spirits. The golden eagle is at home in the upper reaches, building its eyrie either in rocks or trees in some inaccessible spot. Could we say with Robbie Burns that 'Our heart is in the Highlands'?

Notes from a cadet's log book include the following:

Evening relaxation was available in the NAAFI, a large log hutment, with a few casual tables and chairs and a counter for serving tea and buns. Jimmy Shand type of music constantly flowed from a loudspeaker, spilling out its sequence of Scottish reels, marches, strathspeys, pibrochs and songs on an accordion. Many tunes I can recall today whenever I think about Glenfeshie.

Teams of huskies were driven along the rough tracks, wet or dry, pulling a sledge of considerable weight, long whips cracking overhead and sometimes thunderflashes exploding alongside.

One evening the Canadian sergeant in charge strode into the NAAFI with his favourite husky. It looked more like a male lion in size and colour. Rearing up alongside his master the dog planted its elbows on the counter, large mouth drooling he gazed into the face of the unnerved canteen assistant. At his master's request he was served first and lay under the table munching away just like the perfect domestic pet!

I thought that I would go on to include further notes from his diary. Note the events lead on from the first twenty-four hours finding and sleeping in a makeshift shelter up in the woods. But first, to quote from Wordsworth, let me add, 'Bliss was in that dawn to be alive. But to be young was very heaven!'

No 1 Coy HFTC Glen Feshie No 3 Course (September 1943)

Fairly early in the course, we were assembled for a night march, at the end of a normal day's training.

We climbed laboriously up slopes, gradually skirting Carn Ban Mor. The weather closed in, with rain and mists that became thicker as we approached the mountain tops.

The idea was that we should reach the ridge overlooking the South end of Lock Einich about midnight, and make a 'mountaineer descent' with ropes etc down the precipitous crags of Coir na Caillich with the aid of flares fired intermittently from the loch shore, a thousand feet below.

It was bitterly cold on the top and the thick mist made it almost impossible to keep in touch with the chap in front.

Uneven rock-strewn ground caused stumbling, while a few yards to our right, a chasm yawned.

Things became hazardous, but we were led to the very edge, in preparation for a descent. Verey lights were fired and as they fell, giant stacks like castle turrets were revealed, thrusting up through the whirling mists, while the green spluttering flares lit up an awesome backdrop, worthy of a Grieg epic.

Decision was made to 'stay put' and we bedded down for the

night on what even rock we could find. To proceed would have been suicidal.

Bundled together for mutual warmth, I took my boots off, donned dry socks, wrapping my feet in my dry towel, and strapped the flap down tight, on my haversack, around my ankles. With angora woollen balaclava rolled down over my face, I was warm at both ends, and actually slept.

At dawn we were aroused; strangely, I was quite snug, until I rolled over to get up, and disturbed the water around my rump, which my body had 'warmed'! Surrounding cold water flooded in and I was soon 'up and about'!

The mist was still hanging but thinning. We did some exercises in pairs, to get the circulation going and resumed picking our way along the ridge, northwards.

By this time we were beginning to feel the misery of the night, and a sense of lost direction. Our sojourn had seemed interminable, as if we were doomed to tramp blindly through mountain tops for ever.

At last we began to descend, and suddenly we emerged from the mist – the clouds, like curtains, lifted, and as we halted to make breakfast on the high slopes, we were amazed as brilliant sunshine lit up the grandeur of the panorama spread out below us. The Spey, a silver serpent winding down the Strath, interspersed with forests and sprinkled with lochans, stretching away to the hills of Duthil and Rothiemurchus, gladdened the eye!

The warmth of the sun, the aroma of bacon, and the taste of hot tea, created a brief Paradise, then refreshed, it was 'Bash On!' – 'Again!'

G.W.W. Halnan

John Downton, a company commander at HFTC and later to be a housemaster at Gordonstoun, puts it well when he says,

If you ask anyone who went through HFTC what he remembers most strongly, you are almost certain to be told about the remarkable spirit of cheerful commitment and the strong feeling of mutual support. There was an atmosphere of being in it together, of seeing each other through, of playing down one's own discomforts for the sake of the team effort ... Circumstances were not infrequently unpleasant – discomfort, pain, exhaustion, even plain terror were also there, but we showed that we could stretch ourselves further than we had ever dreamed possible.

There was certainly plenty of battle inoculation – Duncan Chisholm, fixing with the aid of a telescopic lens on, say, a party crossing a lake, would target the shots close enough to cause a draught as they passed by! Signal pistols, smoke bombs, cakes of gun cotton, anti-tank grenades, thunderflashes were all part of the armoury. Dawn raids, night attacks, ambushes, daylight 'dummy raids' which caused discomfort and disruption such as the non-arrival or disappearance of rations, abseiling down sheer rock faces in full kit, all-night marches, plodding through bogs, approaches waist high in a river – the daily, and nightly, menu for living was never lacking in variety if, at times, revoltingly indigestible.

Alertness was imperative because the cadet could be called upon suddenly to conduct the proceedings himself. The aim was to push back the boundaries of what one could do; to be confident in oneself.

The 'Devil's Ride', as it became known, or 'Death Slide', was a spectacular test of nerve. The student dipped his 6-foot long toggle rope into the waters of the Feshie in order to get it thoroughly wet, then climbed the high left bank and a yet higher Scots pine. Near the top he saw an instructor perched near the launching platform. A thick rope ran from the tree to the base of another tree the other side of the river. The student placed his toggle rope over the thicker rope, grasped the smaller with both hands and launched himself into space. If all went well he arrived a few seconds later safely on the far bank of the river; if the main rope was slack, he found himself suspended above or in the river.

One day I jotted down an idea on the back of an envelope, which became the exercise I called 'Fit To Drop'. This involved men in full kit with rifle standing in the back of a moving lorry and at a given signal taking a running jump out of the back and on to the ground, preparing to roll back on to their feet, rifle at the ready. Needless to say, the speed of the lorry was restricted.

The course lasted ten weeks and as you may have guessed, at

the end of it I put on a stage show. I know you will forgive me if I quote the following from the local newspaper, the *Badenoch Record*, as it might convey the fun and excitement that a show can create. Lots of local people, two busloads from a nearby hospital, truckloads of personnel from ack-ack units from miles around, Women's Army and nurses, RAF crews on stand-down, plus our own cadets and staff all converged on the hall, which was, of course, blacked out. In those days we were all thrown together and this bred its own spirit. Remember, there was, of course, no television and radio programmes were somewhat restricted.

The Badenoch Record, 31 July 1943

'Never a Dull Moment'

The Victoria Hall, Kingussie, was filled to capacity on Thursday night at both performances of the musical revue, 'Never a Dull Moment,' presented by students of the Highland Fieldcraft Training Centre. Appreciative audiences witnessed a production that lacked nothing in the way of sparkle, originality, or spectacle, due to splendid team-work on the part of these amateur players.

A novel introduction kept the audience guessing, as a chorus appeared from the wings to start the ball rolling with a rollicking sea song. The revue gathered momentum when a nautical dancing number was followed by Jock Scott portraying an enthusiastic Boy Scout. 'Morning in the Manse', a short sketch, put the house in the right frame of mind for 'Children of the New Regime', which compared hiking and cycling and demonstrated that both have their disadvantages. Michael Royou, baritone, was well received when he sang 'This is Worth Fighting for' and 'Because God made thee mine'. Another sketch, 'His Wife', proved that wives cannot be trusted. In 'Acte Superbe' a Victorian atmosphere was obtained when four 'muscular' giants gave amazing demonstrations with a barbell.

By this time the audience had settled down and fun sped fast and furious as four lightning sketches were put over. It was illustrated that medical students and painters have a little in common, even if it is only white smocks. 'Room 392' showed that the tenant is always right! 'Sporting Events' brought popular sports meetings to the stage

Lieutenant Colonel Lord Rowallan MC, TD.
(Camera Press, *London*)

à la BBC, and the final flash – 'Gangsters All' – gave one a glimpse into the private life of mobmen. Pathos was introduced in a busking scene from which an impression was obtained of an episode in a Cockney busker's life. 'The Voice of Inexperience', Arthur Baxter, gave a realistic impersonation of BBC star Oliver Wakefield, with topical subjects in clever original patter.

The first act reached a crescendo with a musical number 'Song in my Heart' that had the people singing and tapping their feet. During an interval J.C. Brown and P.S. Drake entertained on the piano, and the second half got a rousing send-off with the novelty 'A.T.S.' chorus, 'The Kingussie Kickers', who bewitched the audience with their 'feminine' charms and daintiness (?) that would have made a Metro-Goldwyn scout look twice. A popular turn was a clever bit of nonsense and whistling by Smudger Smith in 'Strike a Light'. Next on the programme was Ken Johnstone, whose serious monologue, 'Amongst those Present', described the greatness of the Regiments of the Line.

Many of our exercises started up through the glen itself past Glenfeshie Lodge and on by the side of the Feshie and beneath Mulloch (3,338 feet) or we cut away above the camp beneath

'The River Feshie' (Murdo MacLeod, Edinburgh).

Meall Dugh (3,268 feet). Ben Macdhuie (4,296 feet) was, of course, the highest peak, with Loch Etchuchan beneath it, and probably the most spectacular setting was amidst the Torridon Hills and when 'bashing on' through the Larig Ghu.

Fitness became the watchword. A man's feet and his shoulders (where the straps of his pack could dig deep) were barometers of his condition. We were in a world of our own where fitness and character were our currency and attitude was all.

In order to avoid the heavy snow lying on the metal roads it was decided to move for the winter months to the area of Torridon and Gairloch in the West Highlands. Gairloch is the parish name of the country between Loch Torridon and Guinard Bay of Loch Broom. Within its bounds are Loch Maree, which is twelve miles long and world famous for its beauty, only to be rivalled by Loch Lomond and Loch Awe, neither of which has a mountain with so powerful a presence as Slioch, nor the Scots pines and heather that grace the shores of Loch Maree, where deciduous trees happily alternate with coniferous.

Gairloch itself is a village whose population is now augmented by a number of holiday homes or bungalows for full-time residents. The road strikes east over a barren moor until it falls away to the village of Poolewe at the estuary of the River Ewe, where it surges into Loch Ewe, which in itself is twice the size of Gair Loch, fully eight miles long and two miles wide.

The day before war was declared HMV *Guardian* suddenly arrived at the mouth of the loch and was seen to be laying a boom net. A German plane was reported as flying in low, dropping three bombs and then disappearing. This area was code named Port Alabaster and it became a secret and vital focal point for the entire war effort. A fleet of cargo ships regularly brought vital supplies across the Atlantic, escorted by the Navy, to this vast loch. *Renown, Repulse, Dunedin, Exeter* and *Gloucester* were all included in the list of some fourteen warships which conducted these all-important trans-Atlantic convoys. The skippers, after exhausting days and nights on the bridge, usually went to the Loch Maree Hotel for some well-earned sleep. Obviously a network of anti-aircraft posts sprang up and there was increased security.

It was around Poolewe that we established ourselves and after the relatively friendly arrangements of Glenfeshie, were confronted by a much bleaker prospect for administration purposes. The fine Canadian-built huts of the glen were exchanged for Nissen huts vacated by ack-ack crews and other personnel. The Officers' Mess was in a much smaller house than Glenfeshie Lodge. We built an assault course next to it on the edge of a small lake, but this lacked the freedom of movement which we had in and out of the river at Glenfeshie. All this is not to detract from the standard of the course held at Poolewe, but from an administrative point of view it was more complicated.

It is the humid climate that gives the Highlands such a variety of colour so relatively absent in lands of the sun. The West Highlands are notoriously wet and this at once added to the challenge. There was also the nature of the landscape, especially on the island of Skye. Two rocks predominate on the Cuillins: a coarsely crystalline gabbro dear to the heart of mountaineers because it is tough and reliable, and a smooth basalt which can become very slippery when wet. The two rocks are present in equal surface quantities and few of the Cuillin summits can be reached without rock climbing. We were most certainly not into that activity. However, Bruach na Frithe, 3,143 feet, can be reached without rock climbing. The descent, after incidentally one of the best views in the Cuillins, ends in the grassy slopes of Fhionn Choire, which lead back to Sligachan. We also worked on the path up to the Bealach a' Mhaim leading to Glen Brittle on the west side of the range. The north Cuillins can be seen very clearly from here. Lower Glen Brittle is farmed and ends on the great bay of Loch Brittle. We made good friends with the Morrisons, the farmers, and I enjoyed a happy post-war reunion with them.

The Sligachan Inn is reputedly one of the best hotels in the Highlands and, post-war, was run by Ian Campbell, a former cadet at the Highland Fieldcraft Training Centre, until his death in 1996, but the family continue to run it.

Naturally Skye, in particular, lent itself to all manner of alluring exercises. It has to be appreciated that at both centres we were working in an area of Scotland where identity cards had to be carried by all members of the public and all vehicles, including police cars, had to have distributor caps removed when not in use. There was always a real awareness of German parachutists arriving. The danger of spies was far more accentuated in this part of the world. All this led to fair game, for instance, in an 'exercise', where 'The Infiltrators' are being hotly pursued by 'our forces'. It can well be imagined that a party of determined cadets, some in disguise and with a larger party of cadets equally determined in pursuit can lead to all manner of dramatic incidents: such as the Broadford ferry to be seen moving out to sea in a most erratic manner on a hitherto unheard-of route; a small country telephone exchange suddenly being taken 'captive' with a resulting havoc; a lieutenant in the Home Guard indignantly declaring, 'I will not be given orders – I was formerly a General in the Indian Army, sir!'; a red-faced police sergeant saying, 'I only left my car for a few minutes!'

Two people remain clearly in one's mind: Ben Forbes who ran the YMCA in what is now the Poolewe House Hotel – and incidentally was great on the banjo – and Nancy Dumas, then a bright-eyed young schoolgirl helping in the village post office, who was later to run the Poolewe Inn. Nancy still lives in the village and always attends our reunions.

There was an undoubted strain in taking on such challenging conditions and terrain. A cadet in another company unfortunately died of pneumonia when almost within sight of the Sligachan Inn. There were also anxious times waiting at some rendezvous for people to turn up. It should be appreciated that our equipment was not specially adapted – for instance, our boots were ordinary army issue but we had extra windproofs.

In all the activity there was little time for proper, if any, reconnaissance before a company commander had to take on an exercise, or 'scheme' as we called it. I was, for instance, to take the company up Slioch, 3,217 feet, which is named after 'Sleagh' meaning a spear. There had been no previous reconnaissance so I elected to climb by its south-east ridge. The four principal summits are Slioch, Beinn Lair, Meall Mheinnidh and Beinn Ciridh Charr, 2,593 feet The view from above as we climbed embraced a vast tract of rocky mountains; south to Torridon and Flowerdale Forest; east to the still higher peaks of Fannich Forest and north into the wildest region of the Scottish mainland, the forest of Strach na Sheallag and Achaniasgair. We were on a continuous mountain ridge bounding Loch Maree's north shore. It was indeed spectacular.

We worked our way towards the summits of Beinn Lair and Airidh Charr, which buttressed the north side with a fair amount of snow underfoot, but on moving suddenly into the shadows of the north side, the surface changed to ice without warning. The leading sections found they could barely stand and several individuals lost their balance entirely. As more of the company were moving up the slope and also encountering the icy surface, I called out, 'Stop – watch for ice.' Then, 'Get down off the slope – go carefully.' The NCOs also called out such orders.

Naturally, men suddenly floundering on an icy slope want to get off it and regain their balance as quickly as possible and some began to sit on their haunches or glissade the short distance down to the snow, where we were regrouping, As soon as possible, as ordered, everyone got together again on their feet, but unfortunately one of the cadets, Gibson, trying to regain his balance, slid and caught his head on the side of a snow-covered rock. On reaching him I decided that he had a neck or head injury as one might find on a rugby field and he had to be got down the mountain and carried full length carefully. Working in teams the lads did a marvellous job in holding him as securely as possible and I sent two runners forward to find any form of makeshift stretcher. A loose gate was later produced, another runner was sent ahead to alert the big naval hospital at Gulmarg, and a reserve went with him. When we eventually reached the lower ground, we found walking in a river bed caused least upset. Finally, after about four hours since we began the descent, the ambulance crew from Gareloch Naval Hospital took over. It was now dark. Poor Gibson, who had strained ligaments in his neck, did not complete the course and the last I heard he was in practice, post-war, as a dentist in Scotland.

Billy Rowallan appeared to be much less relaxed than he had been at Glenfeshie and his short break at home midway between the course certainly did not appear to help. The nature of the terrain and more complicated administrative arrangements created many problems.

For my part, I was on my third course at HFTC, which was one more than had been originally understood, and I began to feel that I was on borrowed time. For something like a year and a half I had been going really flat out – in the sub-Arctic, at battle schools and at Glenfeshie and Poolewe – with precious little leave and I was admittedly now feeling the strain. However much the starting up and development of the HFTC had been an enormous challenge, it also had been extremely demanding. So much was left to oneself as a company commander. I had requested to have a move, even at the start of our course at Poolewe, but of course I realised that I was now well out of touch with either my Battalion or whatever interesting prospects my War Office Battle School sojourn as Chief Instructor would have brought. Still, on the other hand, it had been a terrific experience at HFTC. I might have been tired, but I was basically enormously fit. I felt that I had made a contribution to its success in my own particular way.

Leadership comes in various brands and is founded on discipline. Xenophon asked Socrates what was the basis of discipline and the answer given then will be the answer 10,000 years from now: 'Discipline is founded upon respect for the officer and confidence in him.' And, as the text goes, the soldier asked again, 'And what are the qualities of such an officer, his fundamental characteristics?' Again the old philosopher answered – and his words are everlastingly true – 'Such an officer is one who has at heart always the best interests of his men.'

My belief – especially with a set-up like the Highland Fieldcraft Centre – was that it was essential to breed as much self-confidence as possible into the men themselves; a belief that to have enthusiasm is absolutely golden. To have a sense of loyalty to your mate and unit is another, but something else is required – an inward confidence – 'You <u>can</u> do it! So – just do it!' That is the maxim.

Of course, in this way one built up a fairly potent head of steam over the ten weeks. 'You <u>can</u> do it!' enlivened the mind, sent the pulse racing. That was one's remit and whatever dynamism I had was directed at achieving as much as possible along these lines so that at the end one wanted to see these guys straining at the bit, ready to show their paces. Of course, like the fizz in a bottle, the cork would in the end come flying out and that is why my company gained a reputation for its 'grand finales' at the end of a course. Witness the departure on the last day when they finally left by train, as individuals, from Kingussie station. With the Commandant smiling and speeding them on their way and the train slowly pulling away – out came the thunderflashes. To cheers, waves and harmless explosions the Company gave its final salute.

The course over in Poolewe in the Highlands ended after ten very hard and physical weeks still with the Company on a high – 'You can do it!' and they did.

I was striding on my own along the road past the little Post Office at Poolewe. It was a moonlight night. Suddenly there was a rush of feet. I was, in fact, 'kidnapped'. Rushed to the little jetty, my pockets were emptied and then down I went into the black waters. Almost the moment I surfaced a boat was alongside. I was at once hauled on board. Towels and a hot toddy and soon dressed again, and to the accompaniment of three rousing cheers, they sang 'For He's a Jolly Good Fellow!' It was an unusual ending to an unusual army experience.

In the autumn of 1976 Major General Philip Ward took over as Commandant of the Royal Military Academy at Sandhurst and wrote to Lord Rowallan, 'Now we need to give the new RMAS Company an appropriate title. May we call it Rowallan Company?' It was the first time in the history of Sandhurst that a company had been called after an individual. In the following March, Major General Ward wrote, 'Rowallan Company is proving a tremendous success. The pilot scheme finishes on 2nd April and we will then take on twice the numbers for succeeding courses.'

This had all come about because the Ministry of Defence had been so impressed by the results achieved at HFTC that it had been decided to incorporate this kind of training for some of the cadets under consideration to be commissioned as officers. It has proved very successful. A Rowallan cadet has won the Sword of Honour and Rowallan officers have won much respect. I have often thought that such training, but of a non-military nature, could be adapted for civilian use for some of our young people. Australia, New Zealand and Canada could help provide the right natural background and the investment in our youth could surely also warrant the cost of transport. The Duke of Edinburgh's Award Scheme and the Outward Bound Schools have pointed in the right direction, but some investment in youth on a much grander scale is needed now that National Service has faded into the past. Much more imaginative thinking and action are required to combat present-day violence and drug taking amongst young people.

After the war ended Lord Rowallan wrote to me and apologised for his sometimes testy attitude at Poolewe when under strain. He said that he looked forward to meeting me at scout conferences in the future.

It so happened that our first meeting after the War was at a scout conference at Filey. It was on a Sunday and in the *Sunday Times* of that day there appeared a feature about him which I had written under a splendid portrait of him by Karsh of Ottawa. I wrote among other things that he had the eyes of a sergeant major but the heart of a Chaplain General and wished him God speed on another world trip etc. Of course the *Sunday Times* sold like hot cakes at the conference and who should I find myself sitting next to in the camp bus that morning but the Chief Scout himself. Instead of congratulating me on my article as I expected, he glared at me. 'Aren't I in enough hot water without you putting your oar in?' he demanded. Sometimes one just can't win!

Strange that a man who so inspired others should have such a turbulent family life.

The spirit of Glenfeshie and Poolwee lives on in the highly successful Highland Fieldcraft Training Centre Association. Thanks to a line of imaginative and highly responsible members of its officers, it flourishes with a present membership of some 175. In 1993, Jim Barnes, a former cadet, edited a splendid 'Golden Book' resplendent with the Association's crest – antler horns with the words 'Air Adhart Au Buaidh' – on the front cover printed in gold, or 'Bash on Regardless!' as members might interpret it.

Each November there is a reunion in the superb setting of the RAF Club in Piccadilly. Previously we met at the Services Club at Hyde Park Corner and after one such gathering I had about seven crammed in my touring car on my way late in the evening to continue our celebrations at my house in Victoria. I was in no state to drive and my 'chauffeur' was Peter Merritt, aged 23, from Vancouver who was staying with me, having been to the Commonwealth Games in Wales. When a bobby held us up – a shocking state of overcrowding, I am afraid – Peter said cheerfully, 'It's all right, officer, they are just a bunch of war heroes.' We were permitted to proceed on our way!

Talking of war heroes, Peter's father, Lieutenant Colonel Cecil Merritt's war had lasted only six hours, but long enough for him to win the Victoria Cross for his heroic leadership at Dieppe. The Dieppe Raid in 1942 was subsequently judged a military disaster and needless waste of lives, especially Canadian lives. Even so, it was a terrific fight and those who survived looked back on 19 August as a day of awesome courage and sacrifice.

The military purpose was to gain experience of an opposed landing and the capture of a continental port in anticipation of launching a second front in north-west Europe. There were also political factors. The Western Allies were under intense pressure from Stalin to 'do something' to draw German reinforcements and aircraft away from the Eastern Front in Russia.

The United States Chiefs of Staff believed that a cross-Channel invasion was feasible in 1943, but Winston Churchill and his military chiefs knew this would be premature. A large-scale raid on the French coast was therefore proposed as a response in spirit to Moscow and, incidentally, a means of demonstrating to the Americans the immense difficulties a full-scale invasion would present.

There was also a Canadian factor. When Britain faced invasion in 1940-41, Canadian troops had been rushed across the Atlantic to strengthen the country's defences. Now that danger had passed, the Prime Minister, Mackenzie King, declined permission for these troops to be diverted to North Africa – a place of no interest to Canada – but was anxious they should be seen making a current contribution to the war. Therefore Canada provided the bulk of the troops for Dieppe.

Some 5,000 men of the 2nd Canadian Infantry Division, 1,000 British Commandos and 50 United States Rangers comprised the landing force. The original plan envisaged a devastating naval bombardment and extensive support by ground-attack aircraft, but both were significantly scaled down. This was to minimise civilian casualties and avoid rubble in the streets impeding the landing force advance A frontal attack on the town was thought preferable to an encircling manoeuvre on the grounds that the operation would be judged a failure if the port were not taken.

Two experienced British Commando units (Numbers 3 and 4) were assigned to land before dawn to destroy German heavy gun batteries on promontories east and west of the port, a task in which they were largely successful. Two Canadian battalions were scheduled to land at the same time to the immediate east and west of Dieppe to give landward support to the attacks on the guns and form a secure perimeter for the main force to land. The right flank Canadian battalion assigned to Green Beach was the South Saskatchewan Regiment commanded by Merritt. His objectives were Pourville, west of the port, then the cliffs above the village.

His force crossed the Channel in Royal Navy destroyers, transferred to landing craft ten miles offshore and reached Green Beach on time, in near darkness and unopposed. But the main part of the battalion was landed on the wrong side of the River Scie estuary and faced crossing a narrow bridge through Pourville in order to approach their objectives on the cliffs.

By then alert to the situation, the German defenders targeted the bridge with machine-gun and mortar fire. Initial Canadian attempts failed to storm the bridge, leaving it covered with dead and wounded. Merritt led the next rush forward, waving his steel helmet with the rallying shout 'Come on over. There's nothing to it!'

His audacity took the enemy by surprise; one group of men followed him over the bridge and others used the girders to cross. Merritt soon had most of his surviving men on the far bank, but shortage of mortar ammunition and lack of communications to the destroyers to call for supporting fire made any further advance impossible.

Meanwhile, the company landed on the west bank of the Scie had reached its objective and sent a success signal to the operation command ship. This and one from Lord Lovat's Number 4 Commando were the only two success signals sent in the entire operation.

Finding all moves towards his objectives blocked by concrete 'pillboxes', Merritt led an attack on each in turn, personally killing the occupants of one by throwing grenades through the enemy's firing ports. When the last enemy strongpoint had been silenced,

Merritt had been twice wounded and his battalion reduced to fewer than 300 men.

He held on to an improvised perimeter nevertheless, and kept contact with his section positions by moving from one to another after his runners had been killed. When the time came to move back to the beach, Merritt coolly gave instructions for an orderly withdrawal and announced his intention to hold off the enemy from a rearguard position in a small bandstand near the beach to cover the re-embarkation.

'Cec' Merritt was a tremendous character. I had a great evening dining with his vivacious wife, Grace, and him at their home in northern Vancouver. I met Peter briefly again on that trip. He was married and working with a firm of solicitors in a town in north British Columbia. 'Cec' had a very distinguished law practice and was a Member of Parliament. He died on 12 July 2000 aged ninety-one.

We have, of course, our own proud holder of the Victoria Cross, Richard Annand, better known as Jake. He was for a time on the staff at HFTC and was in my own regiment, the DLI.

On 15 May 1940 he was in France with his platoon in position on the south side of a bridge that had been blown when at about 11 a.m. the enemy launched a violent attack. Undeterred he launched his own lone attack hurling hand grenades amongst the enemy with great effect, and then returning for more supplies and again attacking enemy positions. 'It was like giving cream to an elephant,' his Sergeant Major observed afterwards.

He was wounded and discovering that his batman had also been wounded, he somehow got him back to the safety of their own lines with the help of an old wheelbarrow.

News of his heroism followed by the award of the Victoria Cross on 23 October 1940 for conspicuous gallantry came at a time when the nation was under enormous pressure and it acted like a national tonic. We are always delighted when Dick and his charming wife, Shirley, join us at our reunions.

To return to our annual meeting. On the same day there is a lunchtime 'get-together' at the Bag of Nails in Victoria. The Officer Commanding Rowallan Company, together with the Sergeant Major, are always guests of honour at the dinner. The reunions around the country are great successes, but, of course, the pièce de résistance is when every two years we are drawn inevitably to Glenfeshie and Poolewe. At Glenfeshie our headquarters are the Duke of Gordon Hotel in Kingussie. At Poolewe members are dispersed between the Poolewe House Hotel, the Poolewe Hotel or in Gairloch.

On a pile of stones at the head of the valley up the glen stands a cairn of remembrance, 'The Glenfeshie Memorial', with a simple inscription:

Highland Fieldcraft Training Centre
1943-44
In memory of those who gave their lives for their country.
Erected by their friends who trained with them in this Glen
and at Poolewe, Wester Ross

(There were forty who were killed in action or died of their wounds.)

We are admitted on to the private road into Glenfeshie and after we park our cars by the river, somewhere in the ethereal background one can almost hear the sound of marching men and snatches of song and banter borne upon the wind. Each of us has his own memories of a remarkable period in our lives. There is a memorial to Lord Rowallan in the Highland Park near Kingussie.

We have marvellous regional reunions, of course. There was one held in Cornwall, where at the time I had a cottage in the village of Portloe. It was huge fun and I remember setting a trail along the clifftops. It was perhaps rather demanding in view of our advancing years. The object was to reach the bay where my cottage stood on a headland. First home was a tall fair-haired man. He was Bill Shaw and, as I watched him romping home, the years flashed back to the same blond Bill, twenty something, who was so enthusiastic that he spent one short leave intent on seeing even more of the glen on his own.

I was chairman of that reunion in Cornwall and decided that the men should wear dinner jackets, and it has been the same since. Most of those attending stayed at the Idle Rocks Hotel at

Meet the Millichaps.
Ever since the
Highland Fieldcraft
Training Centre
Association began, its
reunions have been
attended by the
Millichap family,
shown here at the
reunion in the
Cotswolds, 2000.
2nd Row: Martin,
Nigel, Rebecca, Mark,
Nicola, Denise and
Oliver
Front Row: Sammy,
Jill, Rhiannon, Ken,
Abigail, Anne and
Richard.

(Photograph by John
W. Kinchin)

174

St Mawes. I had the piper arrive for the dinner by boat so that, romantically, we first heard the notes of his pipes across the water. I remember next morning when we were all aboard at the quay ready to cast off for a trip upriver, two dear old ladies arrived and joined us at the last minute, thinking it was the local ferry. It was too late to ask them to leave. As we sailed on past the riverside house where Agatha Christie once lived, it seemed as if they really were characters who had just stepped out of one of her novels; or one of Daphne Du Maurier's marvellous stories, for she lived not far away at Menabilly. What possible dark deeds and twisted story line lay ahead, one wondered. Perhaps the day would unfold an exciting mystery!

The late Ted Bindloss, formerly a company commander who had retired as a master at Tonbridge School, lived nearby and came sailing up the creek next day to join us. I remember the grand finale when we had a riverside barbecue and left in two coaches for the Ship Inn at Portloe. Even the locals, who usually inhabit one corner of the bar and regard the visitors with ill-concealed disdain, joined in. With our own Fred Smith at the piano, it seemed that 'For those three hours at The Ship Inn at Portloe everyone sang'. (Apologies to Siegfried Sassoon!)

CHAPTER VI

In Search of a Posting

A<small>FTER A LEISURELY FEW DAYS LEAVE</small> at home in Newcastle upon Tyne I brought my mother to London where I was awaiting details of my next posting. I was in a billet at Olympia and for the past three days I had anxiously observed the list of names posted on the main board.

On the previous day I had a remarkable experience. A tall man in civilian clothes approached me in the main hall and asked if he could have a word. In fact we had coffee together and to my surprise he asked me if I would care to call at an address in Victoria later that day. His mysterious manner intrigued me and he was obviously beating about the bush, as they say, but he assured me that the appointment had something to do with the Army.

Accordingly, I made for a block of flats behind the cathedral in Victoria. If I remember rightly, I think it was in Ashleigh Gardens. There was an inter-communication phone which I used and I was asked to make my way to the third floor, where I was met by a thickset, though slightly tubby man with a ruddy complexion, aged about thirty. He was, I remember, wearing a worn tweed jacket and slacks, rather suggestive of a country type. Intrigued, I followed him into the flat, which appeared to be mostly unfurnished, and sat down opposite him at a plain table. To my amazement, apart from introducing himself as John, he began to talk non-stop in French for several minutes and then, after a pause, he broke into German. My blank expression caused him to stop in full flow. 'You don't understand me?' he asked.

Mystified, I nodded, whereupon he began to speak again, rather more slowly, in German. Again, my blank expression must have caused him to give up because, smiling, he reverted to English.

'Just testing,' he said, adding, 'look, first I wanted to find out your languages – I mean if you understood French or German ...'

'Well, I have a little French …' I broke in, obviously looking mystified.

'Don't worry, I'll get to the point of all this. I want to talk to you about coming to Scotland for some special training.'

My mind began to whirl. Was I hearing right? 'Scotland? For some training?'

'To come to the point,' he went on, 'we're going on the offensive as individuals – in a sort of secret army. If you came in with us, we would have you up in Scotland for courses in handling explosives, unarmed combat, radio drills and so on.'

There was a pause. Then – I remember it well – he leaned forward and said in quite a matter-of-fact voice, 'We would parachute or fly you into some point in Europe and you would meet others to help you on your way …'

'To do what?' I remember asking in a rather strangulated voice.

'Well, whatever the assignment. It could be to get into the local power station and blow it up. You know the sort of thing!' He gave me a comforting grin as though he were suggesting a game of golf.

'Excuse me,' I interrupted, 'who exactly are you?'

'We are known as SOE, Special Operations Executive. We get tip-offs from the unit here in London where you are awaiting posting, of any suitable personnel, so we thought we would have you along for a chat as you seem to have the right background. We could have you ready to be flown in somewhere after about eight weeks.' He sounded like a salesman.

'Except for the language difficulty,' I broke in.

'Yes,' he agreed that it was a snag, but two months of tuition would be possible. 'You could latch on to sufficient phrases, but maybe you would need a few months longer if there was time.' The 'if there was time' bit sounded ominous.

My gut reaction was that it would be very exciting. Yes, I was wonderfully fit, I could quickly master the finer points of how to kill and so forth, nor was I afraid of the project, but there were two obstacles. One, the language problem. I would surely need several months to get hold of, say, enough 'native-like' French, but my main worry was about my own nature for such an assignment. I was obviously too 'hail fellow well met', I had a certain kind of laugh, an unmistakable 'give away', and I was certainly not a loner, someone who would not take easily to hiding in dark cupboards and attics and that sort of thing.

We discussed it further. The parachuting would be no problem. In fact I was keen on that having done most of the basic training. 'How to kill' techniques were no problem. But I was by no means a loner, my whole Army life had been on learning to lead, on team work, and the 'lone ranger' idea never appealed to me. At the back of my mind also I remember feeling that it all seemed strangely haphazard and casual; jolly good show if it worked, too bad if it didn't!

Later, I joined my mother and we wandered around watching the swans on the Serpentine until it was time for me to see her back to King's Cross for her journey to Newcastle upon Tyne. I did not discuss my dilemma, of course, but we vowed to come back and see the swans when it was all over.

Immediately her train pulled out I made for Olympia again to see if my name was up. It was and when I read my brief posting details I literally froze on the spot. It was not possible. I was seeing things. I was posted to Nigeria! And my duties ... wait for it ... to run a wing of a battle school on jungle warfare. Jungle bloody warfare ... I had never been in a jungle in my life. I stormed at the wretched duty officer. 'Typical of some silly office-bound half-wit at the War Office,' and the rest of it.

I lost no time in sending off messages asking for help. Lord Westwood, a friend on Tyneside, with whom my mother and I had dined only the night before at the Great Northern Hotel next to King's Cross Station, two brigadiers in my regiment – Andy Ricketts and Peter Jefferies.

My old unit was stuck in a wood in Norfolk where they were to remain for more than a year before going over to Holland and they were, in fact, already full. It is one of the disillusionments of army life that you can be away from your unit for some eighteen months and then come striding back to pick up where you left off with a new CO and half the mess full of strange faces.

I managed to get a message to Nigel Poett, at one time my CO in the Durhams. He was with the new Glider Pilot Regiment and I got word back. 'Sorry, we are full!' So I missed out on Arnhem.

The author, 1940.

There followed what were without doubt the worst days of my life. Olympia for those few days became a prison. To have gone off to see my old Battalion in Norfolk to see if I could get back would have risked being court-martialled. Forty-eight hours later we were at Southampton Docks ready to embark.

Time seemed to drag on a slow voyage out to Africa, arrival at Accra and thence to a camp named Olokomeji deep in the jungle or bush, as we called it, which consisted mainly of a collection of bamboo-built huts. The nearest habitation was Ibadan, a busy trading town some 10 miles away.

Everything about the place at first revolted me. Once known as 'The White Man's Grave', West Africa is certainly no sun-kissed tropicana. It is sometimes very hot, almost stifling, and there can be an unhealthy dampness in the atmosphere; one becomes very sticky and lethargic. Yellow fever and bilhartzia – the latter could be caught in river crossings – were the real enemies. Mosquitoes were the dive-bombers! I resolved, at once, that I would keep up a programme of fitness whatever the conditions.

At first I wondered at the apparent easy acceptance of life by some of the officers and white non-commissioned officers, though they were, let's face it, only doing their duty as detailed to them: just as in India, for instance, there were thousands of British officers and non-commissioned officers also making their various contributions to the war effort.

I saw little of the civilian population, but those whom I met were always courteous. Those from the north, the Hausas, were the most impressive, especially the soldiers. They were tall, usually heavily marked on the face, unquestionably proud and their whole background made them of a warrior class.

I was in a position now where there could be a return to my rank of major in due course and a nice little number in allowances and food billets, but I felt that it was an abomination. My spirits were rock bottom. The only saving grace to it all was that I really took to the West Africans as soldiers. They were always spotlessly turned out, willing to have a go and, particularly the northern Hausa men, excellent 'in the bush'. For tracking, camouflage, fieldcraft, patience, stamina and unfailing cheerfulness in adverse conditions the Nigerians, like the Gold Coast Regiments, were in my experience good value. One secret, apart from their background, was their own NCOs who exerted sharp discipline and it was best to look away if one of them decided to take an African private soldier to task in 'the bush' as we called the surrounding areas to the camp.

Many of the men I had to train were urgently required in Burma for the Chindits. Orde Wingate had a high regard for Nigerians. Although for security reasons his force was officially known as the 3rd Indian Infantry Division, it did not, in fact, include any Indian soldiers. All thirty battalions were British except for three Gurkha, one Burma Rifles and the three Nigerian battalions. In the overall operation there was, of course, the vital and extensive support of the No 1 American Air Commando.

Time could drag with relentless monotony. The officers were cheerful enough company, but to me life had missed a gear. One kept as fit as possible, though organised sport was difficult. I had to fight with myself to keep up my spirit. Accra was a long trip for a prawn supper or an occasional dinner party. The African soldiers called their sexual adventures 'jiggi jiggye', mostly at the weekend. 'Everybody, Everybody, Everybody Likes Saturday Night' were the lines of their favourite marching song. One very enjoyable break, though, was a visit to Achimota College in Accra. Dedicated to Christian teachings, the College was opened in 1927 and the inspiration of the Frasers ensured the success of this centre as a vital need to train Africans in leadership qualities.

There was a wonderful social custom in West Africa and that was the occasional Sunday lunch parties thrown at different messes. Ground nut stew was served after a liberal introduction of drinks and this was guaranteed to stiffen any man's sinews. The ingredients of this fantastic dish were in particular gin, hot peppers and tomatoes, meat and ground nuts with peanut butter and spinach or sometimes, instead of the meat, fresh fish sweetened with spices. Sometimes both meat and fish figured in the dish. The special culinary expertise in presenting this mini banquet was a source of much pride for the unit doing the entertaining and the cook and all his staff were paraded afterwards for fulsome praise, which they enjoyed enormously.

So there I was. Marooned, though for how long? I at once recommended my campaign to get to Burma. Once again I sent off cables asking for help. The weeks dragged on and then suddenly an order came through. Peter Jefferies, a brigadier in Burma whom I knew as one of my regiment and whom I had tried to contact before leaving London, had apparently asked West Africa Command for me.

My spirits were high as I boarded the aircraft in Accra. Now at last I was on my way! We landed at Freetown in Sierra Leone and as we trooped off the plane for what appeared to be a regulation stop, I had little warning of what awaited me in the shape of a rather fussy staff officer who requested me to accompany him.

Puzzled, I followed him into the airport reception area where he at once turned and said, 'Captain Johnstone – you are to remove your kit off the plane, please!'

I stood staring at him in disbelief What the hell was going on?

'Look here,' I said, gulping, 'I have my flight instructions, you try and stop me!'

'Captain Johnstone,' he replied testily and with what I felt was undue emphasis on my rank, 'our latest orders are that no officer under the rank of Lieutenant Colonel is entitled to be flown out individually to India.'

'I don't believe it,' I stormed at him. 'I've been trying to get to bloody Burma so hard and at the last moment I am marooned in – Freetown, of all places.'

I glared at him. 'I request an interview with the General Officer Commanding.'

At this he shrugged his shoulders. 'Please put that in writing and it will be dealt with,' he replied in the detached monotone of the typical official ducking all responsibility. At this he turned on his heels and left me to deal with the Transport Sergeant and my personal kit.

Stuck in hot, sticky Freetown! I remember the vast tree opposite the YMCA became a place of benign shelter as I took to searching the horizon like a stranded mariner in search of a ship. For a few days break I went to the Gambia and on a fishing expedition we landed a huge crocodile whose skin I still have – it was sent home for me afterwards.

The relentless pressure by me went on daily. In fact when the staff in the General's office saw me coming they either fled or buried themselves in their files. Finally they – and myself – were put out of our joint misery with the arrival of the *Almanzora* bound for Bombay. But even that had an anti-climax – she broke down in the middle of the Red Sea! The heat was atrocious and if the ship did not actually sink, my spirits almost did. I occupied myself by getting a stage show together from the troops on board, though there was an ENSA party travelling out to India. Its star was Heather Thatcher, so I got a soldier in drag to put on an act named 'Feather Snatcher' and wrote and presented a revue which was a huge success. Of course, I asked the ENSA party beforehand if they minded the idea and they all said that they thought it great fun and like the good troopers they were, came along to the performance.

When we eventually arrived in Bombay it was most amusing to see how the Africans measured up. Many of them huge in stature in comparison with the Indians, they were soon enjoying themselves riding in rickshaws and to see an African NCO in his perfectly pressed green battle dress, probably possessed of gold teeth like a portable Fort Knox and impressive tribal markings on his face, ordering about the staff at the rail station, including the Station Master, was hugely impressive. It was history in the making for it was the first time that Africa had ever gone to the aid of India.

Before leaving Bombay, the Africans, of course, encountered the extraordinary begging fraternity, something they had never seen so blatantly before – the young and old who appeared to have life-crippling diseases and those seemingly physically able but desperately poor. Babies in arms were often apparently pinched by their mothers to make them cry or at worst had been maimed at birth. Multiple amputees paraded about seeking sympathy and, of course, money. The continual and persistent demand becomes an irritant despite the colourful panorama of life in this densely crowded city.

In contrast, the Bombay traffic police presented a smart and colourful display in their dark-blue uniforms and I was impressed by them immensely. They had plus-four breeches just over the knee, bare legs and black sandals called 'chaplis'. They wore black leather sashes and holsters and belts with heavy brass clasps. Around their necks they wore white lanyards and whistles and from wrist to elbow detachable armbands. On their heads they wore a blue pill-box hat, trimmed in red and kept in place with chin straps. The showpiece, however, was the large white umbrella firmly planted in a holster attached to the belt and held in place higher up the shaft by an attachment to the sash. Thus equipped, they were able to keep the traffic moving whilst being protected from the midday sun. Bombay being well inside the Tropic of

Cancer, for several months in the summer the sun is directly overhead. The Africans were clearly impressed and stood watching them in action.

Strict instructions were given to the troops about the many brothel areas in Bombay, including the revolting and notorious 'cafes' in Grant Road. The 'call girls' of the Taj Mahal Hotel were, of course, safely out of price range.

Medical examination was given higher importance than ever and woe betide any soldier found infected. Condoms were issued and lectures given, though the inadequate sizes of some of the condoms caused unconcealed mirth on the part of the recipients.

I took advantage of an offer to visit the Parsee Towers of Silence. Here I saw high on a slope several very tall circular stone towers with metal cages on top and inside were remains of corpses which were already attracting the vultures. Visitors and tourists are not now admitted to these gardens and the Towers are jealously guarded at all times. The Parsees arrived in Bombay as immigrants towards the end of the seventeenth century from Persia in order to escape Arab occupation. Their Zoroastrian religious beliefs refer to earth, fire and water as being too important to defile. For this reason the bodies of their dead are laid high up on the Towers on grills by burial squads who are themselves not Parsees. The theory is that the grills are so made that the vultures are able to consume the flesh, but not carry away the bones, which then drop into the wells at the base of the Towers. The Parsees, who live mostly in Bombay, are among the most successful businessmen in India and these include the well-known Tata family.

It should be noted, incidentally, for visitors' peace of mind, that in 1881 the three large reservoirs which supply the water to the city of Bombay were covered up and are now safely under the terraces of the Hanging Gardens which were designed, constructed and largely financed by the Parsee community.

It was a rushed visit. I was, after all, not on a sightseeing tour. However, it was very refreshing to receive this local hospitality before rejoining my party to see them off at the very English railway station in name and architecture – Victoria Railway Terminus.

By sheer perversity I was finally – would you believe it – put on a plane in Bombay to complete my journey to Calcutta!

Whatever the impact of a crowded Bombay had been, Calcutta, a city teeming with life and incredible diversity in its array of uniforms of multi-national fighting forces, was enough to blow the mind. Once described as the jewel in the crown of the Indian Empire, the clamour of its streets never ceased: even at night the place was alive and restless.

The impressive Grand Hotel was the Mecca for officers on leave and a favourite ploy, because the rooms always appeared to be fully booked, was to get into the spacious lounge sometime before or after midnight and grab as much 'shut-eye' as possible in the easy chairs until the spacious and elegant breakfast room opened early in the morning, at which there was a wild scramble for tables and, in answer to the question 'Room number, sir?' any old number was trolled out!

There were some startled guests when it came later to settling their account. I hasten to add that I was not guilty.

Again, I was fortunate to find a transport officer with my sense of urgency and within two days I was on my way – by air again, would you believe? This time my destination was Chittagong on the Bay of Bengal. At last I had arrived in Burma.

Things began to move quickly for me. I was kitted out in 'jungle green' and soon on my way to a posting to the Divisional Reconnaissance Battalion. Their high reputation had already reached me – they were considered to be a really hot outfit. I set out in high expectation.

I went south of the Chin Hills by truck, moving in a convoy along extremely bumpy 'roads' towards the vast back-drop of the Arakan Yomas. Two days later I was dropped off at an assembly point and taken by jeep on a ride of some two hours deep into the bush and reached the headquarters of the Division's Reconnaissance Regiment. The unit was obviously proud of its own special character. They had fashioned their own skills as a kind of cavalry of the bush. The very words 'battle school' would clearly be anathema to them, so I resolved, perhaps uncharacteristically, to keep my trap shut!

Some of the officers were Rhodesians, one or two titled, and they all looked very bronzed and tough. Their mess, though deep in the bush, had a certain air about it as if a copy of *The Times* would arrive at any moment. Mostly they used the native language when with the troops.

But I had, at least, arrived. Without more ado I was out on patrol next morning and face to face with my first Jap. He uttered no sound and made no movement. He was dead. 'Steady, sir,' the Sergeant warned me as I began inspecting the body. 'The bastards sometimes strap a primed grenade on the back of their dead.' The Jap was a deep brown colour and not yellow skinned as I had expected.

Every now and then we came across signs of very recent Jap occupation – personal items like letters and photos left scattered due to hurried departure, in fact, so hurried, that our arrival was no doubt being observed. They, too, had their reconnaissance out.

Two days later I was in the thick of it with live ammunition hitting trees around me, throwing up dust lines and though there were no hits to our patrol, the undergrowth and foliage obscured any successes we may have had. There was the question of my seniority. I was, as I have mentioned, a war substantive captain, which meant that I could not be reduced from that rank unless, of course, by some ghastly misdemeanour. However, it became clear that I was blocking promotion for one or two other officers who had already spent some time with the unit in the bush. It was, after all, a very distinctive type of outfit and though I felt no animosity on their part, I had, as I discovered, been recommended by the Brigadier who had got me out there in the first place – always a tricky situation in these circumstances – and I had no wish to appear to be given preferential treatment. I was, in fact, that unusual animal known as 'a special case', and 'a battle school wizard'. Ugh!

I therefore readily fell in with the suggestion that I should move to the 7th Gold Coast Regiment, also in the vicinity, where there was a need for a company commander. Accordingly, I moved over and quickly fell into the routine of bush life. They were charac-teristically cheerful. Some of the officers were 'old timers' and could speak the Gold Coast tongue fluently. One of them had been in action in Burma day in and day out for more than two and a half years. He had enormous side whiskers, by permission, and was hugely reliable, a marvellous communicator, being an old

'Coaster' and when at last he was persuaded to be relieved and fly out – he had to be practically dug out – he was awarded the Military Cross.

Another outstanding officer was Seth Anthony, who was also later to be decorated with the MC. His patrolling record was absolutely outstanding – he never seemed to be at rest – as was his ability to command the total respect of his men, whom, of course, he knew by language and custom. Later to represent his country as their first Ambassador at Lake Success, he was an absolute charmer.

It was a happy unit. The men were well disciplined and excellent on the march, adept in handling extra equipment either on their backs or head or as muleteers, at which they excelled. And there was their faith in one's orders, their cheerfulness, self-discipline in fighting a white man's war in a brown man's country against a yellow man. They fought well for 'King Georgey' and one wonders post war whether their contribution was ever really fully appreciated. Orde Wingate, for one, extolled the virtues of the Nigerians. He insisted on having them in his Chindits and they were the only non-Europeans except for the Gurkhas and the US Air support.

Clearing villages was a regular chore – there seemed to be endless gatherings of dwellings reached by different paths through the bush. Some of these villagers must have been sorely perplexed by the changing scene of 'Japs in', 'Japs out', 'Brits in', 'Brits out'. On the whole they were reliable, but one had to be careful through our Burmese interpreters. Hunting for possible booby traps was, of course, essential to be undertaken after the first careful recce to ensure that there were no Japs still lurking around. Business, though, was not overlooked as villagers attempted to sell the men chickens which were sometimes revealed as dead dogs by the size of their limbs.

Every so often there would be a sudden fight with pockets of Japs and the possibility of snipers was an ever-present menace. Some villages proved to be armed traps to catch our patrols. Force 136 was made up of Burma Intelligence and others and were excellent in giving local information to us, particularly with the language difficulties. Where a village headman proved to be working against us by hiding Japanese, he would be shot. Japanese mortars were much in evidence. They could be unpleasantly accurate.

After I moved over to 7th Gold Coast Regiment, the working situation was clearly different. Whereas the recce boys used jeeps covering wide areas, the GCR lads moved mostly on foot, often using mules for heavy baggage such as radio equipment and moving deeper into the hills. On patrol with African soldiers one had to get used to the punctuation of doubt which usually came halfway though a whispered message at the side of a track, such as when the scout, having gone ahead to do a recce, returns taking elaborate cover. 'Sir,' he says softly, 'I go down the track to look for Japani.'

'Yes,' you say tentatively. Then he gets closer, adding usually in a whisper, 'Well I go look 'im.'

Here he pauses and you feel a tightening of the stomach muscles.

'But I no see 'im!' he adds reassuringly, with a big smile. (Well – not always!)

When the presence of water was found by the 'medics' we used our issue of two tablets – one to cleanse the water and one to take away the abominable taste.

Termites, also known as white ants, were a nuisance – they built huge nests as hillocks sometimes to a height of several feet, riddled with galleries of smaller insects, held together by their excrement. They were thought capable of destroying virtually everything except metal. Then there were the mosquitos. (What a pity DDT had not yet been invented!)

Mepacrine tablets were issued. This was a synthetic drug which did not actually cure, but kept at bay such as fever and malaria.

Of course, much of the jungle (or bush as I still preferred to call it) was damp and overhanging. Leeches could be a confounded nuisance. They fastened onto one's skin until they were satiated with blood, then attempted to slide away. Their bite cannot be felt and the use of a spot of salt or a cigarette end released them, though scratching at them was bad as it could cause a sore and infection. They only appeared at certain points where the jungle was thickest. As for the dreaded scorpion, which happened to be our divisional sign, one was careful to shake out carefully whatever one was to lie on. Fortunately I did not encounter one. Mostly there were non-poisonous green snakes in evidence. One would awaken sometimes covered in tiny bites from flying insects.

Prickly heat was an exasperatingly regular condition, while diarrhoea could be almost unbearable in the hot conditions. If contracted when on the march, this became a private hell. I suppose that general inertia, blisters and foot rot made up a regular 'medical menu', mostly having to be attended to oneself, but full marks to the hard-working medical officer and his very capable African medical orderlies. They were invariably patient and extraordinarily skilful.

On the 'plus' side, West Africans excelled as cooks under all manner of conditions – their speed in getting something cooked was quite remarkable. In addition to the ubiquitous 'K' rations, which were air dropped to us periodically, we were fed rice cooked in all manners of ways considering the conditions.

Our West African signal units were superb. Communications were vital as maps were not plentiful and usually unreliable. Of course, the absence of map reference points as used in Europe – church spires, crossroads, etc. – now made for more reliance on compass bearings and estimated distances with plenty of radio contact.

Indian Air Force planes kept us well supplied, first informing us of agreed dropping zones and giving us time to make safe and clear the area. One day one such drop included a small parcel addressed to me. It contained a new pair of brown leather gloves with a note from my great aunt Mary in Bilston, Staffs sending her love and saying that the gloves would be nice for church parades! Of course she hadn't the slightest idea when she had mailed it many months before that her present would reach me in such circumstances.

There was the night of the dance. This followed an almost unbelievable dispensation of regulations as a reward to the units concerned. A huge bonfire was lit. There would be no hiding it from the Japs in the surrounding hills, of course. Suddenly, signalled by special chants, about 200 completely naked Africans formed a circle around the fire. There began the slow beat of the drums and the dancers began to gyrate, slowly at first, and then at a gathering pace, all the while repeating their cries in unison. As the dust rose it formed a curtain on this unforgettable scene.

There had been a well-regulated dispensation of wine and as a result the dancers' efforts were soon galvanised. The pitch of the drums rose and fell; the chanters, increasingly inspired, set the pace. A veil of dust hung in the air as the bodies, now glistening with sweat, moved in Terpsichorean rhythm. West Africans were kicking Japanese arse!

Everything resumed next day as before following this brilliantly devised 'treat for the troops'. I was to take over from Scotty, a Londoner and former schoolmaster, with whom I had formed an intellectually invigorating series of discussions at odd moments because he was one of the first 'intellectual' socialists I had ever encountered.

We were dug in along the tree line of a series of small hills. He and his radio operator occupied an excellent dug-out, well covered with soil and lined internally with logs. 'Mac', a sergeant, also a Londoner who was on his way out back to the UK on leave, joined us. He was to be flown out along with others in the morning. Scotty was to become second-in-command of the Battalion whilst I took over the Company next day. He was very proud of his well-fortified, equipped command post, which unfortunately had only room for two. It had a flat soil-covered roof upon which Mac, the Sergeant, and I were able to kip down for the night. I suppose the area we occupied out in the open under the trees would be no more than about ten feet by six feet wide.

Mac was a roof tiler back home in London and he spoke excitedly about seeing some of his old mates, watching the Arsenal, visiting his local and seeing his parents again. I suppose he was about twenty-three, a mixture of innocence and experience. He had no opinions, it seemed, on the rights and wrongs of the War. It was just something we had to get on with. He had joined up in the Ox and Bucks, been drafted to the West Africans and he was genuinely proud of them. He had been more than two years in Burma and here we were suddenly brought together lying in a hole in a sandbagged arena in the middle of the jungle.

'I'll have a last fag before I get some kip,' he said and then as he fumbled for his packet of cigarettes he began to tell me in a wave of nostalgia of some of his more glamorous adventures with what he comically kept calling his 'Porksword'. This really made me laugh as I had heard this part of the anatomy described in various ways, but never as a 'Porksword'!

'There they go, the little bastards!' he said as the Jap guns suddenly came to life. They used to pull these guns up through the bush under cover of darkness and then open up, firing at intervals at each of our four hill-top positions which we occupied as a Brigade.

The intervals between firing differed as did the order of the targets, probably with the idea of causing as much confusion as possible. I suppose they were sited about a half a mile away in thick bush and the bombardment usually lasted for about an hour before our patrols could track them down, by which time they had invariably packed up and disappeared.

'Boom-boom' was the first indication that they had opened up and, after an interval, 'Boom!' where the first shell landed. Tonight was probably a reprisal for our 'War Dance' of the previous evening.

'And bollocks to you,' I heard Mac murmur half asleep as a shell exploded on a nearby hill.

What happened next I will never know. I have long since given up trying to grope my way back through the tunnels of my mind to that awful night. There was a shattering noise – that I can vaguely remember – but of being catapulted into a bunker way down the hill on top of a startled soldier and being drenched in the blood of mules sliced by shrapnel and hearing their terrible squealing failed to register on my mind. I know only what I was told later. Fortunately, Scotty and his signaller survived the direct hit intact. My wounds were quickly bandaged, but I lay in a very confused and detached state, drugged against pain so that I only vaguely heard the mournful notes of the bugle next day as the sound of 'The Last Post' drifted across the trees. Poor fragmented Porksword was on his way to his final leave.

Two days later, my mind still a vacuum, I was air-lifted to Madras where after rest in a hospital, the CO kindly prescribed me three weeks sick leave.

I remember the splendid old fort and sea front of the city where I was able to sit and relax.

Another air lift as far as Delhi and then a seemingly never-ending rail journey much disturbed at night because all India seems to move overnight by train. Stations are crowded with sleeping figures who on the approach of a train suddenly leap into clamouring life, causing sheer bedlam until somehow those arriving and departing disentangle themselves. The train eventually departs, usually with 'passengers' jammed inside and outside.

Still feeling withdrawn and dazed, I was on the last lap to my Shangri-la. I eventually alighted at Rawalpindi and was directed to a motor coach that appeared to have escaped from a scrapyard. It was already crowded, but a window seat had fortunately been reserved for me. Then we were off on what turned out to be the most perilous coach trip of my life. The passengers – a motley lot – jabbered away incessantly. A live chicken kept escaping and squawking wherever it landed – twice on my lap as it happened. The coach rocked and shuddered its way up mountain gradients only to race down the other side and around hair-raising bends. There seemed to be complete disregard as to any approaching traffic or whether the bus itself could stand all this strain.

At last there was deliverance from this private hell. Shattered, I was just able to stagger off the monster, only to be besieged by a group of about half a dozen muscular, turbaned young men, all demanding to know which was my personal baggage. Eventually, one huge young fellow produced a superb-looking pony and beat off all opponents to secure my bag. Shouting encouragement, he ran alongside, my bag on his head whilst I at last began to relax astride the sturdy animal as we set off through the woods.

I shall never forget the sheer ecstasy of the mountain air. There was a pervading smell of eucalyptus – a scent of such gentle fragrance that one wanted to sing for joy. After the hell of the last few weeks, heaven, it seemed, was just around the corner.

Suddenly the track widened and levelled and there burst into view an almost English setting of rolling fields surrounded by a wood with, unbelievably, the sound of bells. It was not a dream. It was real. I was in Kashmir and as far as I was concerned, it was Shangri-la.

It was, in fact, Gulmarg and in truth one could only describe it as a large meadow with ample borders of wild flowers, three kilometres in area, dotted with hotels and guest houses, dilapidated huts and ski slopes. This is now India's premier ski resort. The name appropriately means 'Meadow of Flowers'.

I stayed at the very atmospheric Nedou's Hotel and almost immediately felt relaxed. The very air one breathed seemed to cleanse and rejuvenate one.

Isolated in a high valley of the Himalayas, Kashmir has over the centuries developed its own independent culture and historical tradition. Buddhism was established at a very early stage. By the time the British partitioned India the predominately Muslim state of Kashmir was ruled over by a remarkable man, Sir Hari Singh, a Hindu maharajah who saw his state as neutral, a kind of 'Switzerland in Asia'. He would entertain with elaborate dinners, after which he liked to play martial music and the British National Anthem on the gramophone. Alas, his determined independence and his love of the good life at his two-storey palace with its idyllic setting beside Dal Lake was to be short lived. Two months after partition, in October 1947, thousands of armed Muslims crossed from Pakistan into India and headed for Srinagar. There was no hope for the Maharajah. He signed over Kashmir in exchange for military support and five decades of conflict began. Now there is the clumsy arrangement of India administering 65 per cent of Sir Hari Singh's princely ideal and Pakistan controlling the remainder.

In 1989 the people of Kashmir demanded their right to be consulted. There were split loyalties. Some wanted accession to Pakistan and others autonomy. India brought no less than 700,000 security forces into the valley and blatantly helped to ruin the lives of the people. Then in reprisal Pakistan sent soldiers and armed militia over its border and the two countries were locked in one of their fiercest battles since Independence: and it is to be noted that both are nuclear-capable. When at last Pakistan withdrew it unleashed an incredible wave of Indian jingoism. There have been barbaric examples of disappearances and mutilation of people and four Europeans have also disappeared.

I am glad that I saw Kashmir when it was safe enough for me to revel in its beauty and there was no serpent in my Shangri-la.

Gulmarg is about 50 kilometres from Srinagar and the road passes through rice and maize fields. In the present surge of world tourism the unfortunate absence of Kashmir because of unrest as a place to visit is a huge loss, quite apart from the local welfare, of course, which would have been enormously enriched instead of the present desperate poverty.

On Dal Lake at Srinagar a few miles away, amidst breath-taking mountain scenery, there are the famous houseboats and the superb Moghul Gardens. However, in the town itself, filth did really test tolerance when I was there.

The houseboats originated in the Victorian era as a superbly British solution to a tricky political problem – and have, of course, become famous. The British Raj loved to escape from the heat and dust of the summer on the plains. However, the Maharajah wouldn't allow them to own any property. So the Brits took to the water in the form of houseboats, many of them quite palatial in their appointments.

I loved the life on board even if it was only for a brief spell. The traders regularly came alongside with all one required and in the constant daytime sun it was pure heaven. When I was there the lotus flowers were in full bloom. The floating gardens were quite beautiful.

Incidentally, since that time Peter Thompson has designed a golf course at Gulmarg, one of the highest outside courses in the world at 2,652 feet.

I must explain, by the way, about Kashmir tea, a fragrant, delicate brand flavoured with cardamom and ginger, probably the best in India. It is brewed in a samovar with grated almonds and usually drunk without milk. Incidentally, the Kashmiris also make a good blend of camomile and cardamom tea which can be recommended for tummy upsets.

Let us hope that an original bad and loose political settlement festering once again into military clashes can resolve itself into a peaceful settlement between India and Pakistan.

But with all this pontificating about politics I haven't related how I got on during my leave, which was desperately short, of course. There were a number of officers of various nationalities and units at the hotel so that we had a pretty boisterous time. A big blonde woman in her late twenties or early thirties was also there, something of a mystery. She was christened 'The Baroness'; it was hinted that she was German although she insisted, 'I am

Swedish.' She seemed to turn up all over the place on a huge dappled grey.

Breakfast at Nedou's was hilarious. The main topic of conversation was about the previous night, mainly concerning who had bedded the Baroness. And I was supposed to be on sick leave. The mountain air and relaxed company had done the trick. I began to think properly again.

A lively session with a bunch of US Air Force guys led to an invitation to join them on a flight back to Calcutta. They were leaving next day.

I was ready very early next morning. There was in fact only time for a snatched sleep for a couple of hours before my lift to the airfield. What happened next would certainly never appear in a flight manual. The Dakota appeared to be ready for take-off from the makeshift airfield almost as soon as we arrived. The crew was in great form and anxious to get going. There were about a dozen other passengers from various services.

'Let's go!' came the yelled instructions as we boarded her and the engines raced. Then, almost deafened by the noise, we were told, 'Hang on, fellers!'

There was a further roar and the aircraft began to advance clumsily along the very uneven terrain optimistically called a runway. We stopped and slowly turned whilst the engines revved again. It was all so frighteningly casual and I began to wish that I had elected to return instead on the crazy mountain bus and the long train journey south.

Then came the urgent instructions, 'Get the kit forward. We've got to get the God darned tail up. Everybody forward! Quick, let's go.'

We grabbed items of kit and scrambled forward whilst the plane, like some crazy horse of the sky, strained to be off. We began bumping and swaying interminably along the ground – surely to God there could not be more ground? We lay sprawled over our kit as far forward as possible. Would that tail never rise? At last, with little ground left to spare, we wobbled up into the sky. 'Bye, bye Shangri-la.'

I rejoined the Battalion after three and a half weeks sick leave feeling much restored in health, but with little or no memory of that terrible night, and thankfully it was taboo in conversation.

There was a big push to join up the 81st and 82nd Divisions and finally knock out Jap resistance. It was arranged that my unit would be the link-up and that it would be a night operation with orders to maintain complete silence throughout. I was to be in command of the centre movement.

Moving in the dark in silence was an eerie experience. The villagers often kept fires blazing out in the open all night and it was necessary to give them a wide berth. The pariah dogs roaming at will were a nuisance, too, because of their barking. It took about three hours to get close to the appointed area and one felt the anxiety of keeping on target and also keeping in touch in the darkness. After all, we were in the lead of the first echelon of the Division. What if we missed the link-up? It could lead to chaos. What if we came across Japs? Our instructions were to remain silent and avoid clashes.

I was moving slowly on my own in the darkness when suddenly the long grass in front of me parted and I could just make out in the half-light the figure of a Jap officer. I froze. He must have done likewise. 'Hello, how are you?' he said in fractured English, obviously startled. We were so close I could feel his breath on my face. In a matter of seconds we were wrestling with one another. I hoped to God he had not got a knife handy. I had one on my belt and I was trying hard to reach for it, but suddenly as we twisted round and round in the darkness I got both hands free and grabbed him round the throat. I had never choked anyone before. Desperately I pressed. In all this long, tormenting, shitty war he was to be my one awful memento. He shuddered and then lay still.

I saw figures moving on the skyline nearby across a valley. Concentrating hard and using night glasses, I tried to make them out, meantime moving a Bren gun team up to take a bearing on them. It was what can be described as a pregnant moment. Ours or theirs? There are times when one can feel very lonely and this was one of them. Suddenly I made up my mind. They were ours. The 51st Division, in fact. Objective secured.

Ages later, I can't remember when, I got a note from Brigadier Peter Jefferies saying how good to note that the DLI had been so prominent in the link-up of the two Divisions. It must have been written up in some form of despatch.

Some two weeks later we reached Henzada, a small town on the Irrawaddy in the south-west of the country. Actually I had arrived there a day or two earlier to arrange for places to billet the Battalion.

The local people kindly put on a reception for me. In fact, I remember standing on a verandah by the flickering light of swinging oil lamps helping myself to some tasteful tit-bit with my outstretched right hand whilst conversing with people on my left, when suddenly I realised that an enormous Chinese-looking guy with gold teeth standing next to me was using the same plate for the items he had discarded. Ouch!

Henzada people were mostly Karens – the Burmese Christians. Right from the start our time there was a great success. Our Commanding Officer left us for the UK and I was now in command of the Battalion and I determined that after all the rigours and unhappiness of the Jap occupation we should show the other side of the coin to these people.

I instructed the men to be cheerful and to be helpful. We started a club room for the townspeople. I helped to clean out a church which the Japanese had used as a stable and in this a young subaltern named Stuart Booth, grandson of the founder of the Salvation Army, took a leading part. The townspeople responded readily. I started a scout troop and I still remember clearly the leader, who was a fine local lad named Saw Edison.

Amongst the African soldiers I had a nickname – 'Booga'! 'Major Booga-Booga.' I must say that when they chorused 'Booga-Booga' it sounded very impressive. So much so that many of the townspeople of Henzada adopted it.

It was all so constructive after the soul-destroying skirmishing and fighting. The Army has, however, a trick of always producing a regular officer out of the hat when it comes to commanding a battalion. My brief sojourn, which I enjoyed hugely, was about to come to an end. I was, of course, a TA (Territorial Army) officer and a regular officer of suitable rank was found to be appointed CO. I was instructed instead to report to 82nd (WA) Divisional Headquarters at Gyobu Reservoir, some eighty miles north of Rangoon, totally unaware why I had to report.

On arrival Major General Hugh Stockwell interviewed me and

kindly congratulated me on what had been achieved at Henzada. Then he told me that I was to be appointed to what was known in the abbreviated form beloved by staff wallahs as ADAWS. That meant Assistant Director of Army Welfare Services. As the Director, South East Asia Command was stationed at SEAC HQ in Ceylon it meant that I was to be responsible for the welfare of most of the troops in South Burma, some 35,000 at a guess.

I will always remember taking leave of Henzada where in such a short time one had made so many friends. I had to cross the Irrawaddy to start on my journey when leaving the place and as the boat pulled out a great chorus of 'Booga! Booga!' came up across the water. There must have been half the townspeople in addition to our soldiers lined up along the shore line.

There began an almost non-stop but absorbing programme. I had the use of a small Auster aircraft and pilot and my jeep driver, Festus, known as 'Swan Vestas', who never seemed to stop grinning, became an indefatigable member of my team. I seemed to spend half my life in that jeep.

This work brought me, of course, to Rangoon, which was struggling to sort itself out after the very recent Jap occupation. The mightily impressive Shewe Dagon Pagoda, a massif of gold, stood reassuringly undamaged, but there was much chaos in the city. Rangoon was steadily filling with all manner of forces personnel.

At last one could see the Burmese capital for oneself. It was not too badly damaged. To understand something of Rangoon one has, of course, to appreciate the nature of the Burmese and the country itself.

The Burmese are so diverse that there are something like twenty-one major ethnic groups with over 100 languages. These people mostly live within the deep river valleys of the Irrawaddy, Chindwin, Sittang and Salween. The greatest of their rivers, as we have seen, is the Irrawaddy which rises in the southern Himalayas, moves through the Kachin Hills, weaves its way across the Shan Plateau and crosses the arid central plain and on into the Andaman Sea. Once years ago the Irrawaddy Flotilla Company ran as many as forty steamers on it, trading up and down and Burma meant enormous business in timber and oil – one of the richest parts of the British Empire.

Rangoon had become Burma's capital in 1885 when gunboats completed our conquest of the country. The city was transformed into an imperial capital and it became a major port. In fact it became the world's largest exporter of rice due to its strategic position facing the ocean and served by a river navigable for 900 miles. It was a station for KLM, Air France and British flying-boats.

The vast distances meant, of course, that Rangoon so far south was a capital that few Burmans in the north ever visited. It was the colonial administrators who mostly kept up the connection and the 'Thakins' – the name for the English, meaning bosses – who made the long journeys to and from the capital. Mandalay in the north therefore became increasingly important.

In the streets of Rangoon there were the vivid colourful checks of the Arakanese longyis, the 'skirts' worn informally by both men and women, and the 'ingyis', scarves worn by the Burmese ladies and usually of a delicate shade of pink. The half-naked, brown, lean bodies of the men were in evidence, of course, usually with their black bunch of hair knotted over the ear.

Taking and giving bribes was a way of life in Burma and the struggle to live in Rangoon. Of course, as always, the rickshaw wallahs were much in evidence. The cry 'Pike-san-pay-like' meaning 'Give me the money' was constantly heard. 'Jaldi hi!' was the universal cry to urge on these sweating rickshaw men. 'Change money. Give clothes!' called out the street urchins. Of course, the orientals were much in evidence trading and providing food as ever, regardless of the nationality or politics of their customers.

Just before I moved into Divisional HQ at Gyobu Reservoir in early June we had the rainy season. 'Coming down in sheets' is indeed a true description of a Burmese rainstorm. It comes suddenly as if a switch has been thrown. One moment it's blinding hot, then with a crash the rain arrives, pouring down in cataracts and in the brief intervals the sun flares fiercely again and the mud beneath one's feet cracks and steams. But it is so exhilarating after the tension of the baking heat that, at first, you stand hands upraised letting the rain sluice around you whilst you are drinking it in from your cupped hands. However, I am bound to add that after twenty-four hours of this non-stop deluge the exhilaration wears off.

The heat in Rangoon meant that it seemed to be always tacky. Even walking made one's boots feel more as if one were wading. Around midday there was less incentive to move about or even do anything. The Burmans called it the time 'when the feet are silent'.

The Strand Hotel, built at the end of the century by the owners of Singapore's Raffles, was certainly an outpost of character and quality. Once known as 'the wardroom of the Royal Navy', this was the place where the British administrators, the busy buyers of teak and the visiting wives of plantation owners, plus members of the Colonial Service, many on leave perhaps from up-country stations, had stayed in pre-war days. It was where one could now, at least, get a cool drink in the long bar: but I liked to be out and about meeting the Burmans and carrying out my HQ duties, which were really demanding.

Of all the ethnic groups of Burma I moved most easily with the Karens, largely because of my unforgettable experience with them at Henzada and naturally because of their Christian beliefs.

Rangoon, of course, filled with forces personnel. There was the joyous meeting with the ever-cheerful Duggie Gibb, an old school mate and long-time scouting friend from Newcastle upon Tyne, who sought me out. He was a Flying Officer in the RAF. He it was who christened my driver, Festus, as 'Swan Vestas'. When visiting hospitals I came across old friends, including two from HFTC days in Scotland.

I worked out more suitable programmes in English for Radio Rangoon and had a regular spot myself. We were also busy fixing up transportable bamboo staging so that we could get shows out to units in the country. Then I started to get together our main stage show. There was Charlie Lines and his band for a start. They were a lively sextet and proved a great success. I tried out a number of volunteers for the show and some 'pressed' men. Visiting a unit up on the Irrawaddy where they were busy building rafts, I was particularly taken by a very amusing impression of a speech by Churchill given impromptu by one of the officers after dinner in the Mess, and back in Rangoon I arranged for him to come for an audition. He was a most engaging personality and I thought he had huge potential as an actor. He certainly had – his name was Lieutenant Lionel Jefferies of the Oxfordshire and Buckinghamshire Light Infantry. Lionel wore an aged pair of suede shoes and a quite dashing cravat to set off his green uniform, and saluted in a slightly curious manner, which enabled him to peep at you through his fingers. He had a huge sense of humour and was always helpful; being so adaptable on stage made him a great asset. Little did he or any of us know at the time that he would go on to star in Hollywood and the English stage.

Quite soon we had a promising little team together: an excellent tenor, a couple of northern lads who were great tap dancers and all together about eight in the show – just right for some sketches, solo acts and chorus numbers – plus about half-a-dozen crew to set up the bamboo stage (under all sorts of conditions, I might add), run the lights with our travelling dynamo, take it down and travel on to the next camp. I used to compere and act as stage manager-cum-producer.

Then I helped the Chinese get their show on the road, though mind you they were so lively and enthusiastic that they needed little help, that is if one did not get mixed up in any row between the actors. On one occasion, travelling way out in the country to some remote unit in order to do a show with about half a dozen Chinese in their own truck, I was the only non-Chinese present. Suddenly on a remote track a mother and father of a row broke out amongst the cast of the show. I sat there holding on tight wondering when it would quieten down until suddenly, yelling and screaming, they all – including the driver – chased one another into the bush leaving me on my own in the truck. Thinking it best to wait until they quietened down and returned, I settled down for a quick nap. A group of Burmans appeared looking tentatively at the apparently deserted truck. Hearing the noise I awakened with a start and must have inadvertently pressed something, for the huge dragon in the back of the truck suddenly lighted up, flames spurted off its tongue with the result that the Burmans let out a concerted yell and they, too, took to the bush, leaving me alone with a roaring, spitting dragon with smoke belching out of its nostrils.

The Africans were more self-conscious, but I got an act going with their own songs and one chorus number by them was particularly good for the big show.

One local Burman I introduced in time for our production at the spacious Rangoon Theatre was a huge success. We billed him as 'Ka Slo', if I remember correctly. With his longyi hitched up around him like a loin cloth, he would lie on his back on stage with a huge barrel balanced on his bare feet and manipulate this up on its end, spin it round, kick it alarmingly high and catch it, still on the soles of his feet – and all to stirring music. When the twirling barrel lit up as a finale to his act, it nearly brought the house down, as they say.

Like most forces shows put on by the units themselves in wartime, ours was an all-male show – the chorus line in drag being traditionally a riot – but I was able to discover and successfully introduce a couple of good singers from the nurses' ranks for the Rangoon Theatre show.

Incidentally, on one occasion of a visit by an ENSA show, I am afraid I made what I may be bold enough to call an uncharacteristically rude remark in public – though I am told that it did not come over quite like that. It was when Tommy Trinder was in town with an ENSA show. I could not get to the theatre in time to take up my reserved seat in the front row and so I came in as unobtrusively as possible just after the start of the show. But Tommy would have none of this. He stopped his act and pointed me out. 'You, sir!' he barked. 'You, sir – you're two minutes late!' It was a great line and brought a big roar. What could I say? Except – in slightly comical vein – 'And you, sir, are two years late!' That brought an even bigger roar from the crowded house, but at the end of the show in my public appreciation of their visit I made it good for Tommy by saying that my remark was only, of course, a joke and that we appreciated him and ENSA enormously. Funnily enough, years later I heard this story recounted by someone who didn't recognise me as being the person concerned.

I visited a number of Burmans in their homes, making friends in particular with the Harbour Commissioner and his wife and family. I was delighted to be able to entertain their son after the War when he was a pupil at Harrow School by taking him to dinner in London. I am bound to say that the rice served up by my hosts in Rangoon revealed a delicious taste and quality not experienced with rice served back home.

When I met the surprisingly young Major General Aung Sang, who had been head of the Burmese Army of Liberation, we hit it off so well together that we became good friends, meeting many times, sometimes on our own to play tennis or have quite serious discussions. He was a strong personality, built like a rugby forward, gleaming white teeth, ready with a smile, but readily taciturn when it suited him.

His was a remarkable story. The Burmans had been calling for independence since the start of the century. As a young law student he became obsessed with the idea of helping his country to strike out on its own and became really the leader of the movement. He was contacted by the Japanese and, together with twenty-nine young fellow nationalists known as the 'Thirty Comrades', he was invited to Japan for military training. He quickly adapted himself and accompanied the Japanese invasion of Burma in 1941. He was a tough, natural soldier and leader, entirely intent on his country's freedom. His cause as he explained to me was not that of Japan. He saw the British as his rulers and as a young politician yearned for complete freedom for his country and the Japanese were merely an end to this. In fact, when their promises of Burmese autonomy seemed to be getting nowhere, he switched his allegiance and began rapidly recruiting Burmese forces in support of the Allies.

Burma became a devastated cockpit of war and in the end Aung Sang was not only a remarkably young Major General, but, as Burma's war hero, was considered the man to lead his country after the end of the conflict. He told me that he would like to see an independent Burma as a member of the British Commonwealth.

I went to a party he gave to celebrate the birth of a daughter. She was Suu Kyi, destined to become a national heroine in her own right.

Before I left Burma I went to wish him well and he asked me to come back and visit him sometime. Alas, that opportunity did not arise for on 19 July 1947, not long after as Prime Minister he had negotiated independence, he was assassinated, along with the rest of his cabinet.

One day I received an urgent call from our Divisional HQ

instructing me to attend a dinner in the Mess the following evening. It was marked 'Top Security'. I did not get back until late the following afternoon with just time in which to get ready and arrive for dinner, where I at once noted a more than usual contingent of Regimental Police in the background. A band played, dinner was served and then the General got up to make a speech. What he told us literally brought gasps of surprise from all but his immediate staff officers, for it was in fact a farewell speech. A bombshell amongst us for it had come about very quickly and obviously was of top security. What made it all the more dramatic, and indeed sad, was that he was immensely popular. He thanked us all for our loyalty and hard work and praised the men of his Division and then he told us that he was to immediately replace General Sir Miles Dempsey as Commander-in-Chief of the Middle East. He would leave soon after dinner.

He spoke movingly of the Arakan campaign and his deep regard for the officers and men of the Division. We filed past him, shaking his hand and each having a brief conversation with him. He, like us all, was obviously moved. He told me, 'You've been a great asset and done a good job – and always so cheerful.' Then the band played 'Will You No Come Back Again?' and we followed him out of the tent down to the edge of the Irrawaddy. It was a night charged with emotion. In no time, it seemed, he was aboard the Short Sunderland flying-boat, the searchlights lighting up the river as the great bird turned, swept past us and took to the night sky. I discovered afterwards that in his thoughtful way be had left me the following testimonial, addressed to me privately:

To Whom It May Concern

Major K. Johnstone is an officer of integrity. He has drive, energy and a charm of character. He is tactful in his dealings both with his seniors and his juniors.

I can strongly recommend him for any position of trust, particularly where independence and personal initiative are concerned.

H.L. Stockwell
Major General Commanding
82nd (WA) Division

S.E.A.C.
21 May 1946

In 1956 Sir Anthony Eden's decision to link up with France in military operations in the Canal Zone was to bring General Sir Hugh Stockwell into prominence as Commander of the British Land Forces.

CHAPTER VII

Postscript to Burma

On the road to Mandalay
where the flyin'-fishes play
An' the dawn comes up like thunder
Outer China 'crost the bay!
                    Rudyard Kipling

RELAXING IN A CANE CHAIR under a shady canopy on the observation deck of the aptly-named river cruiser 'Road to Mandalay', she watched with amazement as the sun set on the countless deserted stupas in the ancient city of Pagan. The legendary Road to Mandalay was not a road at all but the Ayeyarwady (Kipling's Irrawaddy).

'Yesterday,' she said, 'I saw Shwedagon, a pagoda whose roof was fashioned from gold bullion encrusted with 6,500 diamonds and rubies.'

She was one of the visitors drawn by 50-page glossy brochures to visit Burma.

They now come to this land of golden pagodas and flaming red sunsets where the air is perfumed with incense, no doubt oblivious to the fact that behind the cynical welcome is the misery of slave labour and one of the cruellest regimes in the world.

They call it Myanmar, but to the rest of the world it will always be Burma. In 1987 there was a sudden brutal and unprovoked attack by soldiers when thousands of unarmed protesters were gunned down Chinese style in the streets of Rangoon.

The economy was in ruins and for a brief interlude there were active political groups.

Then the military struck again and following a bloody coup, all international help was frozen, but this was followed by what the military rulers fondly thought would act as lip-service to democracy. They tried to kid the rest of the world that they were democratic. It was a deliberate policy of subterfuge. They held elections which they thought would be a matter of little consequence – but to their consternation, the vote was a huge majority for Aung San Suu Kyi. We know her, of course, as the daughter of my friend, General Aung San, Burma's national hero, who was assassinated in 1947 soon after becoming Prime Minister.

When 82 per cent of the votes were cast in her favour in these elections, held in 1980, the military rulers hurried to place her under house arrest. Her British husband, the late Michael Aris, whom she had first met at Oxford University, was permitted to spend only a few days with her at her house on the lake, which I know. That was in May 1992. When asked her views about her own possible departure she replied, 'It is not negotiable.'

He was a Tibetan scholar, aged fifty-three, and a don at Oxford. An identical twin, he was born in Havana, Cuba and educated at Worth School and Durham University. From 1980 to 1989 he was research fellow in Tibetan and Himalayan Studies at Wolfson College, Oxford. He and Suu Kyi met and fell in love when she was studying in Britain in the 1960s. The courtship was of a literary nature – Suu Kyi wrote 187 letters to him before they married in 1972.

Suu Kyi did not herself become embroiled in Burmese politics until 1988 when she returned to the country to nurse her dying mother. Suddenly, as Aung San's daughter, she found herself at the forefront of a popular movement to oust Ne Win's regime. He had so misdirected the government of the country with his isolationist policies that from being a prosperous exporter of rice across Asia, Burma rapidly became one of the poorest countries in the world. Now the people voted by a huge majority for Suu Kyi to be their leader, but she was arrested.

Then Michael was taken seriously ill with cancer. He was not expected to recover, but the authorities at Rangoon refused to let her have a visa to permit her to go and see him in the United Kingdom. He died soon afterwards. In a statement issued on behalf of herself and her sons after Mr Aris's death, Miss Suu Kyi said, 'I have been so fortunate to have such a wonderful husband who has always given me the understanding I needed. Nothing can take that away from me.'

She had been awarded the Nobel Peace Prize in 1991 and at least her husband and sons had been able to travel to Stockholm to receive it. Alexander and Kim, the two boys, make up a family that has been martyred by the military junta in Rangoon.

What would some of the tourists think if they knew even just a little of the devious planning by the present rulers of Burma? The murders and beatings. The Death Railway where a total of some 120,000 people were literally forced to build 110 miles of embankment in almost inhuman conditions. Forced labour has been used to restore some of the tourist sites, such as Mandalay Palace, and to upgrade the infrastructure – railways, roads and airports. Amnesty International has released particularly damning documentation of conditions in prison labour camps in September 1995, and the horrific number of deaths through exhaustion and beatings have caused the United Nations General Assembly to pass their fifth consecutive resolution on Burma deploring the continued violation of human rights in the country. But all have seemingly been of no avail.

The number of Burmese seeking refuge in neighbouring countries has increased dramatically over the past three years, with conservative estimates claiming over 150,000 refugees now living in the bordering countries of Thailand, Bangladesh, China and India. Between 50,000 and 100,000 may have fled into Bangladesh. Some 30,000 have fled to China. Several thousand have sought refuge in India, while over 60,000 are living in camps along the Thai border. Those in prison face the most barbarous tortures quite unbelievable in this day and age.

Only away in the north the gallant Karen military detachments have tried to maintain running battles with sections of the Burma Army in the bush, but it has been very difficult for them to maintain supply lines.

In Burma military personnel certainly continue to rule the roost. They are allotted land at mere token prices. For instance, Myanmar Golf Club in Rangoon required more land in time for the awaited tourist influx. At first the Army blockaded the area in an attempt to intimidate the people living there to simply move out. When this failed, the SLORC – the governing body – simply arrested one member from each household and sent them without trial to Insein Jail. The remainder were then moved to a satellite town 25 km out of the city – an area subject to flooding. They were not, of course, given the slightest compensation. Their relatives were finally released some ten days later.

There are now as many as ten airlines operating in Burma on domestic and international flights. One is the national company, Myanmar Airways, which is mostly under military financial control – and the remainder are Thai Airways, Silk Air (Singapore), Air China, Beman Bangladesh, Myanmar International (half Burmese and half Singaporean), Lao Aviation, Pakistan International Airlines, Indian Airlines and Air Mandalay. Tourism is now the world's largest industry with 567 million people travelling in 1995, a figure expected to rise to 937 million by the year 2010. But the tourist industry does not actually manufacture anything – it makes money by turning people and cultures into commodities. The SLORC, though, is hoping to make billions of dollars through tourism, as their neighbours have done, and believes that the construction of hotels and communications of an international standard will turn Burma into a modern nation. What they seem to choose to ignore is that Burma, like Iraq, Eastern Timor and Serbia, is now a pariah country. I have written to all tourist companies pointing all this out and saying, 'Don't visit Burma yet.'

The most disgusting and barbaric practices are being followed in Burma in using slave labour. Total and Premier Oil are two companies investing heavily in Burma creating finance and credibility. They will argue that they are not strictly breaking the law. The European Union could, however, make a real difference by following the example of the US Government and barring all new investment in Burma by companies in member states. Premier Oil – to whom I have written in protest – refused to allow the matter of barbaric conditions in Burma to be raised at their AGM. They say that they work within the European Union's regulations, but what I ask them to do is to make their own moral decisions.

The European Parliament has called on the Commission and the Council to implement full economic sanctions against Burma and to prohibit any investment until the Rangoon regime has stopped these serious violations of human rights. Total and Premier Oil may be helping a few thousand people in its community programmes, but this is of scant value in a land of 47 million people brought to its knees by a plundering military regime.

Moreover, the traffic in drugs in northern Burma now being tolerated is a world menace. Rory Maclean has written a most revealing book about Burma called *Under the Dragon*, which he describes as 'Travels in a Betrayed Land'. He learns about the economics of the disgraceful heroin trade and the tragedy of child prostitution. He meets the courageous and imprisoned Aung San Suu Kyi. Writing in a decaying Rangoon, he puts it thus, 'To me Burma was a paradox, a land of selfless generosity and sinister greed stitched together by love and fear. Its people persevered while accepting life's impermanence, its rulers deified their former leader yet imprisoned his daughter.'

I have referred to the SLORC. It means, incidentally, the State Law and Order Restoration Council. Their executives nearly all have military titles. The Army, Navy and Air Force officers get first pick on land development and opportunities in business. The newspaper, *New Light of Myanmar*, is always careful to get the rank right as it reports the goings and comings of millionaire soldiers and a very small rich middle class.

The national coach company now whisks tourists from place to place. The real condition of the people is hidden from visitors. There is a new private overnight road service to Mandalay suitable for businessmen and visitors. It is the Leo Express. Ordinary people are not really catered for. It is all becoming like Thailand and no doubt some of the flotsam and jetsam of filth now residing in that country will find its way here, too.

Of course I long to see again this land of wild Conradian beauty, flaming sunsets, far snow-capped mountains, great winding rivers, the rice paddies and even the relentless bush. To hear at dusk the sound of tinkling temple bells. To meet again these modest, diverse and, as I knew them, cheerful people – but reality might now be too distressing. Sometimes it is better not to disturb one's memories.

CHAPTER VIII

European Journey

IT WAS 20 NOVEMBER 1947. I was in a London full of gaiety and pride. It seemed that the War just ended was momentarily forgotten, if that were possible.

I stood amongst the crowd, said to be fifty deep along The Mall and down Whitehall. Many had slept there overnight. How we cheered wildly as the King and his daughter drove to Westminster Abbey in the Irish State Coach escorted by the Household Cavalry, resplendent in scarlet tunics and mounted on black horses.

The bridegroom was listed as Lieutenant Philip Mountbatten RN on the order of service, but at a private ceremony earlier in the day he had been given the title by the King of Prince Philip, Duke of Edinburgh.

The congregation of 2,500 at the Abbey, we learned later, had been one of striking contrasts. There were Heralds, Gentlemen-at-Arms and others in uniforms vivid as playing cards and all around in the pews people in their daytime grey suits. The ceremony itself may have been simple – as one of the presiding prelates said, 'The same as for any cottager getting married in her village church in the Dales this afternoon' – but the occasion was indeed glittering, such as the nation had not seen for more than a decade.

The bride's beautiful ivory coloured dress was embroidered with flowers of beads and pearls. Her tulle veil hung from a circlet of diamonds. It was designed by Normal Hartnell who had taken it to the Palace himself the night before in a six-foot-long white box.

To me, an unabashed romantic, every detail, every picture stirred me. In fact, everything about the day was thrilling. How the good old USA would love to have a Royal Family. Well they would, wouldn't they? However much Tinsel Town holds court to its 'monarchs' of the moment – take for example their regard for the tragic Kennedy family – the American public have always sought a true centre point.

More than ever one had this sense of wonder at the resilience of the British people – this extraordinary ability to adapt. After all, only two months earlier the sun had set on the British Raj. Two new dominions, Pakistan and India, had been born out of Britain's vast Indian Empire on 15 August.

I wondered about the other countries in Europe. How were they faring? That morning in The Mall I had a sudden resolve to go and find out. That was it! I would simply take off and meet the people.

Back home on Tyneside I put it to John Grey, Editor of the *Sunday Sun*, and he jumped at the idea to have me write a series of articles on a European Journey. I lost no time in making a start.

It was by now early 1948. First I stayed for a few days with friends in Paris. Here, on a racecourse on the edge of the capital, I heard the lanky, hook-nosed General de Gaulle address a packed meeting where he called for a general election and a new constitution for France.

Back home the hit song was 'Maybe it's Because I'm a Londoner', typifying much of the general feeling of the day. The Government pushed through an order 'to defeat spivs and drones' and in New York, Tennessee Williams had made a hit with the opening of his play, *A Streetcar Named Desire*.

The BBC had become extremely serious about morals and writers and producers of the then immensely popular radio play *Dick Barton* were issued with a series of rules designed to protect Dick's upright character. Only clean socks on the jaws would be tolerated: there was to be no swearing, Dick never lied and sex was definitely out.

In my notebook – and I had already learned most of them off by heart – were standard phrases in French and German such as 'How are you?'; 'I am glad to meet you'; 'I am just travelling on foot to see your town and meet people'; 'Is there a hostel near?'; 'Is there a cafe near?' and so forth.

Fortunately it was fairly mild weather. I had a stout fleece-lined jacket, well padded around the lower part of my back, and I wore a thick pair of cords – but not 'long johns' underwear as I don't like them, though I had had to wear them in the sub-Arctic. I had a second pair of thick socks, a cardigan, long scarf, two spare shirts, medical kit, toilet bag, a pair of slippers, dictionary (English to French and German grammar books) and what maps I could find en route. Beneath my pack I had my faithful Grand Hotel – my one-man tent – and roiled up securely in stout waterproofs my fur-lined sleeping bag. Finally, my boots had thick soles and, very important, were not new but already well worn.

Money was, of course, restricted and I had to be frugal. The £35 allowance at that time would be about £350 now. My idea was to avoid information bureaux, military headquarters, 'Ministries of Mis-Information' – I wanted to meet the people, to sink as inconspicuously as possible into their midst.

My maxim would be:

'I am part of all that I meet
Yet all experience is an arch wherethro'
Gleams that untravelled world whose margins fade
For ever and for ever when I move.'

A member of the French Government to whom I was introduced gave me a marvellous send-off to my journey when he drove me from Paris to Strasbourg. Then, after showing me around the lovely old city, he drove me across the Rhine and left me on the main route to Frankfurt and the north. I stayed overnight in a transport cafe hostel and soon after breakfast the next morning I got the first of the countless lifts of my trip.

I suppose that my real passport was my smile. I am sorry if this sounds rather smug, but I just happen to look on the bright side – to smile because I really like people – so here I was with my pack and my bonhomie extending the right hand of friendship. But of course there had just been this goddamned war, and all that it meant in destruction and misery and now here comes a guy like a kind of happy wanderer – and he is English, too. Who said we were all rather reserved?

I was to find on this journey that students would suddenly appear and want to talk to me. They were, after all, victims of this tragedy, captive in a madness that was not of their making, eager to make friends, to ask questions. Of course this was not holiday time. The terrible War had not long ended. There appeared to be so many of them, their young formative years already fractured by circumstances far beyond them.

It was students who reacted first. When I got off the truck later on that first day a few miles south of Karlsruhe and hit the road on my own. I began to meet people – at first a wave, then a nod and a smile, next there would be a couple of students alongside me, then more, until I arrived in this small town like a kind of pilgrim. They were so friendly to this English guy with a rucksack. Soon afterwards they escorted me to what appeared to be a hostel and once inside offered me a cup of coffee and some cake. After a short discussion among themselves they offered to take me on a short tour of the centre of the town, which was really a small agricultural community.

Later, back at the hostel, I met a tall pale young man who was introduced as the manager. He had heard about me already, he said, and would I like to stay for a few days? Naturally I at once agreed. He paused, ready to allot me a room. 'Homosexual?' he enquired. I shook my head. Then, with what I thought was a slight air of disappointment, he consulted his list again before leading me to a small room which he indicated was for my own use.

News got around quickly and I was soon meeting more local people. One of them, a middle-aged professor eager to practise his English, became my guide and philosopher and two days later when he called on me he was obviously very excited. He had, he told me, gained special permission for me to visit an old castle just outside the camp. It was presently being used as a kind of prison. So next day in his ancient car he drove me up the hill to the gates of this austere-looking building and, after some interrogation by an official, we were admitted.

There followed some extraordinary interviews, carried out with the professor as interpreter and a rather bored-looking German officer in attendance. To my amazement, when they took me to meet one of the detainees, he turned out to have been at one time Hitler's chauffeur. His accounts through the interpreters – I had actually two now because the professor and the officer/guard were competing with one another to show off their English – were fascinating, particularly when, in a burst of animation, he told us that Hitler regularly farted when standing up in the vehicle taking the salute. Did he, I wondered, defecate in tune with the heavy brass in the band?

Another detainee was Prince Wilhelm, better known as 'Little Willie', the son of the ex-Kaiser, Wilhelm II, who had died in June 1941. He appeared delighted to meet me, adjusting his monocle and putting his hands on my shoulder with unexpected bonhomie. Fortunately, though, he did not attempt to kiss me! Soon he was recalling great times in London society. How he used to love Ascot and the Derby, and staying at the Ritz in Piccadilly. He asked after members of the Royal Family, at which I had to explain rather lamely that I didn't see them that often.

The professor appeared to regard me as a kind of trophy and soon I was meeting all manner of local folk. I did not feel there was antagonism towards me. The people seemed too intent on trying to put their own lives together. They had not lost their capacity for taking pains. Whatever the state of their clothing they made the most of it although they were mostly neat and respectable. Careful improvisation was to be seen in damaged shops and buildings. People went about in an orderly, if chastened, manner. The struggle to survive occupied their attention rather than a debate on how they had got into this mess.

It was the food, or lack of it, that was most evident. The typical day's diet meant ersatz coffee and a couple of slices of dry bread for breakfast. Some more bread and a little cheese made up a 'second' breakfast and for a midday meal it was usually soup, tomatoes (black market willing) and two slices of bread. Around 4.00 p.m. a cup of tea and perhaps a piece of cake and at 7.00 p.m. some fruit – fortunately and surprisingly not difficult to obtain – and seemingly the ever-available soup made up of anything they could lay their hands on for stock. Sometimes, though, there was a little fish and this was always welcome. On Sundays whole families contrived to get together to spend their meal tickets at what appeared to be very reasonable prices and meat and fish sometimes appeared.

I made it a rule to be very careful not to accept food too readily as I did not want to take anyone else's ration and this worried me a little, though I was assured that I was not depriving anyone else.

After a week I thanked them all and moved on. Sometimes I took a bus to help me on my way, or hopped on board a train – they were beginning to run to time again with typical German efficiency.

One afternoon I was invited into an old farmhouse, just off a country road along which I was walking. They were a family of four and after asking me to stay for a meal they produced a photo album of their son. He had been killed in action in the Western Desert. They seemed to feel that I would have got on well with him. He was apparently about my age. Strange that it seemed to be a comfort to a family to meet and show their dead son's pictures to a man who had been their enemy. They insisted on having me stay for the night. I had this feeling that they were stealing glances at me not as a former enemy, but as a kind of illusion of the son they had lost.

It was early February 1948 and I had reached Prague. It undoubtedly deserves its title as the 'Hundred Spired Golden Praha', the Rome of the North. It was the chief city of the old kingdom of Bohemia and the cultural centre of Europe in the fourteenth century, enriched by artists and architects from Germany, France and Italy. Although it never reached such heights again, there was a new wave of artistic expansion in the age of the baroque, which has led to the sometimes expressed comparison with Rome. Certainly, like Rome, the skyline is a fairy-tale scenario of domes and spires.

I lost no time in visiting the beautiful facades of the baroque palaces after walking slowly through the Mala Strana. The Abbey Church of Oboriste was another on my list of places to see and also the Abbey of Loreto where Mozart once played the organ. Here I met up with a lively bunch of students who revelled in practising their English and in no time practically adopted me. They took me to visit the baroque library in the Strakovsky Klaster and the Narodini Gallery.

Next day we all visited the royal gardens of Kralovska Zahrada and the fourteenth-century Nova-Mesto. Having such enthusiastic guides was sheer heaven, enabling me to really take in this beautiful city.

It was evident that there was a growing restlessness among the people. An unmistakable feeling of sadness, too. Here and there along the streets were many small photographs, some pathetically faded and creased, pinned to doorways or nailed to walls. Sometimes a wreath surrounded them, for these were the faces of Czech boys and young men who had bravely fought in the capital's streets against the Germans during the November revolution.

They were remembered and honoured where they fell.

The Communists had suddenly seized power. In the new government they and their allies, the left-wing Social Democrats, now held almost every important post. No-one quite knew what President Benes thought of these developments for every time it was announced that he would make a speech it was mysteriously cancelled.

Klement Gottwald, 52, a joiner by trade, had become the new Premier since his Communist Party had slipped into power on what was 33 per cent of the vote – though this was questionable – two years before. Prague students, however, still retained the liberal traditions of the early years of the Republic and my new-found friends were very much involved in the fight against Communism. In fact, when Erik their leader invited me to stay in a little room above the bakery run by his father where he himself worked part-time, I discovered that it was next door to the Resistance headquarters! Before I knew what was happening I was involved in clandestine political meetings, in between hearing some of their lilting folk songs.

Slowly the Czech genius for vigorous planning had been harnessed to the deadening policies of the Russian so-called 'pro-prosperity' sphere. The first move was to legislate for the compulsory nationalisation of all enterprises employing more than 500 workers. A huge Ministry of Industry was set up divided into no fewer than twenty different departments. It controlled 10,125 industrial enterprises with a total of more than a million workers.

I have a deep suspicion and dislike of Communism and I only wished that I could have understood what the students were saying. But I admired their tenacity. Consulting my diaries years later I noted that whilst Prague was in tumult, the news elsewhere for the remainder of the year included the following: the new state of Israel was born; the British National Health Service came into being; Freddie Mills became the undisputed World Champion, beating Gus Lesnevich on points; Don Bradman bowed out with a duck; Lester Piggott won his first race aged twelve years; London held the 'austerity' Olympics (Germany, Soviet Union and Japan didn't make it); a young singer named Julie Andrews sang for the Queen and a new star was born; Harry Truman became President of the USA; Mahatma Gandhi was shot by an assassin; and on 15 December 1948, the first-born child of Princess Elizabeth was christened Charles Phillip Arthur George, to become better known as Prince Charles.

But to get back to my adventures in Prague.

About two weeks after my arrival my friends suggested I accompany them to the Kinsky Palace where there was to be considerable activity later that day. This proved to be the understatement of the year. When we arrived a mob several thousands strong, and apparently hastily bussed in from factories and villages on the outskirts of the city, was surging around the Palace. They were calling for Klement Gottwald. By the time he came out on to a balcony to address them, the whole place was in ferment. Somehow he quietened them down and made his speech.

Meanwhile the students, who had gathered on the outskirts of the mob, began to press forward chanting slogans and shouting. As more of them arrived the situation became explosive and fighting broke out. Soon there was uproar all around me. I was pushed to the ground, got on my feet and landed a yelling Communist a haymaker. Then the police and members of the Works Militia – the Trades Union police – arrived, all obviously fervent Communists wearing armbands and carrying guns.

Erik grabbed me and shouted, 'Ken, you must get out of here!'

For the moment we were parted, caught up in the surging crowd only to be hurled together again.

'It's going to get really bad,' he shouted, as if this wasn't bad enough.

There were renewed shouts from the students of, 'On to the President's Palace.' 'Down with the Communists.'

A number of them began trying to regroup in order to march to Hradcany Castle in the old city. Soon the idea caught on and as more students began to form up, the police moved in again, waving their batons.

Erik was at my side pleading, 'You might get beaten up or arrested. You'll be in a hell of a spot stuck in a police cell.'

Then he pulled me towards him. 'Ivan, here, is going to get out of this. He's got a bakery round to do. Go with him now, he'll get you on your way. Good luck, we'll not forget you.'

We hugged one another like true patriots. He was right. They knew that I was ready to get on with my journey. It was too dangerous to hang around there.

'Remember me to the others – and good luck – and thank you,' I told him.

My journey was to be a pattern of quick friendships, but surely none more moving than with this wonderful group who loved freedom and their country and struggled against an evil tide that threatened to engulf them.

I stuck close to Ivan as we battled our way out of the crowd and walked more freely back to the bakery, where I quickly packed and with a last look around the spot where we had talked and laughed and they had sung songs of freedom, I rejoined him. Soon I was crossing the Danube in the back of a baker's van.

Reaching the Danube was, after all, one of my main objectives of the journey.

The noise of the demonstration receded and soon Ivan dropped me off along a quieter stretch of road. Before we parted, though, he called over a truck driver whom he knew and after some conversation together, a tall friendly looking chap in his mid-twenties offered to give me a lift to the town of Regensburg. Better still, he knew some of the boat skippers there and said he would try and get me a free lift down the river. On arrival he found a friend who agreed to take me on board his small cargo boat all the way to Vienna.

This was the sort of luck any traveller dreams about and when it comes, there is a wonderful surge of elation. It's what has been described as walking on air.

I at once offered to help on board. There was a very small crew consisting of two friendly older men, who had no semblance of English, and Karl the skipper, who had just a little.

We cruised the rest of the day until we reached the Bavarian city of Passau, renowned for its Italianate architecture, which I did not, of course, have time to see at close quarters. After some hours spent loading and unloading, we were off again past the splendid scenery of upper Austria and on to the city of Linz, where we did not stop, and so to Melk, arriving as darkness fell.

I was glad that there were plenty of jobs for me to do on board the little vessel – cleaning down the decks, sorting out the cargo, washing up after meals – so that I did not feel too much of a parasite and Karl seemed to enjoy my company. If he really did like the English I cannot say – perhaps he hadn't met any before – but in the immediate post-war circumstances when his world, like most people's, had been turned upside down, he had learned to pull on his pipe, get on with his job and say little. And I was content not to risk any contretemps ...

So the beautiful Danube became a glorious post-war interlude, any lack of comfort on the voyage being of little or no consequence. After all, the rigours of wartime were still very fresh in one's memory. The Danube like no other European river has shaped the course of history. Romans, Celts, Thraks, Illyrics and Ottomans have all played their part.

In Vienna I saw the statues erected to Russian soldiers – I was to see many more of these as I travelled east – and it made one wish all the more that Winston Churchill's desire that the Allied Forces take part in the drive up 'the underbelly of Europe' had been heeded, although there were no statues to the Western soldiers. Consequently, following spectacular Soviet military successes, Marshal Stalin had arrived for the big conference at Yalta in February 1945 in a strong position. Frontier changes in Russia's favour had been made at Poland's expense and in tacit Anglo-US acceptance of Soviet supremacy in Eastern Europe. This was to prove a great mistake.

Only two months later Marshal Tolbhukin liberated Vienna after several days of vicious hand-to-hand fighting. The Germans, who lost no less than 130,000 prisoners in the battle for the city, made their last stand in the old Jewish quarter, but whilst their casualties were heavy, fortunately little damage was done to the city. Vienna was liberated with almost all its buildings intact.

Hence, I found more and more evidence that Russians were regarded as 'the liberators' and that the Iron Curtain had been slammed down against the West, though paradoxically in Vienna, the Communists had recently been dismissed from the Government. There were unmistakable signs of quite sinister intrigue. People sat close together drinking in cafes, periodically looking over their shoulders. It was a partitioned, romantic city. To walk along the dimly lighted streets made one wonder what went on behind the shuttered windows.

I met a film writer from Hollywood, an assistant to Carol Reed the famous producer and director. He, too, was clearly intrigued by the clandestine atmosphere. 'We're working on it,' he told me.

They certainly were! Two years later Graham Greene's superb screenplay of Carol Reed's classic thriller *The Third Man* was released, in which Joseph Cotten as a pulp novelist comes to post-war Vienna to search for his old friend, Harry Lime, only to be told that he has died. Lime, of course, famously reappears in the shape of Orson Welles, and the sound of the zither became part of film history. I can vouch for it that they really captured the mood and the moment.

And so to Budapest by way of some steady walking and friendly truck drivers.

In fact, I relished the chance to relax at one of its many health spas and in City Park I lost no time in visiting the large outdoor pools connected by a heated corridor and known as Szechenyi. I made my way past a wooden board itemising the spa treatments available, from steam, mud, sulphur and salt to magnetotherapy and 'hygienal massage', and into the men's baths where the walls were covered in exquisite turquoise tiles. Here, clothed only in a small-sized loin-cloth, I relaxed dreamily – most welcome after my hard travelling – until an hour later I was pummelled back into consciousness by a masseur.

The city was wasting no time putting on a brave face with some effort and even talking of resuming its Spring Festival, which had always heralded the emergence from winter to the sound of music from gipsy bands to Liszt and Bartok.

When the Nazis fled the city they destroyed all the bridges and the palace on Castle Hill – subsequently rebuilt – so that the Russians were treated as saviours, but this feeling was noticeably already beginning to be less certain.

The Russians were stacking the grain high in their wagons as they blatantly robbed the farmers of their stock. The vast larder around Lake Balaton, in particular, was being steadily plundered and sent east by rail.

The ancient towns of Buda and Pest, on opposite banks of the Danube, recall the influence of other past invaders, though the parliament buildings appear to be fashioned after the Palace of Westminster. Elsewhere austere Gothic, stately Renaissance, and a mixture of the exuberance of the baroque and oriental decoration present a wondrous panorama of gilded spires. There could be almost a suggestion of Paris with its broad tree-lined avenues, the cafes and restaurants – though these were obviously greatly re-duced in what they had to offer when I saw it and much would, of course, hopefully improve in the days ahead.

Heroes' Square – a gigantic expression of national pride laid out in 1896 to celebrate 1,000 years of Hungarian existence – was thankfully undamaged with, at the top of the square, a column bearing a statue of the Archangel Gabriel and at its base more statues – seven wild men on horseback, the seven chieftains who brought their tribes to Hungary in 896. The Museum of Fine Arts with its dramatic steps leading to an enormous portico was very impressive, too.

The city had released itself from unforgiving winter and the people were out and about as if revelling in a peace that had never seemed to be possible. On the Pest side there appeared to be the most progress and already there were some attractive-looking women to be seen teetering on their platform shoes. The fashion-able bars were struggling to get back in business – Beckett's and Fat Mo's – and a few of the beautiful people were beginning to emerge again under the bright bar lights.

The morning after my arrival I was off early to catch the No. 2 tram at Margaret Bridge. Full of character though, of course, sadly in need of painting, the long, yellow trams had three carriages. I went to Vigado Square where the concert hall had been almost completely destroyed.

It was very moving to attend St Matthias's Church. Afterwards I sat on the edge of the Fishermen's Bastion, an odd nineteenth-century folly, and looked out on the waters of the Danube.

The shops may have had little on display, but the Danube ran full and free and violins played as sweetly as ever in the cafes of Buda. It is the music that comforts these people as a kind of antidote to the fickleness of fortune, and I heard more laughter here than anywhere yet on my journey east.

I must admit that, even in the lodgings I had for a couple of nights in what I'll swear was a bordello, they seemed to play the violin as the beds creaked.

It was time to move on. Much as I enjoyed the city, I had, after all, reached my objective, the Danube, though truth to tell I had always hoped to make my target Constanza on the Black Sea. For a lone walker on very limited funds that presented a helluva task, even though in normal circumstances it would mean more feature articles in the *Sunday Sun*.

Now on the edge of the Balkans in an atmosphere of political upheaval it was a very dodgy prospect.

My first taste of this came, in fact, on my second day out from Budapest. I had arrived in the small town of Godollo to find a distinct atmosphere quite different from anything I had yet met on my journey. It was a sense of danger, a feeling of being watched and yet one was unable to say positively who was the observer. People did not speak freely.

After a night's lodgings in a small inn, I set out early next morning walking cross country following a map as best I could and glad to be free of the atmosphere in the town. Striking out across the hills I at once felt more relaxed. I was making for a place called Miskoli on the River Sajo and my intention was to first reach a rail junction at Hatvani, about two days' hike away, and go on from there. Beyond stretched the Ukraine.

The spring flowers were nodding encouragement as I climbed steadily, beginning to feel more relaxed and gradually forgetting my uneasiness of the night before. In the late afternoon I decided to call it a day and, finding a sheltered spot I put up the 'Grand Hotel' and made a cup of coffee on my small stove and ate a sandwich. I had covered a fair distance and rolling out my sleeping bag I decided to have a spot of 'shut-eye' for an hour or two. Suddenly I awakened with a jolt. I was being roughly shaken.

I sat up rigidly and was half hauled to my feet. I was startled to find I was looking down the barrel of a rifle. Three Russian soldiers stood facing me. One had a rifle in his hands. I was motioned to get to my feet. I was physically held and searched bodily by another soldier who must have once been an all-in wrestler. After all, I had been until recently a major in the British Army and I didn't take easily to some grotty-looking private soldier in the Russian Army roughing me up. I glared at him all the while muttering 'English! English!'

My rucksack was upturned and the contents slowly examined. It seemed to take ages and every now and then they spoke to each other in low tones and looked across at me. I decided it was best not to appear to be furious, but to try and be calm.

It was, of course, difficult to convey what I was doing there. I suppose a dotty Englishman out for a hike, far from home, wouldn't get to first base as an excuse! I showed them my passport, but they appeared not to understand so nothing was said further as they moved off with me in the centre of the patrol, having at least been allowed to repack my tent. Soon we reached a track where they motioned me into the back of a waiting truck. Thoughts raced through my mind. Could I be arrested as a spy? Would I be imprisoned? Any kind of charge could be trumped up. Certainly I got nothing but scowls as I searched the faces of the soldiers.

We bumped along in silence for about half an hour until we reached a village and pulled up outside what was clearly marked as a police station. Fortunately the Hungarian police sergeant could understand a little English. He asked me to show him my papers. After studying them for some time, he spoke quietly to the Russian officer, whom I could now see looked surprisingly youthful, and they both kept frowning across at me, obviously uncertain what to do next. At length the Hungarian police officer seemed to want to clear everything up amicably. He came over to me and explained that the Russian army patrol was out looking for people who were trying to get across to the US Zone in Austria and they had been following me. After about a quarter of an hour the air cleared. The

Russians departed and the police sergeant, visibly more relaxed, made out his report. I spent the night in a cell following a cup of coffee and a half stilted conversation about football.

In the morning all seemed quiet. I had slept fitfully. They brought me a cup of coffee and a slice of bread and margarine and I began to wonder what was to happen next. There was an awkward hour or so during which I could only sit and hope. Then my passport was returned to me and confirmation that all was well came when the police sergeant, all smiles, suddenly produced a battered old copy of a magazine in which there was a picture of the wedding of Princess Elizabeth and Prince Philip. He indicated to me that I was free to go – an enormous relief, as I don't mind admitting that I had a pretty disturbed night. There was always the possibility that I could have been held by the Russians and carted off to God knows where.

Some months previously President Truman had called it an outrage when he accused the Russian Army of helping the Communist minority in Hungary in order to force changes. Now I had indeed seen the presence of Russian troops for myself. I certainly felt safer with the Hungarian Police and having decided that the Balkans were too dangerous, I jumped at the offer to have a lift back to Budapest.

Once there, however, I decided to change plans and go on to Bratislava, where I had two contacts. One was through my friends back in Prague and the other was someone who had given me a lift in his car one day about a month before. As it happened, the contact through Prague did not answer when I phoned, so I wrote him a note and posted it from the railway station, but the other call struck lucky. The gentleman, whose name was Pierre Caleja, at once remembered me and when I said that I was on my way back to England he insisted that I join him at Zlin for a few days. It seems that I had, in fact, just caught him before he left and he would be round to pick me up outside the railway station in an hour. This was the kind of good luck that sometimes happens once you hit the road.

And so I came to Moravia, surely the name for a fictitious country in a musical comedy, but in reality a hilly area located amidst the Hostyn Peaks and the White Carpathian Mountains in the south of Czechoslovakia. Here I was to discover, to my delight, the special spirit which had taken this once poor Valassko (Wallachian) region into breathtaking economic development since the 1920s. In Zlin itself the 'economic miracle' was most evident and had given rise to a modern industrial community in hitherto one of the most backward parts of the historic countries of the lands of the Czech crown.

It was this spirit of enterprise and business flair that had enabled Zlin to recover from the repercussions of the Thirty Years War, establish small business enterprises based on local crafts and markets, and to flourish after two world wars. When the sister and brothers, Anna, Anton and Tomas Bata, for instance, opened their shoe factory, it not only marked the surge forward in development of the town, but the start of the amazing rise to fame of Tomas Bata, the youngest member of the family. That was in 1894 and it wasn't long before this remarkable young man was to create from virtually nothing a dramatic advance in the Czech shoe market. The supply of boots to the Czech Army in the First World War helped all the local shoe makers, including Bata, but Zlin was to suffer an economic crisis. Bata managed to survive this, partly due to his daring tactic of cutting all prices drastically, thus winning the support of hundreds of thousands of customers and virtually conquering the Czech footwear market.

Tomas Bata died in 1932, but not before an extensive factory compound had been erected on the western outskirts of the town. Here, equipped with state-of-the-art machinery and equipment, the company began to flood world markets with millions of pairs of shoes, backed by a determined sales policy. Shops were opened on virtually every continent. Zlin itself boomed architecturally with a go-ahead building plan which embraced modern functional designs then unparalleled in Europe and which are still most impressive.

Building activity was, in fact, brisk during my visit. There was, for instance, a collective twelve-floor block of flats with various layouts, the work of Architect, Jiri Vozenilek. It was a residential architectural style pioneered from 1930 by left-wing Czech architects. It distinguished itself, among other things, by the positioning of technical and cultural facilities concentrated on the ground floor and the terrace. Given that in the inter-war period this form would have been totally unacceptable for ideological reasons, its implementation in this specific environment in a later period appeared to be rather paradoxical. Naturally, with my English background, it was not all to my liking, but this did not take away from my admiration of the verve and drive behind it.

I found the independence and spirit of the place most attractive. I was introduced on arrival to a few people and in no time I had invitations to stay as a guest and even work at the Bata shoe factory. I must say the two weeks' pay was a welcome aid to my now greatly depleted exchequer.

Amazingly, only two years before this the whole district had suffered a heavy US bombing attack and, of course, occupation by the Nazis had stifled progress, but their resilience and independence was wonderful to behold. Now they were bracing themselves to deal with Communism, but the nature of their terrain and their character would ensure their resistance, even though they had to tolerate temporarily the name of Gottwaldow – but they persisted in referring to Zlin!

The Bata company's administrative building, a fifteen-storey, 77.5 metres high structure which had been completed in 1938 and was the highest building in Czechoslovakia, boasted a curiosity – the office which had been used by Mr Bata measured 6 × 6 metres and was located in a lift.

The company now operates from the Bata International Centre in North York, Toronto, Ontario, where Thomas J. Bata, who was so kind to me on my visit to Zlin, is now the head of Bata International.

So good luck to Zlin. Attacked by the Germans, bombed by the Americans and menaced by the Communists; and still they remain optimistic, hard-working people, full of artistic, avant-garde ideas in commerce, architecture and film production. My kind of people!

All journeys have to end somewhere and I thought it fitting that my European journey should end here in Zlin. It is a story of hope. The once poor Wallachian region has undergone breathtaking economic development since the 1920s. The phenomenon known as the 'Bata' spirit appeals to me greatly, and I was coming home wearing a new pair of boots.

CHAPTER IX

Kemsley Days

ONE DAY AFTER THE WAR HAD ENDED, I received a letter from an old friend, Denis Hamilton. In it he said that he wished to repay a good turn I had done him in the past. He was referring to the time when having been invited pre-war to take up a commission in the Territorial Army (TA), I asked if my friend Hamilton could also be considered. I was informed that there were no further vacancies which meant that he would have to await his call-up into the ranks in the normal way. It so happened, however, that I was able to bring up the matter again and this time the Brigadier relented and agreed to see him. The result was that Denis did get his commission in the Durham Light Infantry and therefore a head start into his career in the Army. At no time since had this been discussed or referred to between us.

Traditionally you got a commission in the TA because you were a friend of the Colonel or the Colonel's family, or you had been at public school, or played a good standard of rugby, or whatever. It was considered an honour to be commissioned into a county regiment, especially the Durham Light Infantry. What really happened, I believe, was that the Brigadier said, 'We must get Ken in – he's a good chap,' as I was, I suppose, well known through scouting and the Gang Shows. Anyway, the day I was embodied, Hitler declared war – maybe he heard the news that I had joined up and lost his nerve! I reported to the Drill Hall at Birtley, County Durham one evening and by the next day we were all out digging slit trenches as though Jerry had already landed. There was little opportunity for me to do basic training and drills as I was almost immediately dealing with new recruits myself. I had to swot up and get the Regimental Sergeant Major to give me a few tips.

Denis was a reporter on the local newspaper at the time, aged twenty, just a year older than me. He was later to become a wartime brigadier and win the DSO whilst still in his twenties, which led to his immediate post-war appointment as Personal Assistant to Lord Kemsley, head of Kemsley Newspapers in London, the largest group of newspapers in Europe.

On returning from war service, I found that Cut-Outs Limited of Newcastle upon Tyne, who had kindly continued to pay me a small basic allowance during the war years, now wanted me to go and work in London for them as their sales representative. They had no office and little or no connection there. I was grateful for the thought, but I was not attracted to it. I therefore had to rely on some sales agencies of my own on Tyneside, but I was finding it difficult to work out my future.

I had been invited to become Chairman of the Young Conservatives of North Newcastle upon Tyne constituency. It had nearly always been a Conservative-held seat, though in some years ahead it was to change, largely because of the many young voters who moved in and the drift away from the right. However, in the immediate post-war years, things went along merrily in the constituency and I must say that I was able to help generate great enthusiasm amongst the YCs – all this in addition to my scouting.

The next thing that happened was that Wallsend-on-Tyne constituency Conservatives came to see me and asked me to stand as their parliamentary candidate. The constituency was made up of Wallsend itself and surrounding areas – all mostly Labour – but also Gosforth where I lived. Except for the mid-1930s, when it had a Nationalist MP (Dame Irene Ward), it was traditionally left because of the high population percentage in Wallsend, where ship-building and coal were the main industries. The Socialist majority was about 19,000.

My adoption meeting appeared to be a huge success. I particularly enjoyed speaking down in Wallsend with all the hectoring, though I remember one lady supporter from Gosforth hearing me speak there thought that I was too coarse in my language.

Life was very hectic indeed, but with scouting and politics I was doing little about earning money and my future. So I went to work in newspapers in London because of all the contacts and prospects it would mean, but with the intention that I would still continue to nurse the constituency. My other interest at the time was the construction of a new scout hut at Kenton which was in the capable hands of a parents' committee who would, I felt sure, want to get on with this themselves as it was, in fact, their own enterprise. The troop had a new scoutmaster, Joe Copp, and I was satisfied that it was going along well. My sister, a widow, lived just a few miles away in Ponteland from my mother who was, of course, set up in the house I had bought, so she would be all right. She had my old wartime dog, Brinjie, with her as companion.

On joining Kemsley I became assistant to Angus Burnett-Stewart on the *Daily Graphic* and then I graduated to the title of Assistant General Manager of the newspaper. At first I stayed at Roland House, a hostel in Stepney which was owned by the Boy Scouts Association. My intention was to try and help in the poorer part of the East End of London on some evenings, but I soon saw that this was not possible. Any time I could get away was needed for my trips to Tyneside and my constituency, with the odd game of rugby and training to keep fit.

I had joined the Saracens Rugby Club whose HQ was at Southgate, but I had little time for training. I must say, though, that their pot pie suppers after a match were hugely successful and probably my best meal of the week. One never left the clubhouse, of course, until the visiting team had been duly entertained and departed.

I also loved visits sometimes with Denis to see his wonderful family at their home in Bishop's Avenue, North London. There were four children, all boys, including one set of twins. I had first met Olive with Denis when at what we called back home in Newcastle upon Tyne 'The Hoppings' or 'The Fair' on the Town Moor. I was the one who did the whistling to attract her attention. I was known as 'Uncle Boom' to their young family.

The headquarters of the Kemsley empire looked most unimpressive, being located in a war-damaged office block surrounded by a bomb site in Gray's Inn Road, WC2. There were two entrances. The smaller of the two in Coley Street was used only by members of the Kemsley family and very senior staff. Here the commissionaire would receive a telephone call at about 9.45 a.m. that his Lordship had left Chandos House, his beautiful home in

Entertaining a party from the Imperial Staff College, Camberley at Kemsley House, London.

Queen Anne Street, and was on his way. The lift was then held for his arrival. Sometimes he would first take a short walk to see if newsagents were carrying stocks of the *Daily Graphic*.

My introduction to one of the great dynasties of the newspaper world was most revealing. Lord Kemsley's christian name was Gomer, his family name was Berry, and Lady Kemsley was formerly Edith Dresselhuys – a very fine-looking woman who was a divorcee. Gomer was the son of a Merthyr Tydfil estate agent and his first job had been as assistant in a haberdasher's shop in Merthyr Tydfil, though in later years he would never refer to these origins. His elder brother, William, had first become an apprentice on the *Merthyr Tydfil Times* and then at the ripe old age of eighteen left Wales and moved to London where within four years he launched the *Advertising World* from a room which he shared on a third floor in Fleet Street. There was a third Berry, a boy called Seymour, who became an industrialist. All three of these lads from quite humble origins in Merthyr Tydfil were to become multi-millionaires and peers of the realm.

Bill and Gomer worked hard to build up the circulation of the *Advertising World* and sell advertising space. They sold out at a handsome profit four years later and then started *Boxing World* and other periodicals. By 1915 they were even ready to buy their first newspaper, the *Sunday Times*, founded in 1822.

Just look at the expansion of their empire once the First World War ended. That was in fact their great opportunity and in 1924 they bought the former Hulton Group of Manchester newspapers from Lord Rothermere and, with Sir Edward Iliffe, formed Allied Newspapers, which organisation later acquired Hulton's *Daily Sketch* and *Illustrated Sunday Herald*, followed by newspapers in Glasgow, Sheffield, Newcastle upon Tyne, Middlesborough and elsewhere. The boys from South Wales, together with Edward Iliffe, within only a few years controlled no less than the Amalgamated Press, Kelly's Directories, the *Financial Times* and, in 1927, the *Daily Telegraph*, which was sold to them by Lord Burnham. It was a terrific success story. William Berry was elevated to become Lord Camrose, Gomer Berry became Lord Kemsley and Edward Iliffe became Lord Iliffe.

The Kemsleys eventually acquired a vast estate out at Dropmore in Hertfordshire and both there and at Chandos House in Central London they would entertain lavishly. Lord Kemsley parted in business from his brother and Lord Iliffe in 1937, six years after his second marriage, his first wife having died in 1928. They had six children.

The *Sunday Times* had virtually become the official newspaper of the Conservative Party and many of the party leaders would be amongst the thirty-two guests who would sometimes sit down to dinner at Dropmore in the lovely dining room designed by Adam.

All this time cabinet ministers and leading national figures came and went through that unprepossessing doorway in Coley Street. Who said that Tony Blair invented Public Relations? The power and ramifications of the press never ceased to amaze me. I remember once I was deputed to meet the Marchioness of Huntley and Gordon at King's Cross Station and see her safely on her way via Waterloo to catch a boat train at Southampton. She was

Pamela, the daughter of Lord Kemsley, married to the Marquis with a seat on the board of the *Aberdeen Argus*, the two-centuries-old newspaper owned by Kemsley. The arrival of the party at King's Cross, complete with staff, was nothing short of royalty and I was involved getting them all safely on their way. When Lord Kemsley did visit part of his domain at Manchester, for instance, he had to be carefully schooled beforehand who were the long-serving members of the staff who were to be presented to him and indeed to be reminded of the names of others whom he would meet, who were, in fact, running the place for him.

Incidentally, I once had to plan how Lord Kemsley could get his *Times* and *Sunday Times* without delay when he was at his house in the Bahamas. I remember that it must have been the world's most expensive newspaper delivery bill. I arranged that a first edition would leave by motorcyclist to Heathrow in time to catch a plane to New York, where the package would be at once handed to another motorcyclist, who would speed to New York's other airport to catch a plane heading for the Bahamas, where, finally, they would be rushed to his house. I shudder to even try to remember the cost of this daily operation during the month or so he was over there.

The all-powerful pride of the group was the *Sunday Times* and beneath its title, and every Kemsley newspaper, appeared the emblem of the group. In post-war Britain this clearly raised the hackles of the Socialists and Herbert Morrison brought the matter up in Parliament so that this helped to bring about a Royal Commission on the press in 1947 which was to last for the next two years.

The Kemsley editorial plan was an endeavour to give weight to the good things the group could achieve. It was expensive but successful and Hamilton worked hard at it. It was entirely his idea and was expressed in the Kemsley Manual of Journalism, the first of its kind. Scholarships were offered, especially throughout the Empire and hundreds of Kemsley juniors were trained at centres up and down the country. Hitherto journalists had learned their trade the hard way. When a contingent of Empire journalists arrived under the banner of the Kemsley Empire and Common-wealth Scheme I was sometimes involved in taking them to meet national leaders such as the Archbishop of Canterbury, members of both Houses of Parliament, trade unionists and some business leaders.

I began to get pressure from Burnett-Stuart, the General Manager, about my visits to the North-East to see to my constituency, Wallsend-on-Tyne, and I am afraid I did get extremely tired. On one occasion, when visiting friends in Southampton, I packed up with exhaustion and had to go to bed in their house. Somehow – I can't think how because we were not in regular contact – my brother heard of it, dashed down to Southampton and I suppose he thought that I was 'overdoing it'. Next I knew he was in touch with Walsend Conservative office and as a result, before I really realised what had happened, it appeared to be a 'fait accompli' that I would withdraw and the press up there got hold of it. Naturally I was disappointed, but there it was. I had not let anyone down and we had put on a large number of new members.

In Manchester, Belle Vue I staged a pageant called 'Johnny Manchester' on behalf of Kemsley's Manchester papers. In it I featured John Howard Davies, then a child film star. My mother joined John's mother in Manchester to attend it.

Now many of my readers will be of an age, glory be, not to have experienced or be familiar with some of the events that occur in my story. Others, I hope, will revel in the nostalgia. Those who remember the radio show, *ITMA* – the wonderful characters, jokes, situations and, above all, the infectious catch-lines – will recall that when Tommy Handley died on 9 January 1949 his death so stunned a worldwide radio audience that 6,000 people lined the streets around St Paul's Cathedral where a crowded congregation attended a memorial service as the nation mourned his passing. The Bishop of London said, 'He was one whose genius transmitted the copper of our common experience into the gold of exquisite foolery.'

For ten years the public had enjoyed *It's That Man Again* – the title taken from the general reaction by members of the public to bombing by the enemy: 'It's that man again'. Just before war was declared the BBC Repertory Company, consisting of about fourteen variety artistes and actors, together with the BBC chorus and orchestra, arrived in Bristol to do the first series of the radio show,

It's That Man Again. It came from Clifton Parish Hall. The opening lines used to go something like this:

Announcer: 'This is the BBC Home Service.'

Trio and Band: 'It's That Man Again. Yes, that man again. Yes, sir, Tommy Handley is here. You know the guy. He plays "I Spy". With Furtive Funf and here's mud in your eye.'

The characters became household names. Tommy usually played Mr Funf; Dorothy Summers was Mrs Mopp, the Corporation Cleaner, whose lines usually began with what was to become the famous 'Can I Do You Now, Sir?' Sydney Keith was Sam Scram, always selling saucy postcards. 'Claude and Cecil' were really Horace Percival and Jack Train with their exaggerated, 'After you, Claude – no, after you, Cecil!' Jack Train as Colonel Chinstrap had his famous line, 'I don't mind if I do.' Jack was a West Countryman and very popular. Then there was Horace Percival's 'Don't forget the Diver' and Maurice Denham's Mrs Tickle. It all enriched the lives of millions. Ted Kavanagh, the writer, collaborated closely with Francis Worsley, the producer, and there were many other characters such as Clarence Wright's chirpy commercial traveller and Dino Galvani's Signor So-So.

Now, why I mention all of this is because soon after Tommy died, the *Daily Graphic* announced that there would be a Tommy Handley Memorial Concert. It was on a Sunday evening at the London Coliseum and guess what? Yours truly was to organise it. I only had about four weeks and whilst other members of the newspaper and theatre staff saw to publicity, tickets and house arrangements, I had to round up the company and work out the programme with Francis Worsley. It was certainly a headache, but wonderful to get in touch with those mentioned above and also Hattie Jacques, alias Ellie Phant and Sophie Tuckshop; Deryck Guyler, alias Sir Short Supply and Percy Palaver, and others, including Molly Weir as Tattie Macintosh, Fred Yule as Norman the Doorman, oh, not forgetting 'Bigga Banja'. It was a bit scary getting it all together in time, but it is a splendid theatre, there was a good audience and all went well on the night.

Another *Daily Graphic* idea was the National Youth Orchestra. I wasn't too keen on this, not being a music nut, but naturally I had to get on with the organisation. It came at the time of the Tommy Handley Memorial Concert, so I had my hands full. A special Tommy Handley aria was, in fact, written for it. The performance of the concert was in the Royal Albert Hall, no less, and as the final rehearsal came round in the afternoon it was clear that we were very short of certain young musicians for the performance that evening. There is a spot in London – it's around Archer Street in the West End – where 'resting' musicians gather in search of news of jobs, what they call 'gigs'. I had to organise a quick raid in two taxis to enlist three or four unsuspecting musicians to make up the orchestra. Fortunately these somewhat grey-haired or balding members of the 'Youth' Orchestra thus recruited were able to be suitably camouflaged.

But the biggest production I was to undertake for the *Daily Graphic* was the reunion of the Eighth Army at which I was to write and present a pageant and be directly responsible to Field Marshal Viscount Montgomery. He was very anxious for it to be a big success.

Permit me to digress for a moment.

Well before Alamein had marked the progress of the Eighth Army in the desert a private of the Welsh Regiment named W.J. Jones had spent his spare time drawing pictures of his mates in the Army. By the time Monty's men got to Tunis, in fact, everyone knew this stocky, cheerful Welshman as 'Jon', cartoonist and creator of what he called 'The Two Types' – two mustachioed characters dressed with careless abandon, full of resilience under odds, and always slightly surprised that anybody might find them strange. I got together with Jon as soon as I was asked to stage the Alamein Reunion Pageant and found him a wonderful, lovable guy. Together we found two actors to fit his two famous army characters. In the days of the Eighth Army Jon had become everybody's favourite. General Sir Bernard Freyberg even loaned him his car and driver for three weeks. *Everybody's Weekly* of 8 November 1952 carried a big illustrated story written by Peter Lewis headed 'Ten Years After El Alamein'. It read as follows and versions of it appeared in the national press, who gave considerable space to it:

Monty liked to plan the lighting for his entrance.

They came again – the veterans of Alamein – to London for their own reunion: from city offices, from banks, from factories and from coal mines: from town and country.

And there were Jon's famous two characters – two actors on this occasion. Each wore the famous shoes known in the Army as 'Brothel creepers' and their rakish scarves. London welcomed the heroes of Alamein on this great night. They came from every walk of life, bound by comradeship and a wealth of memories. In their thousands, with wives and sweethearts, the men of the Eighth Army streamed through the turnstiles at the Empress Hall for the tenth anniversary of a battle which changed the whole course of the War. Attractive green uniformed WRACs gave each man a free complimentary packet of ten cigarettes, and a complimentary programme, and to the soft music of the Band of Her Majesty's Coldstream Guards the great arena slowly filled as the veterans moved quietly into their divisional areas.

A few minutes after seven o'clock the arena lights were dimmed and for half an hour we watched the pageant of the old and the new Elizabethans – 'Our Heritage' – written and produced by Ken Johnstone.

The pageant, with a cast of several hundreds, took us briefly through the years of England's greatness, including Queen Elizabeth on a beautiful black charger, and then we found ourselves at Alamein as the curtains on stage swept back to reveal a giant map of the impassable Qattara Depression. The voice of the commentator, Lionel Gamelin, took us back over the Divisions of the Eighth Army at Alamein, and as he spoke the divisional areas were illuminated, and on the flanks of the map the spotlights picked out the divisional signs.

As each area lighted up, the veterans of Alamein cheered and clapped their 'own crowd', and what more fitting than the loudest applause should go to the 7th Armoured Division – the original 'desert rats'. Then, as the giant map disappeared from view, we heard the sound of marching feet, and from the rear of the stage came a platoon of the 8th Army Infantry.

Up a flight of steps and down again on to the stage, they marched and we heard once again the music of 'Lilli Marlene' – German maybe, but a song we shall never forget.

In their khaki drill the men of the desert army came from the past and they brought with them memories of the past. Our thoughts went back over the years to Alamein. We heard again the thunder of a thousand guns on that October night and saw again the men who followed close behind that mighty barrage.

We saw the dust and smoke of battle and heard again the rasping squeal of tank tracks in the crisp October morn ... and for us all there were personal memories. Of fear, exhilaration, pain, perhaps and thankfulness that God had given us the strength to strike such a blow for England.

Then from behind the stage we suddenly heard the swirl of bagpipes. There were the kilted pipers of the 2nd Battalion Scots Guards. This was, indeed, fitting for who will ever forget the sound of the pipes at Alamein when the men of the 51st Highland Division got to their feet and with bayonets fixed walked steadily forward into No Man's Land?

It was indeed the greatest of all Alamein Reunions and we shall remember Mrs Churchill leaning over and brushing the lapels of her husband's coat before he walked out into the arena to make his speech ... Field Marshal Earl Alexander putting his fingers to his ears a few seconds before the toy gun went off with a terrific bang in the parade of the toy soldiers.

There was also a stirring finale to the pageant entitled 'Our Heritage' in which Sir Francis Drake was played by James Hayter. It culminated with the lights picking up the statue of Sir Francis and beneath it stood Peter McKendrick, a fifteen-year-old school-boy, the son of the then Secretary to the Lord Mayor of Newcastle upon Tyne. Peter stood facing the statue of Drake and slowly took off his jacket and rolled up his sleeves. This brought an absolute crescendo of applause and who shall deny us once again the joy, the chorus of 'Land of Hope and Glory'?

All great stuff, of course, and it fitted the mood of the moment. When it was over I was introduced to Mr Churchill by Monty. It was a warm handshake and he said quietly, 'You did it very well.' Then I met Earl Alexander of Tunis, General Matthew and Mrs Ridgway and Viscount Freyberg – each of whom was most complimentary. I could see that the Kemsleys were delighted and, of course, the Hamiltons, so that I suppose it was quite a triumph sealed by Monty's quiet word, 'Well done, Ken.'

A former bandsman in the Army was living in a caravan at the time. I got him in the show with a trick car that kept falling to pieces. He was Norman Wisdom (now Sir Norman). The Jovers were a family comic act who also helped. Jack Train ('I Don't Mind If I Do') famous from the *ITMA* shows, the Welsh Guards Choir and Marion Harris Jnr, who was formerly Marion Williams of the famous Desert Rats Concert Party, were all in the show, but what gave me the biggest thrill was to have on stage Esmond Knight, whom I had last met when I introduced him to radio in Iceland after he lost his sight in action: and there was Ralph Reader to lead some rousing choruses.

It was the seventh anniversary of Alamein and as always Vera Lynn sang for us – a reminder of how much she had meant.

This was, in fact, the third of the Alamein Pageants I had produced on behalf of the *Daily Graphic*. They had each become a platform for a speech to the nation broadcast by the Prime Minister. This lasted about ten minutes. It gave him a strong patriotic setting. Even the nine o'clock news was delayed on one occasion.

I had one or two amusing conversations with Monty in my preparations for producing the next three or four annual Alamein nights. Once when he arrived late for my lunchtime appointment with him at the United Services Club – it was during the time he was Chief of the Imperial General Staff – he called out with a laugh, 'Sorry I am late, Johnstone, but I must get a quick wash, I've been closeted with Shinwell all morning.' (Shinwell was HM Minister of Defence at the time.)

Another time, when I was going over my list of official guests I suggested inviting Douglas Fairbanks Jnr who had served with the American Forces, 'Oh no,' he said. 'More Americans. I expect he'll have salad cream [medals] all over him. No thanks!'

There were other remarks he made which were really amusing, but perhaps out of place to repeat here.

I got the idea of having the original singer of the famous song 'Lilli Marlene' over to sing at one of the reunions. After all, though it was a German song, all the troops knew it and it was, of course, an international favourite. I traced the original singer, Lalla Anderson, to a club in Denmark where she was appearing. Her manager was very agreeable. It would secure big publicity for her, of course. One morning soon after I had included her in my proposed programme notes I had a phone call from Downing Street. I was told, 'Mr Churchill asks me to say that he will not have this woman sing to his men.'

Vera Lynn told me, 'Never mind, I'll sing it.'

Both Churchill and Monty obviously relished this annual platform to address the nation backed by the memories and pageantry of these Alamein reunions. Monty told them, 'All over the world the nations that want liberty and freedom of the spirit are engaged in a battle to defeat the enslaving chains of Communism. During the past years the battle has been fought defensively. But recently we have come to realise the full extent of the threat and we now see an urge to fight back to maintain our common heritage of freedom.

Last-minute consultation with Monty and Eric Caswell, Secretary of the Alamein Reunion, on the morning of the show.

One of Jon's famous characters (it was either Norman (now Sir Norman) Wisdom playing the part or Tommy Jover) in the arms of Freddie Mills.

A last-minute consultation with Lord Kemsley and Monty.

'It is quite certain that your ideal of a free home will have enemies and its chief aim today is the decline in respect for other people's liberty. So long as there is tyranny our home is in danger.'

Their message reads loud and clear in my mind, though I was not a political animal. The force that had been behind my efforts at Wallsend, which had resulted in such enthusiasm for me to be adopted as prospective candidate, was my hatred of Communism. I regarded it as a real threat to the country.

At Gray's Inn Road I had discovered to my chagrin that the print unions were growing in belligerence. They refused to rationalise their nineteen different union organisations with their sixty-five separate 'chapels' or branches. I once had to act as the go-between with the journalists' chapel, who were temporarily based in the canteen – I think our crime reporter was the chairman or 'Father of the Chapel' – and the Management, who were gathered elsewhere in the offices.

Early in 1978 industrial disruption seriously affected newspapers, especially *The Times*. Tens of millions of copies were being lost with readers never sure of receiving their newspapers. Advertisers were being thrown into turmoil. Unions employed unbelievable practices known as 'Spanish customs'. People signed the wages book as 'Gordon Richards of Tattenham Corner' or covered up for other employees who just failed to turn up. Wages were in some cases very high, but value was not always being given. Unbelievable deception was encouraged on all sides by workers. It was not possible to go and print a newspaper just anywhere for the other unions would have acted to kill distribution.

Arthur Scargill was on the horizon and the move to Communism was highly dangerous, Fleet Street was the centre of almost incestuous employment practices. *The Times* newspaper locked its doors on 30 November 1978. Pickets appeared. Other newspapers at once put on extra copies. By April the losses at Kemsley alone amounted to no less than £30 million. In the end Rupert Murdoch carried the fight over the last of the old printing technology with its old die-hard union structures. He bought *The Times* and the *Sunday Times* with its supplements and as we all know, he beat the anarchists.

Mrs Thatcher, of course, took up the fight with trade union reform. Murdoch speedily assembled his plant at Wapping, or-ganised his own road transport company for distribution and proved to be a brilliant operator. Roy Thomson bought the Kemsley Group with its mostly strong provincial network of newspapers. A Canadian and an Australian had shown the way.

Police entered into what we now call Public Relations manage-ment in earnest after the Second World War, prompted by the new Civilian Commissioner of the Metropolitan Police, Sir Harold Scott. The first 'realistic' police film on TV was shot in a semi-documentary style and was called *The Blue Lamp*. Not surprisingly, police cars and stations co-operated in it wholeheartedly. PC Dixon was killed within twenty minutes, but was resuscitated by Ted Willis for television and his avuncular manner became a symbol of what the public hoped was police behaviour. *Z Cars* was a popular hyped-up TV spectacular set in and around Kirkby, Lancs, part of Liverpool.

Then a real detective, ex-Chief Superintendent Robert Fabian was himself made into a TV star. Bob and I became very good friends. Following his retirement from the Metropolitan Police Force, he liaised with the *Sunday Empire News*, a Kemsley newspaper, on the weekly stories based on many of his cases, which led to the highly successful *Fabian of the Yard* television series.

Bob attended Kemsley House most days. At one time Tony Armstrong Jones had a flat on the top of the building and he also kept an eye on that arrangement. Bowler-hatted Bob in his dark, well-tailored suit, complete with hard white collar and white shirt – which incidentally he always changed at the office at the end of a day's work – was an impressive figure and much in demand as an after-dinner speaker. 'Fabian of the Yard' rivalled the fictional detectives for his infallible powers. We would go out together and he would take me to meet the gangsters – 'some of the villains' as he called them – at their various watering places in the West End. With him I met the last two men to be flogged in Britain – I think if I remember correctly they were two ex-public schoolboys who broke into Cartiers in Bond Street and beat up the manager in an attempted robbery.

Once I was with him in New York and heard him speak at the Dutch Treat, a morning breakfast club for journalists. Eartha Kitt was also there. I don't think that Scotland Yard were too pleased that he appeared to have retained copies of the files of so many of his cases.

He was a great 'wag' as they say. Once we were lunching with prospective buyers of my house in Petts Wood. They were delighted to meet him, of course, and hung on his every word. Especially when he kept bunging in the name of a race horse favourite for, I think, the Derby. It's name was Dry Rot! I had told Bob beforehand that I was worried about a small sign of this at my house, 'What's the name of the favourite, Ken?' he would tease me. 'Oh, I've got it, Ken – Dry Rot. Yes, it's Dry Rot,' and so on.

Bob, in his talks, would debunk the pedantic language of the Law such as: 'From information received we had reason to suspect an occupant of Number 10 "Such and Such" Street whereupon we proceeded to gain admittance and apprehend the said occupant warning him ...' What actually happens, he would say, 'We got it on the wire to proceed to the given address early in the morning, gained admittance, rushed up the stairs, burst into the accused's bedroom, slapped him on the backside and said "Get up, Ginger – you're nicked!"' He said that about 3.00 a.m. was a good time to catch them.

When we sometimes went down the East End together we would have a drink in the notorious Blind Beggar pub where the Kray Brothers held sway and on to The Horn of Plenty in Globe Street, also full of atmosphere. One of the Kray Brothers ran a highly respectable night spot near Hyde Park Corner known as Esmeralda's Barn. Here I would sometimes meet Bob Boothby, then MP for Aberdeen, who was a regular visitor and friendly with Ronnie Kray, who, incidentally, hosted many well-known visitors at this establishment.

Now from crime to films.

I must pay tribute to a very wonderful person I knew at the *Sunday Times*. Dilys Powell at eighty-eight still reviewed five films a week. Dilys walked into the *Sunday Times* in 1924 and asked for a job. She says, 'The Editor was an old gentleman and he took a fancy to me for some reason. Anyway, he said, "Here's a book – review it," and I worked for them ever since.' She told me that she tried not to read pre-release film hype. 'Watch first, read afterwards.' And she never took notes. 'One of the things that has changed in films, apart from the growth of violence, is the loss of what you might call charm. Now you sometimes admire a performance as a work of art, but you don't want necessarily to know the actors. Jack Nicholson is a very good actor, for instance, but he does not have charm of that sort,' she told me.

At the Young Conservatives National Rally and Conference at the Central Hall, Westminster on 23 June 1951 I led the community singing from the platform before Anthony Eden spoke. He was to be made Foreign Secretary in Churchill's cabinet four months later. He was, of course, the epitome of the polished Englishman and exuded charm. We had quite a long chat afterwards and he introduced me to Clarissa, Churchill's niece, whom he was to marry the following year.

I undertook a number of speaking engagements on the Speakers' Panel of Central Office in and around London. I once introduced Sir Alec Douglas-Home from the back of a lorry outside Shepherds

Introducing the Rt Hon Sir Anthony Eden at the Young Conservatives National Rally at Central Hall, Westminster, June 1951, after I led the audience in a five minute 'sing-a-long'.

Bush underground station and I remember a note of hilarity when on being constantly heckled by a member of a crowded audience in the East End of London, I got a huge laugh when I told her, 'Please don't interrupt, Madam. I know you're a Communist because you've got snow on your boots.'

One weekend I was at a Conservative study group in Kent. We occupied a wing of a building which was also run as a Girls' Finishing School. On the Saturday evening Denis Thatcher arrived in an old Jaguar and he invited me to join him and Margaret Roberts, who was also on the course, to go off and relax around some local pubs. I had my eye on a beautiful blonde student and asked her to join us. It was great fun. I might add that I had two or three times been down to Dartford where Margaret was the candidate – the Socialists had about 19,000 majority – to act as a 'warm-up' before she arrived. (My copy of her autobiography has this message in her handwriting, 'To Ken – at Dartford – your warm up speeches – Margaret.')

She was a food research chemist at Joseph Lyons in Hammersmith at about £500 a year. Denis was Managing Director of the Atlas Preservative Company, which made paint and chemicals, at Erith, Kent and which had about this time, I think, been taken over by Shell. He was about ten years older than Margaret. Mad about fast cars and rugby, tall and bespectacled, I remember him as great fun to be with.

So, indeed, was the student! She was called Mette, a beautiful Norwegian aged, I would think, about seventeen. Anyway, I can still remember the clinging dew-laden ivy round the back of the large house to which we had returned quite late. Denis and Margaret had departed, but it wasn't only the dew-laden ivy that was wrapped around me.

Next day I was at St Pancras Station to see her and two of her friends off on the boat train to Norway. There followed a correspondence that was to fluctuate over the years. Messages would reach me here and in Canada, usually asking me to join her on the Riviera. Unfortunately, by the time they caught up with me it was too late. Somehow we didn't get together again. One call did reach me, though. Suddenly out of the blue she phoned my office at AR-TV, 'I watch you every week,' she said. 'You are very good.'

We talked a little and she told me that she was married to a diplomat. I am sure that she would make a very wonderful ambassador's wife. The difference in years between us might have been eighteen, but she really was gorgeous. Maybe – maybe!

I suppose my idol at Kemsley House was Ian Fleming. He was always so elegant and, as Foreign Manager, carried an unmistakable air of worldliness. Sartorially he was fascinating, usually favouring a bow tie with dots and turned-back cuffs with three small buttons, a blue shirt and dark blue suit with a double-breasted jacket. He smoked his cigarettes from a long holder. A product of Eton, he had served in the Navy, but had been trained in the Secret Service before the War, whilst engaged in merchant banking.

His work with Kemsley involved running the international Mercury Service supplying the Kemsley Press with news from his foreign correspondents, but whilst the *Sunday Times* readers lapped this up, provincial readers really preferred local news. It was because of this that Ian had time to spare – when not playing golf, that is – and took to writing the *Sunday Times* gossip column, Atticus, and an idea that had been in his mind for some time, the 'James Bond' story. He even got two months leave a year to work on this in Jamaica.

It was the buzz at Kemsley House that Ian was having an affair with Anne, the wife of Lord Rothermere, who, of course, was often with Lord Kemsley his fellow newspaper proprietor, and this certainly added to Ian's panache. Then suddenly Anne took off and joined him at Goldeneye, his retreat over in Jamaica. It was here that Ian really got down to creating James Bond, refusing to be put off when the first novels in hardback did not sell.

When in April 1950, at the invitation of the Scout Movement, I had been asked to take the British contingent to the American Jamboree to be held in the USA to celebrate forty years of scouting over there, Ian at once got behind the idea with the result that the Scout Movement enjoyed unprecedented publicity. Lord Kemsley also supported it from the start.

Glad Bincham from Kent was the International Commissioner for the Boy Scout Movement in the UK and obviously had a big

The King's Scouts who attended the jamboree at Valley Forge, Pennsylvania, USA, arrive back at Southampton aboard the Queen Mary.

hand in my selection. Eventually we decided on the eight for the contingent. They were Hugh McBryde from 10th Troop East Belfast, who was 17½ and an apprentice with Short Brothers and Harland Ltd; Alan Williams, the youngest, aged 16, a Patrol Leader of the 27th Cardiff Troop representing Wales: John Watts, 17½, the Troop Leader of the 1st Crowthorne Scout Troop, Surrey; from Cambuslang came Scotland's sole representative, 'Drew' Fleming aged 19 of 58th Glasgow Troop; Eric Hudson, 16½ of the 18th Carlisle Troop had recently become an apprentice draughtsman and a 17-year-old King's Scout from 17th Jersey (Victoria College), Pat Massey, had also been invited to the final camp at Gilwell Park, the big Scout camp in Essex, where twenty-six holders of the coveted King's Scout Badge were gathered from all over the UK for a selection weekend. He came through with flying colours, as did 17-year-old John Wenninger, an old boy of Sheffield's King Edward VII School, who assisted his father in his highly successful pork butcher's shop; and from Westminster School came 16½-year-old David Aslett to represent the Sea Scouts.

After assembling on board the famous ship *Discovery*, moored alongside Westminster Pier – I slept in the cabin which had been used by Captain Scott in his voyage to the South Pole – we headed for Southampton, where we embarked on the US Lines' *Washington*. Drew Fleming played 'The Blue Hills of Tyrol' on his pipes as we cast off. We were the first party of British scouts ever to visit the USA. They proved to be a magnificent bunch of lads. On arrival at Ellis Island, off the Statue of Liberty, we were excited to see a posse of press men arrive by dinghy, each having his press badge tucked into the band of his hat just as they do in the movies. The clamour and impact around the dock area, which is pretty well in the city, is truly exhilarating. Soon we were in taxis on our way to the magnificent Grand Central Station with our guides.

We took the train to Paoli in Pennsylvania, arriving at 3.53 p.m. on Sunday, 18 June, to be welcomed by an excited crowd of some 200 organised by the local Rotary Club. Each of our party was to go off with a different family as their hosts and before splitting up I distinguished myself with a little speech in which I advised the lads whatever happened to keep their pecker up. It was only on enquiring why this had caused my audience to double up with laughter I discovered that pecker was American slang for a particular part of the human body.

After a few days of superb hospitality we arrived at the camp site at Valley Forge, a particularly meaningful spot for the British, for it was here in 1777 in the National State Park of Pennsylvania that General Washington and his men camped in the snow before they defeated the British at Saratoga. I had the honour of running up the first British flag to fly there since that time.

We quickly settled in. We had brought over logs ready prepared for a gateway, which we lashed together, surmounting it with a cut-out of the tower of Big Ben. We connected up recordings of the famous chimes so that when required on the hour we could switch them on and have the famous clock booming out. Our camp was next to a roadway and as soon as the public were admitted, we had to get used to cars moving very slowly past in an almost steady procession with the excited occupants calling out comments such as, 'Where you all from?' To our reply, 'London,' they sometimes called back, 'What state is that in?' Or there would be loud observations such as, 'Hey! How can you hold a knife and a fork at the same time when you're eating?'

All good fun!

Came the official opening when General Dwight Eisenhower gave his welcome address to the 47,000 members of the Movement in camp, at the end of which he repeated the immortal words, 'Let 'er rip,' with which as the Allied Supreme Commander he had launched the Channel invasion of Nazi-held Europe on 6 June 1944. This touched off a truly fantastic fireworks display. There was a blazing likeness of the Statue of Liberty and another of the Boy Scout badge and a vast silk American flag which was shot skywards, unfurled and floated to earth by means of a parachute as aerial flares illuminated the scene. We could have done with some of this flair at the Opening of the Dome in London at the Millennium!

Our two neighbours were the contingent of eighty from Colorado – they spoke so proudly of their State: 'You gotta come to Denver' – and, by contrast, a lone representative from Chile who was always unfailingly smart and courteous with a remarkable dignity for his young years. Earlier no less than 8,000 scouts had taken part in a pageant 'Scouting Across the Nations', which included hundreds of Indians and pioneers riding in covered wagons.

After being frisked by security men, I was called up to the main box, where Arthur Schuck, the Jamboree Chief, introduced me to the President of the United States. Harry S. Truman came over as amazingly ordinary, but genuinely friendly. He looked like a keen businessman who ran a medium-sized family store in a small town. He was small of stature and bright as a button. He had, on 19 January 1949, become President against all the forecasting by the media and the pundits that Dewey would win hands down. Only a month before the jamboree he had made the momentous decision of ordering US Air and Naval Forces to go to the aid of South Korea and he was later personally to fire General MacArthur. He shook me warmly by the hand and turned to the man next to him.

'Dwight, I want you to meet Ken Johnstone, Leader of the British contingent. Dwight, this is Ken.' I chatted with General

Eisenhower for several minutes. He was very interested in my lads and where they came from. I was to meet him again when he was a guest at the Alamein Reunion in London the following year. No wonder they liked Ike. He had a big disarming smile.

Then came a huge surprise. A few minutes later I was introduced to the great Rudy Valee, the original and No 1 crooner of them all. Dressed all in white, he was soon electrifying the entire camp with a couple of wonderful numbers and was obviously a great favourite.

After the jamboree we split up, visiting various cities and functions. One of the biggest was when, together with John Wenninger and Pat Massey, I had lunch at the Fort Pitt Hotel, Pittsburgh, with the Rotary Club as hosts. This was probably the largest of the several Rotary organised lunches at which I spoke – the others included Philadelphia and Washington DC.

In Washington DC, as elsewhere, we received wonderful hospitality, touring Capital Hill, attending a session of Congress, travelling in the underground light railway that connects up departments inside the State Capital and even visiting the White House and the famous Oval Office itself. Ian had arranged for the Washington Press Corps to give us a great night at the Embassy and I think they all enjoyed it as much as we did. Around the piano we sang all the old numbers from back home – 'On Ilkley Moor Baht 'At' et al. – and the British press men were, of course, in their element. All this led the UK Ambassador, Paul Gore-Booth, to decide that we were just the tonic needed in the Mid-West, where apparently the British image remained lukewarm.

This was out of my hands as the Boy Scout Association in London and Lord Kemsley were contacted by the Ambassador himself and in no time I was informed that our visit was to include a week based in Chicago. This meant that my old friend, Bob Beuhler, figured strongly in our plans. He had often visited or stayed with me in England, both in Newcastle upon Tyne and London and proved to be a great stalwart of the Scout Movement. He was a millionaire member of the family whose father had introduced the Victor adding machine, one of the smallest then in existence, to the USA, though Bob no longer took part in the business, which was run by his brother, Shorty.

The lads were naturally excited at this news. So was Berkeley Gage, the British Commercial Ambassador for the Mid-West. Based in Chicago, he lost no time in fixing up a full schedule for us. Colonel McCormick, owner of the *Chicago Herald Tribune,* was a prime target. He was noted for his anti-British views and his newspaper persistently angled news against the United Kingdom. He was, in fact, a thorn in the side of the British in the USA.

The morning we arrived at his Tribune Tower in the heart of the city made me feel very proud. Here were these splendid-looking young guys in their uniforms, each shirt, of course, bearing the Union Jack, and soon they were facing the tough old Colonel who had his huge wolfhound sitting beside the blazing fire in his office in the Tower high above Chicago. They well knew by now of some of the outrageous anti-British stories and comments that appeared regularly in his daily newspaper. They certainly gave the Colonel stick, but in the nicest possible way!

Marshal Field III was, on the contrary, a delightful host and personally conducted us around his famous store. I know that it inspired one member of the contingent, Pat Massey, who later joined Marks and Spencer and was to climb high in executive status.

After relaxing at 'Shorty' Beuhler's country estate, we left Chicago with regrets. Concerts at Ravena Park, hearing and meeting Sarah Vaughan, the great songstress, and a lot of visits arranged by the enthusiastic Berkeley Gage, made for a hectic week. The Beuhlers had been fantastic hosts.

We returned on the *Queen Mary.* The *Sunday Times* had run a series of articles by me on the American experience. Later when I spoke at various places here in the UK for Foyles, the lecture agency, I was able to introduce some references to this visit. All in all the Scout movement received uprecedented publicity.

There was another scouting experience I would like to recall. It was pre-war days when George M. Carter, a leading Tyneside and Wearside businessman who was also a Scout Commissioner, took me as a young rover scout up to the big Rover International Moot at Monzie Castle, Perthshire. It was about 1938. En route, he booked in at Gleneagles, the somewhat palatial hotel in

Scotland. I pitched my tent in the grounds. In the morning a waiter was to be seen gingerly tapping on the flap of my little tent whilst in the other hand he held my morning tea on a silver tray!

At the camp, attended by rover scouts from all over the world, I acted as an honorary waiter at the HQ Mess and waited on, among others, Prince Chicibu of Japan, Count Teleki of Hungary, the Duke of Gloucester, Beverly Baxter, the English journalist, and some top Americans.

It was to be a visit full of nostalgia. Everywhere the Czech contingent marched they were cheered due to the shameful treatment of their country by Germany. Baden-Powell's recorded voice came over at the camp fire as he spoke movingly from his farm in Kenya urging us all to be strong in friendship. I enjoyed conversations with our distinguished visitors. Within a tragically brief space of time it all changed. Count Teleki had committed suicide. Pearl Harbour had taken place and Prince Chicibu was our enemy. BP was dead.

CHAPTER X

Canadian Journey

FOLLOWING AN INTRODUCTION to Eric Morse, the Secretary of the Canadian Clubs, whom I met at the English Speaking Union in New York, I was invited to Ottawa where I was asked to undertake a lecture tour across Canada. My subject was to be 'I Had to See Canada' and I was to give about fifteen talks, starting in St John's, Newfoundland.

So – why not join me on my Canadian Journey?

'I've just got in from Canada ... What's that? Good ... Meet you at the Newfoundland for lunch. Cheerio.'

I hung up the phone at the airport and paused, grinning, my hand still on the receiver, reflecting on the outrageous statement I'd just slipped out to a most distinguished Newfoundlander. 'Just got in from Canada,' indeed – wasn't this part of Canada? An awesome, craggy sea-girt sentinel to the half-continent I'd just left.

Yet in the next few days I was to realise that there was nothing out of place in my remark. This was Newfoundland; over there was Canada and they made no bones about it. It reminded me of a reluctant in-law still sniffing at a marriage of convenience. Over a hundred years ago Newfoundland cocked a snook at confederation and later Canada gave her the cold shoulder when certain overtures were made, but surprisingly on 1 April 1949, the then Prime Minister of Canada, MacKenzie King, was able to broadcast a welcome to the islanders on joining Canada – an entry confirmed by plebiscite and made possible only because of the genius of two men – MacKenzie King himself and Newfoundland's Joe Smallwood.

This was so catastrophic in the opinion of some that they wore dark armbands, pulled down the blinds as if in mourning and even hoisted black flags in their despondency. The final ballot showed 78,323 in favour of confederation with 71,334 against, and in a previous issue a third possibility had been touted – a customs union with the USA. From 1934 to 1946 the United Kingdom had taken the responsibility of a caretaker commission, taking over at a time little removed from bankruptcy and achieving a remarkably good surplus, but the delegation to Downing Street found to their dismay that Britain, beset with currency problems, had no heart for further dollar charges and advised another ballot, this time without the USA customs union ticket.

The plain truth was that Newfoundland had for all those years lived quite apart from Canada: there never had been an umbilical connection; its commerce had been linked with Britain and the Mediterranean, South America and the Caribbean and, of course, with the United States; its sentiments, breeding and traditions had linked it with Britain. It had little interest in Canada except for a nodding acquaintance with the Maritimes.

The Newfoundlander was a baffling mixture of passion, phlegm, fierce independence and delightful old-world courtesy. He had lived long with adversity, but he had never lost that song in his heart. Ageless, inscrutable cliffs were his garden; harsh, forbidding rock deserts were interspersed with lakes of such wild beauty that their naked majesty brought tears to your eyes; and at his doorstep, his highway, the vast green-blue ocean. Nature so dominating his environment had carved out for him a character of enduring dignity. In a strange dialect of 'Devon-cum-Ireland' he expressed something of the mysticism of the Irish as he span a web of wondrous romance in tale and shanty and I'll wager there were more poets per thousand heads there than anywhere else on earth.

It is the sea that stirred his soul; as a babe he awakens in the small hours to lie listening to its thunder, his playground its silver strand littered with magical jetsam to spark a hundred phantasies and seed his poetry – even his earliest bewildered crawling could be amongst the ordinance of the sea, giant's boots of damp, sandy rubber, hard wet salty rope thicker than his arm; mysterious, endless, wonderful nets to explore breathlessly and always the dominant smell of brine, everlastingly the sea at his door.

Especially was this true of the people of the out-ports, any one of the 1,300 little fishing settlements which cling to the stern slopes of the 6,000 miles of coastline, haunted by the plaintive cry of the gulls, vibrant with the unceasing music of the ocean.

These tiny settlements – only twenty-six of them had a population of more than a thousand and many could barely muster 200 souls – had the biggest families in all Canada. Many had as many as ten children.

After several days of almost overwhelming hospitality and having delivered my talk successfully, I endeavoured to leave on what was to be my first trip in a helicopter. From a point not far from the start of the historic flight of Alcock and Brown we attempted a take-off, but the winds were so fierce and unrelenting that we couldn't get far off the ground and had to give it up. Next day I flew to Toronto by normal air service.

I had received a message suggesting that I carried out the rest of my Canadian journey with a little minx. I had agreed without

Handing over a jar containing water from the Atlantic to a scout of British Columbia to pour into the Pacific at the end of my trans-Canada drive by the old northern route.

A brand-new Hillman Minx, mileage zero.

hesitation. This turned out, however, to be one of the new Hillman Minx D models! It was agreed that I would drive it across Canada on my lecture tour and give media interviews en route about its performance.

I collected the car at Scarborough, Ontario and my next engagement was at Brandon on the prairies.

I took with me my small tent, which I had christened 'The Grand Hotel' and sometimes this became my overnight accommodation pitched beside some wildly attractive lake.

Nowadays the trans-Canada journey is, of course, via United States and fast motorways, but my route at that time was north of the Great Lakes on the old Trans-Canada Highway. In one section, in fact, one had to phone in at the start and phone again when clear after some hundred or so miles.

My talk was about what I as an observer believed to be lacking in Canada – that is, a sense of their own nationality. I traced the story of the early settlers, mainly British, but some French, and reminded my audiences of the wealth of the country in resources, but also in people. The need, as I saw it, to be all-Canadian. How I felt that in the years ahead surely 'greatness awaited them'.

It was all stirring stuff laced with anecdotes and they seemed to like it.

My largest audience was during the Maritimes section of the journey when I addressed over a thousand at Halifax. I got world press coverage when, during my talk, I observed that it would be a wonderful idea if the Queen Mother became the Governor-General of Canada.

Soon afterwards I addressed a much smaller meeting down the coast in Nova Scotia. It was attended by a number of university staff and some students, together with local people. My host, Sir James Dunn, a wealthy mineowner, looked after me superbly. He enquired if I would like to meet his friend, Lord Beaverbrook, and when I jumped at the idea he at once phoned Beaverbrook and fixed up a meeting the following day.

Next morning we flew in his private plane over to Frederickton. There he took me to meet Beaverbrook at his house, but soon excused himself, leaving us together for the rest of the morning. 'I am dead against commercial television in Britain – and it won't last!' Beaverbrook lost no time in telling me. 'We will oppose it in the *Daily Express*.' He was in excellent form and was soon on the phone to Lord Kemsley in the Bahamas. 'Bill,' he told him, 'I've got one of your young men here and we're having a great chat.'

We got along marvellously well and I later asked him what was the most momentous moment in his life. He paused for a while before replying. 'I think it must be the day in October 1936 – it was, in fact, 16 October – when I called on the King to discuss the press and his relationship with Mrs Simpson.' There was a pause and before going further, he asked me to observe its confidentiality and this I must do. He was in excellent spirits as his guests arrived for lunch.

'My Prime Minister,' he said by way of introducing the Premier of New Brunswick. 'My Captain General,' he was an ex-Group Captain and former General Manager of the *London Evening Standard* who was now running the local newspaper, which I noticed carried the same heading as the *London Evening Standard*. Then there was his 'Solicitor-General' and the Head of the University.

He was fairly bubbling over with good spirits at lunch – which was, by the way, laced with superb wines – and he decided before he left that afternoon on holiday that we should all accompany him on a preview of the splendid art exhibition which was to be opened to the public on the following day. He had personally made a great contribution to art in the province. He was obviously very popular and everyone seemed to address him as 'Max'.

So, after an excellent lunch, we set off for a private preview of the art collection which was housed in the university gymnasium a few miles away. En route we were held up for some minutes at a railway level crossing. I was sitting next to Beaverbrook and he turned to the Prime Minister who was behind him and said jokingly, 'Remind me I must have a bridge built here next year.'

'You do that, Max,' was the reply.

So we all arrived in good spirits at the gymnasium where unfortunately we found the door to be closed. There was no sign of a key. Despite some scurrying backwards and forwards a key could not be readily produced. There was no sign of the caretaker. The effect on Beaverbook was traumatic. The elf-like grin and jocular manner suddenly disappeared. The delay changed everything and without a word he was back in his car ordering his chauffeur to get going and scowling at us as he was swept away. His quixotic mood had taken over and I never saw him again.

Next day I flew back with my host to reclaim my car and continue my journey. I had not the slightest notion at the time, of course, that my host's wife, whose portrait I had admired that morning on the staircase in the house in Nova Scotia, would, in fact, become Lady Beaverbrook!

A racehorse owner, philanthropist and a woman of dry and quick wit, she married two very exceptional men – Dunn and Beaverbrook. She was apparently a very determined lady, as one could well imagine. She wrote poetry and tried her hand at painting, but racehorses and her dogs were her passion. I seem to remember a news story about her buying a very expensive ticket to fly her dog to Canada. Had I been a little later coming down for breakfast that morning, I might have met her.

Sometimes, to meet my itinerary, I had to leave the car again and fly north – once or twice by float plane – to keep dates at often quite outlandish places, small logging towns mostly. The onslaught on trees in Canada seemed to be never-ending and is, of course, a huge industry, though sometimes sad to see these giants of the forest crashing down.

At last I had reached Vancouver. Pouring the mandatory bottle of Atlantic water into the Pacific provided another press picture, but also marked the end of the trans-Canada trip. Here I was joined by an old friend, Robert Beuhler of Chicago.

I still had two speaking engagements to carry out on the quite lovely Vancouver Island with its distinct English air, including the superb Empress Hotel in Victoria where time, though not thankfully the staff, appears to stand still.

Victoria is indeed a fitting name for the town. The gardens themselves remind one of home. Bob and I enjoyed an all too brief stay with the Mitchells at their lovely Sea Bluff Farm, where they could for all the world be back in their native Somerset were it not for the distant sight across the Pacific of Mount Olympus rising above the city of Seattle. Bob Mitchell will forever stay in my mind as a typical young Canadian with the world at his feet. There I wrote my report on the performance of the Hillman Minx before handing it back to the dealers with a letter of thanks.

My report placed emphasis on the need for more seals in the bodywork to deal with the at times almost choking dust which, particularly in the prairies, heavily pervaded the interior. Even the contents of my suitcase were covered in it. Otherwise I had no complaints on the performance of the car after the 5,000-mile journey and I was grateful to the distributors. I had done some fifteen radio interviews about it en route, together with Press stories and pictures in which I featured the car.

There was a wonderful camaraderie amongst former Forces personnel in Vancouver and in no time arrangements had been made for me to obtain a working pass for Kitimat. A few nights later I was at the theatre and the moment I had seen Margot Fonteyn and Rudolf Nureyev take their curtain calls I was outside and into my waiting taxi in a hurry to board the coastal steamer which was about to leave for the North.

I watched first the city illuminations and then the lights of the various small islands fall behind with the black curtain of the Rockies as a backdrop to starboard before turning in and at the same time wondering vaguely how I would fare now that the fees and expenses of the lecture tour were at an end. The toughest phase of my journey lay ahead and I was left in no doubt when soon after we had disembarked I was allocated to construction work.

Early next morning I was awakened by the noise of heavy boots clomping about the bunkhouse. Men were mumbling and cursing in what appeared to be a variety of European languages as they made their way to the washroom, which was remarkably basic, though thankfully there was hot water. Nobody spoke except to curse. Few bothered to shave. It seemed as though to some the shock of facing a new day was almost unbearable. The sound and stench of so many ill-assorted human bodies coming to life was enough to prompt the question, 'Is it really worth it?' But there is a remarkable flip-side to all this. Whatever the man's basic tongue, the senses tell all. It is 'Breakfast'.

I pulled on my issue dungarees and grabbed an empty seat at a long plain wooden table. Now I was to meet the flip-side of a night in the North. This was a feast of a breakfast. Plates were piled high with flapjacks, tomatoes, fried eggs, fried bread and there were jugs of juice and steaming hot coffee or tea. Nobody spoke, but clamping jaws and the occasional belch told all.

Then I queued up to be issued with a hard hat and a lunch tin in which there were a couple of huge sandwiches and two biscuits. Outside it was bitterly cold and I pulled my heavy dungarees closer whilst I queued for a very dilapidated-looking bus whose destination board still read improbably the word 'Pleasantville'. Inside, too late to get a seat, I stood and swayed, jammed together with others. It is the way much of the world goes to work, though not perhaps in so raw a mode – we carried lunch boxes instead of briefcases – but I had little idea of what task lay ahead of me. It proved to be simple enough, though my limbs ached afterwards with lifting and piling up planks of wood.

After two weeks of this, in which my muscles were sorely taxed, I was told that I would be moved up to Kemano for a few days. This was where they were building huge generators deep in the mountains.

I flew over to Kemano with Freddie 'the Flying Chinaman', a Chinese Canadian who in wartime had flown bullion to safety for Chiang Kai-shek. The mountains dominated the main camp, a mere saucer of land won from the savage bush, and in the late afternoon the light was so bad that the mountains appeared ill-defined like a picture out of focus.

In the winter the sections of forest left uncovered by snow on the mountainside looked like ink smudges on crumpled white blotting paper. Sometimes it snowed at a mere hundred feet and not at ground level so that you looked up into a white sheet like looking up into a tent top.

Under such fickle and dangerous conditions the boys in the 'egg-beaters' – the helicopters – took to the air whenever possible. They were seldom grounded by the conditions. They had a vital role to play and lessons learned in Korea helped again and again; they were the dispatch riders of the sky when communications failed; they snatched pieces of equipment on one mountainside and dropped them on another; they brought isolated men fuel, mail and equipment, ferried in new men and took out the sick, and once hurried two firemen to an outbreak a mile high. Without the impetus of the air this whole project would have taken nearer ten years rather than two, and much of it would have been impossible.

Kemano was a means to an end. No town would rise in this spot, but a small community would have to be maintained to serve the power house deep inside the mountain, which had yet to be built. The vast area torn out of the inside of the mountain would house the great turbines and waterways and the intricate electrical equipment and generators.

A feature was the aerial runway that ran up and down suspended above the main mountain (named in honour of McNeely Dubose, brilliant hydro-engineer and Vice-President of Alcan).

I walked into its giant 35-ton cage called 'The Skip' and found it ankle deep in snow. We were soon hauled into position ready to be launched on our trip to the terminal nearly 3,000 feet above us and as we lay there in the slips at an angle of about 45 degrees, I hooked my arm around a rail to prevent sliding even in my studded boots.

Then began our curious climb into the night and soon we were out in space suspended far above the lights of the camp. It was a strange, almost eerie experience. The snow span and whirled off the thin wire ropes above us and the forest beneath was stealthy with virgin snow; it was as if we were climbing silently into a white hell and as the other men in 'The Skip' sheltered beneath the rim of the rail, their tin hats clearly silhouetted, I imagined for a moment that we were Infantry in a landing craft heading for an enemy beach; and I thanked God that it was not true.

At 2,600 feet where the camp was terraced on ledges scooped out of the mountain side, I alighted and walked through the camp and into the tunnel. Other tunnels have been blasted for as many miles through rock face, but none as fast, for these hard-rock miners, or tunnellers, who were mostly Americans, created a world's record. I walked alone in the darkness except occasionally for the gangs of men at work plastering a bad fault or wading knee deep in water. It was a strange feeling hearing my steps echoing and re-echoing down this long corridor deep inside a mountain where soon the black waters would swirl and race. The water would fall <u>inside</u> the mountain a distance of half a mile through 10-foot-wide piping, its terrific volume driving the waterwheels which would generate electricity in this fantastic power house cored out of the mountain like the nave of some vast cathedral. Then the electricity would be flung across the fifty miles of corrugated mountain peaks of 7,000 feet and more by the incredible power line down to Kitimat.

Building that power line was the toughest assignment of all and Mark Knight and Russ Madsen, two highly seasoned engineers of the big Morrison-Knudsen Company of the USA, which was handling the Kemano end of the project, had to fight for six snow-blown months with their men before they faced near defeat at the dreaded Kildala Pass.

A defiant six miles to the top, the pass rose at a thousand feet a mile, demanding grades of from 15 per cent to 25 per cent for the road that they must punch through the solid granite before two months of spring thaw hit them with flooding, snow slides and avalanches. If a tractor could make it, other machines could follow.

It was a drama of man's determined onslaught on nature. Albert Charron had volunteered to pilot an International TD.24 Crawley Tractor up the hazardous course and, picking his way up the snowfield, this French Canadian made slow, heartbreaking progress for, although stopping only to eat and sleep rolled up in his special sleeping bag, he had covered barely a mile a day. At one point he crossed a snow bridge under which rushed torrents of green water cascading from the mountains above; the wind shrieked and tore at his tractor and sometimes he doubled over his machine gasping for breath as the razor-edged air nearly cut him in half. Gingerly testing the treacherous surface, he eventually got his tractor to the projected campsite and, his fuel almost exhausted, he had just enough to level off a helicopter landing strip before radioing for supplies. Like a phantom bird a helicopter was soon hovering over him bringing the necessary fuel and he soon levelled off an entire campsite – to be known as Camp No. 10 – yet another camp on this amazing 'Kildala Road' where men wrote a saga unsurpassed by any other industrial exploit.

Then Albert Charron faced the crucial tasks. He had to somehow reach the summit. James Ramsay Ullman writes in his *Kingdom of Everest*, 'That man will reach the top of Everest means little; that he should want to reach it, or try to reach it, means everything.'

For five more heartbreaking days Charron kept at it. Once his tractor slid backwards 400 feet and he hung dangerously at a crazy angle as the whole machine threatened to disappear to certain annihilation, but the French Canadian had the spirit of his ancestors; he hung on and gave the engine the gun, the tractor shuddered, gripped, slipped again and for a sickening moment hung there suspended, but then lurched forward; attacking, sliding, backing again, but repeatedly edging forward. Charron reached the narrow defile and level ground and the trial was over.

Kildala had been conquered.

The transmission line would go through.

I was thinking of this as I tramped on through the tunnel for another two hours. When I came out above Lake Tahtsa the snow had ceased to fall and the stars looked down upon man's prelude to power. This chain of camps, their objective nearly achieved; this water child of eons upon eons of time soon to be trapped and harnessed by the modern age. But not without cost to pocket, limb and heart.

As I stood there looking out across those silent wastes I was thinking of the cost to the heart. I was thinking of a lake called Ootsa, some 80 miles to the east where the latitude is 53 degrees.

It was then only forty years ago that the white man had first reached into those hundreds of acres of waving upland peavine grass where the lonely call of the loon floated across the spruce-rimmed lake. Before that, caribou, moose, bear and goats roamed undisturbed except for bands of Indians. It was a little-known gem sparkling silently in the bosom of the mountains. Then men got through along the trail from Bella Coola on the coast of the Pacific – the very place McKenzie had reached across this same country in his historic journey. The pack trains of fifty and seventy-five head of horses had come a little later over the same trail. Mowing machines were carried on horses, cows driven alongside the wagons and women rode the pioneer trail side by side with their men. Lumber was cut and sawn, cabins were built, little homesteads sprang up and a settlement fringed the silent waters of Ootsa Lake.

Their sons went to war.

The community survived depression because the women could make buckskin into clothing and the men trapped and hunted game and fish. They always had food, for if the larder looked low, they merely took to the hills to kill a moose or caribou and returned to the farm home. They sought no riches for the majesty and beauty of this glorious valley was for them adequate reward.

Came the proud day in 1939 when Lord and Lady Tweedsmuir – then the Governor-General of Canada – came to their lake. Lord Tweedsmuir in his dedication address said that he had never seen a more beautiful place, it was a great honour that it was to be called Tweedsmuir Park and he hoped that it may remain as a great scenic park for ever.

And their sons went to war again.

Came the day in 1948 when surveyors and engineers were seen in the valley; then the rumours of a vast hydro scheme and the day when the families crowded into the little community hall which they had built with their own hands to hear the news of the scheme. Came the land appraisers to arrange compensation and the permit of the Government of British Columbia for expropriation and arbitration of the land. Came – the cold reckoning.

The settlers were well compensated. Many a motel, filling station, fishing camp and new farm testifies to this, but then you can compensate the pocket quicker than the heart.

Now the water would creep up the shores of Lake Ootsa and part of the valley would be filled. It would seep through the green grasslands and swallow whole hilltops and uproot countless trees until the lake became an inland sea and in its bosom would lie forever the gem that the mountains once treasured silently through countless years until man prised it from them, only to give it back to the waters from whence it came.

A tiny community had gone but something of its spirit lived on in that greater community which it had helped to sire and which lay far behind me in the night. I turned and walked back through the mountain.

My work on construction lasted all of three weeks during which the pattern of 'sleep, food, work, rest, food, sleep' became increasingly tedious. It wasn't as though one had the opportunity of hearing some of the stories of the many different nationalities represented. The long hours out in these tough conditions, followed by what can only be described as huge meals – and one must pay tribute to the camp cooks – with the prospect of early starts, meant that most of these guys, except perhaps the inevitable card players – and this was frowned upon as it encouraged gambling – pretty well flaked out early. Let's face it, most of them were in a strange land seeking a fresh start or, if they were students – and some were Canadians – the chance to earn enough to put them through their studies. There were certainly some ugly, tough, bearded specimens – I made a mental note to keep well away from them. It just wasn't an atmosphere for enjoying idle gossip.

After about three weeks of this hard slogging – my aching

Kitimat was situated on a fjord in Northern British Columbia far from any other human habitation except for Kemano, a camp constructed to bring in the power lines. (British Alcan picture)

muscles had now just become dull adjuncts to the body – I was called into the office and told that I was to be transferred down to Kitimat where I was to report to the employment office.

Freddy, who flew me off the mountain, told me that next day he had to fly down to Vancouver, but would return in three days' time. If I was free he would drop me off on the way so that I could visit the Queen Charlotte Islands about which I had been asking him when first we met. I duly made my arrangements with the office and later the next day Freddy dropped me at a lumber camp on the mainland before continuing on to Vancouver, having arranged to pick me up at the same place in two days' time.

I had packed my faithful 'Grand Hotel' so I had no problems about accommodation. That night I crossed the Hecate Straits to the islands in a small fishing trawler and I have to admit I ended up in excruciating agony for these are among the most notorious waters in the whole Pacific seaboard.

But I must tell you of this wonderful character I met over there. He had that semi-mute inherent dignity that I have seen before in native patriarchs. His looks bore the distinction of a senator, his manner the poise of a bishop and his dress was that of a fisherman, but it was his eyes that told of his work and life with the tides and the winds and the deep. Silver hair burst at random from beneath his old cap, his brow was broad and his whole firm face a deep nut brown.

His name was Solomon Wilson and he was the elder statesman of the Haida Indians whose culture had once been unmatched from the Bering Sea to the Gulf of Panama. Their canoes, too, had been the fastest and sturdiest of all.

All that afternoon we talked with a spontaneous warmth and now high above his village of Skidegate in the Queen Charlotte Islands we came to the tiny dam which Solomon was having built on a seventy voluntary hours-per-man basis. It was fantastic that the same description should be applied to this simple undertaking as to the mighty structure I had just left over at Kitimat.

As we moved amongst the towering, lovely trees I began to sense that Solomon shared an intrinsic partnership with them.

'We built our canoes from them. Free from knots, you see, and easy to work,' he told me.

I asked him, 'How large were they?'

'Up to seventy-five feet long with a seven-foot beam. You could get as many as forty people in one that size and about two tons of baggage and trade goods, but of course the average family canoes were very much smaller and more popular.'

I stared carefully at the massive cedars. 'But how on earth did they manage – I mean those canoes must have been a work of art?'

Solomon slid his spine slowly down a tree trunk until he was balanced on his haunches. 'Well, first they shaped the outside of the log, see, and after getting a rough sort of balance the inside was burnt out by means of fire controlled with damp sand and after that they thinned down the shell with their stone adzes and chisels.'

'And how thick was the shell?'

'Oh, about two and a half inches. A bit thicker towards the bow and stern, of course ... and then the log was simply hollowed out and filled with water – and they got the water really steaming by adding hot rocks, but it took a pretty time all this because when the sides began to give easily they had to be stretched and pulled to give the craft beam and a lift to the bow and the stern. Next there was the carving to be done on the stern and prow pieces, then they had to be fitted and last of all the whole thing had to be polished with dog fish skin.'

'I see. I suppose the wealthier families had special carving and their own heraldic signs. Solomon, seeing that you were a young-ster when Christianity first came to these islands, do you remember the war canoes?'

Solomon nodded and spread his legs to make himself comfort-able on a grassy patch. 'Sure. I served in my grandfather's war canoe. There would be ten or twenty of us ranged on either side. Do you know, we could make strokes as one man without causing the slightest sound or raising a ripple on the water? But, once we got the signal, we would dash our paddles into deep water and almost lift the canoe as we went racing for the shore – and the enemy if he was there. And we would be screaming blue murder the whole time.'

He was in his element now for these Haidas are born story-tellers.

'But in a flash we might change to a "Song of Victory" and keep perfect time with our paddles as we chanted, sweeping shoreward again, imitating the flight of an eagle; now two strokes and a rest between, like this, see here, now three strokes and pause – so.'

He leaned back and taking out his pipe, began to cram the bowl full. 'There was mighty strict discipline in those days,' he said, lighting his pipe and punching the used matches into the earth.

'We had to enter the canoes in a certain manner and hold the paddles exactly as taught or else there was terrible trouble. When we were away, even the wives slept to a drill – for when we were going towards the enemy they had to sleep with their heads in that direction and when we were expected back they had to turn round and sleep the other way. They were all together in one lodge under a sort of sergeant-major wife and when the canoes came into sight they knew at once how many men had been lost, for the paddles of the missing were lashed upright.'

He looked straight at me without speaking for a moment and then, taking his pipe out of his mouth, he pointed over his shoulder. 'Do you know, I've crossed the Hecate Strait yonder in a war canoe, in a fishing boat, by steamer and in the air,' and the pipe stabbed my chest in emphasis. 'Ay, and in the War they took me over in a submarine!'

'Heavens, Solomon,' I said, 'you've lived from war canoes to atom bombs.'

I looked beyond him at the giant redwoods again. If Solomon's life spanned his people's first days of Christianity to the days of the atom bomb, these trees spanned history itself, for their antiquity was beyond comprehension. They had given the Haidas their lodges, their canoes, ancient totem poles and present homes and from that sitka spruce yonder, Mosquito bombers had been fashioned for a war in which the white man had utterly emulated the Indian in the art of savage and precise slaughter.

Solomon got to his feet and, men of two worlds, we walked down into the village.

These islands were a retreat, a refuge. Scores of peaks stood sentinel to the west and beyond them the Pacific thundered ceaselessly, drumming and churning the lonely beaches. There were two main islands – Graham to the north and Moresby to the south – and you wouldn't find more than logging camps and the odd seasonal fishing camps down there. The Haidas were grouped between Skidegate village – they were the Methodists – and Massett, where the Anglicans held sway. The only other Haida habitat was 50 miles to the north on the southern portion of Prince of Wales Island, which was once the property of Russia. They were quite Mongolian in appearance, these Haidas – high cheek bones, raven black hair and of small stature; but compared to the inland Indians they were as clean as a new pin.

The logging industry had taken a firm grip of the islands. Queen Charlotte City must have been named by the world's champion optimist, for it numbered but 150 souls – Canada seemed to excel at this exuberant use of the suffix city which was sometimes quite ludicrous. So, Queen Charlotte City lay brooding of its unrequited hope beside the harsh beauty of Bearskin Bay, disturbed only twice a month when the steamer called.

The weather ruled the life of these people, adjusted as they were to the whims of the wind and the sea. When the sun shone, the charm of the islands came true – something new found upon the shore, a fresh trail to discover, another wildly enchanting view, always the tide to take you out and bring you back. Newspapers arrived almost apologetically, hopelessly dated, and the radio as often as not was fouled up by trawlers signalling one another. The telephone system was one big party line – a glorious rigmarole of buzzes and rings and if you were way down the alphabet you were expected to count the buzzes that came belching out of the old instrument to discover if it was for you or not.

Funniest sight I saw were two tall thin men in dark overcoats and bashed-in bowlers whom I encountered halfway between Skidegate and Queen Charlotte City. Each carried a suitcase and an umbrella and they introduced themselves as campaigners for the Jehovah's Witnesses. I left them plodding on down the lonely track like two revivalist ravens.

I heard about another odd meeting. This was between two old beachcombers who lived only 80 yards apart in the middle of a staggeringly long stretch of golden sands. Each had his little hut, but, near as they were, neither apparently spoke, for one was a Scotsman and the other English and they had fallen out two years before. By the time Coronation Day came around there were signs of activity in brightening up the two dwelling places – the Scotsman had a little pathway of stones all painted white and the Englishman, not to be outdone, had been up half the night slapping red, white and blue paint all over his walls. When the great day dawned, the Englishman apparently stepped out to take the air and at the same moment the Scotsman decided on a pipe. It seemed that of all days this was the day to settle the quarrel.

'Mornin', Jock,' volunteered the Englishman, shoving his hands into his trouser pockets and rocking gently on his heels.

'Mornin' to you, Sandy,' came the encouraging reply.

'God Bless Queen Elizabeth II,' ventured Sandy.

'Ye idle Sassenach – aa'll hev ye kna it's God Bless Queen Elizabeth the First,' followed by the slam of a cabin door.

The feud was on again.

Another old-timer I met was Paddy. He was carrying a hay fork and shovel which protruded rather awkwardly. His battered old trilby with turned-up brim surmounted a shock of unruly grey-white hair so rampant that it burst out of his big ears as well. His face was angular and his nose aquiline, red-tipped and watery, but his eyes were soft and sea-pale. He introduced himself with unmistakable brogue.

'Well met, Paddy,' I said with a grin. 'And where's your piece of shamrock, man? Don't you know it's St Patrick's Day?' (And indeed it was St Patrick's Day.)

His head shot up with a start, he gripped his shovel and hay fork awkwardly in one hand and with the other removed his little clay pipe from his mouth and smiled a broad, toothless smile. 'Ah?' he said.

It was as if the Emerald Isle was all about him and I dared not encroach upon his reverie. Then he was back with me again, his eyes blinking as he tried to get them into focus; the clay pipe was rammed back into his mouth, hay fork and shovel were juggled until he could lean upon them, and little lines puckered and edged around his eyes with the effort of concentration. He told me that he had sailed out of many places in England.

'Oi was in the Tyne when the *Courageous* was being built. We used to "coal up" at Dunston Staithes. Oi sailed out of Hull,

Bristol – ay, and South'ampton too, many a toime.' Then he gave a sort of half snort and half laugh combined.

'Paddy,' I asked him, 'will you ever again go back to Ireland?'

He turned and gave me a long frank look and then answered in punctuated thought, 'Mon ... Oi ... Oi don't think so.'

Then, knitting his brow and looking quizzical, 'And are ye sure it's St Patrick's Doi todoi?' I nodded, rather sorry that it was true.

'Dang and begorrah, yer roight!' he said, making his mind up once and for all.

So he bade me farewell and as he marshalled his hay fork and turned to go, I saw a tear start down his coarsened cheek.

The Haidas had a secret source of agelitte – black slate. This was collected by the few carvers left in the village into sacks and broken into pieces which they carved laboriously. Their designs interpreted one or more of a legion of stories passed by mouth down through the tribe. After carving, the slate was polished and the results were quite beautiful. There were only a few carvers left and this ancient art would die within a decade.

Later with Freddy I flew over Moresby in an effort to trace signs of former Haida villages and at a place named on the map as Cumshewa Inlet, we came down to inspect a deserted site in search of totem poles which I could examine for carvings of the various heraldic insignia. The Indians had a freemasonry about their central system and they usually designated fish, birds or beasts, though the Haidas still divided themselves into phratries – the Ravens and the Eagles. (Marriage within one's division was barely tolerated, for an Eagle woman should marry none other than a Raven man.)

Amongst the weeds and grass on the wild shore, where I could just make out the old clearing facing south, there were a few rotting house timbers and some decaying totem poles, but that was all. If only these people had carved in stone, their intricate and beautiful designs would remain today. It is a thousand pities that so many of these magnificent poles have been allowed to rot and decay.

No greatness awaits these Haidas. Their time has passed; but once they demonstrated a primitive culture that was unsurpassed and they showed courage and skill and a democratic community life disciplined more by code than policemen. Puberty rites and harsh physical ordeals, trials of manhood at their great feasts or 'pot latches' – all these were barbaric practices, it is true, but they were great leaders in their day.

When I got back to Kitimat I discovered that I had been moved aboard a magnificent old Mississippi riverboat now docked as a kind of floating hostel. On going aboard I felt at once transported back to 1936. I was watching the lavish musical *Show Boat* by Oscar Hammerstein. Any moment Paul Robeson as Joe and Irene Dunn as Magnolia would come into view! This was a huge improvement in my domestic arrangements. I shared a cabin with Vincent Haddelsey from East Anglia. He proved to be an excellent companion, always cheerful and, despite his travels, resolutely English in manner with his 'Oxford' voice.

Vincent loved horses and had been teaching at a riding school elsewhere in Canada. In later years he was to become one of the world's leading equestrian painters. One of his pictures hangs in my lounge as I write. He gave it to me at one of his exhibitions in London which I attended years later.

When in Kitimat, we had often spent time with a veteran Canadian engineer, 'Mac', whom we both respected. We enjoyed yarning with him and somehow or other the idea was mooted that Vincent and I should make a trek into the interior through some pretty wild country further north. I took it seriously, arranging to borrow a rifle and cartridges and a small two-man bivouac, and went about assembling my kit. There was no such thing as a hiking trail, of course, in northern British Columbia. We were to go through woods and across open terrain in comparatively virgin territory with little in the way of maps to guide us, and we were to make for a railhead some 40 miles away.

Mac, our engineer friend, began to drop a few hints about racoons, coyotes, bears and the odd poison salamander and a yarn or two about men he knew who had gone off on hikes of this kind to find all sorts of unimaginable things happening to them. Well, I thought, what the hell? With a good companion one always feels fairly secure as long as we don't take unnecessary risks. Anyway, it was an adventure. Vincent seemed to be full of it and we did not lack encouragement from others, though truth to tell, apart from a makeshift shooting range, nobody else up there appeared to enter into any extra activities. Anyway, I had a number of free days ahead and so, presumably, had Vincent.

Imbued with the idea of this great Canadian trek – basis for many a future yarn about adventures in the 'Great Out of Doors' – I got all my kit together despite various people who gave me warnings about unbelievable things. And then – would you believe it? – early that morning Vincent was suddenly on the sick list, vomiting and all manner of troubles it seems. So there I was, all kitted out, aware of last-minute tips on how to deal with bobcats, bears, coyotes, rattlesnakes, water moccasins and every other imaginable or unimaginable creatures. It seemed that I was now ready for an adventure which would have to be on my own and in fact there was this small group of well-wishers already assembled. My great lone trek in darkest north of British Columbia was about to begin.

Suddenly Mac rejoined the party. He had, it seems, just received instructions from the management. I was not to go on my own. In fact they had not been keen on the idea of both of us going in the first place.

'Bad luck, Ken.' The well-wishers seemed ready to put me at my ease. I was really fed up, though. The whole trip had loomed larger and larger as one helluva adventure – it had become a challenge to me personally – and now ...

I never did get to the bottom of it, though. Was it, in truth, a wind-up? If so, it was very well orchestrated and Vincent a superb actor.

Also billeted on board the riverboat was the son of Sir Cuthbert Headlam, who at one time was MP for Newcastle upon Tyne North. He had been a pupil at Gordonstoun School at the same time as the Prince of Wales.

There was another Englishman there whom I met again some years later back in London. He was a member of a well-known merchant bank associated with his family. It was the experience of meeting people that always fascinated me. So many nationalities and types. To listen to some of their stories and being interested in them brought quick friendships. People love to be treated with respect, whoever they are.

I got about a dozen of the lads together and we met as a kind of boys' club cum scout troop and the son of the head of the school I made the leader.

When I was moved into the Fire Brigade I had to live on the premises. We spent most of our time practising seemingly endlessly and that became tiresome, but the comfortable quarters made up for it. The heavy snowstorms caused a lot of digging out. I remember the branch of the bank disappearing almost entirely so that only its roof showed.

There was a large recreation centre, but it was not used as effectively as it might have been had I been given the job of running entertainments and sport. I saw the opportunity for putting on shows and would have revelled in it, but the whole tenor of the place proved to be heavily concentrated on work. The authorities were very anti-gambling, which was a good thing, for undoubtedly there were some smart operators intent on relieving some unsuspecting guys of their hard-earned money. In fact one heard tales of some guys who thought they had saved up enough to leave the place and start a new life being cleared out before they could get away.

Men who were on engineering contracts with the company had moved in, some with their families. There were plans for the urban development of the place.

I began to feel that if I didn't make a break, Kitimat would get hold of me and I was, after all, really biding my time before returning to the UK to see what were my chances in Independent Television. At least that was the idea ... remember?

It was a wrench and when all the lads in the club I had started, plus quite a few of their parents and others turned up to see me off to Vancouver in the coastal steamer, I don't mind admitting I had a lump in my throat. Especially when the fire engine and crew arrived on what was allegedly a practice run.

So back to Vancouver. Superbly sited between the sea and the mountains and with the splendid Stanley Park; its setting on the Pacific makes for a natural business bridge to the Orient and it is marvellously sited with the Rockies as background to the great tourism boom now being enjoyed. No longer can there be the snide comments of 'Blandcouver'; be sure it will become one of the greatest cities on the North American continent.

There was, however, to be a final chapter to my Canadian journey, though it must be all too brief for I now wanted to get back to London. My talk on 'I Had To See Canada' had been built on my view that 'Greatness Awaits Them', but that Canada needed to weld itself together more as a nation – sometimes signs of a disparate nature had developed. One would come across whole families engaged in a business such as tourism and they all seemed too often to use their mother tongue, be it Japanese or mid-European. Out in the prairies there were whole communities still clinging to their European origins. I had recalled the history of the early settlers and the prodigious growth. It was a call to wave the flag, the Canadian flag; but there was, of course, this other Canada – French Canada.

So just before returning to London, I decided to visit Quebec even if it would be only for a day or two. There, on arrival, I wandered through the upper part of this fascinating city high above the mighty St Lawrence River. I tried to mentally recapture its history. I thought of the night of 14 September 1759. At six o'clock the previous evening the files of English redcoats marching on the walls of the city across the bare plateau of the plains had observed the first of the white uniforms of the French Army coming up on their left from the direction of the St Charles River. They were platoons of the regiment of Guienne, who, had it not been for the obstinacy of Vaudreuil, would have been in position on the cliffs ready to receive them. General Wolfe's right wing commanded by Monckton had been adequately protected by the St Lawrence itself and the centre, commanded by Murray, was composed of Highlanders, Lascelles' 47th, Kennedy's 43rd and Bragg's 28th.

I stood at the gates of St Louisburg, through which the gallant Montcalm, still on his black horse, had been borne, gravely wounded. He died before dawn. Hours before, Wolfe, who had been wounded twice earlier, received a fatal bullet through his lungs, his body carried to one of the English ships on the river.

History bases this great battle on the so-called 'Plains of Abraham', but the whole setting makes it one of the most stirring of military engagements.

I wandered around looking at the Notre Dame des Victoires, the old Convent of the Ursulines – a brave early outpost of

Christianity – and the churches of the Jesuits and Recollects. Here high above the mighty river brave French missionaries and workers had brought their teachings and trades to a strange and hostile country, which many thought to be Cathay – 'the ends of the earth' – before they later rechristened it New France.

I stayed at the Chateau Frontenac, the hotel with its spectacular position high above the St Lawrence where Major General Orde Wingate, still in his jungle kit, had flown direct from Burma following his daring operation in March 1944 when his large Allied force had been landed 200 miles behind the Japanese lines. Churchill had invited him there to join urgent talks about the campaign.

CHAPTER XI

Bath Days

I HAVE ALREADY DESCRIBED MY FIRST TIME in Bath when at the age of fifteen and a half, though supposedly at least two years older, I was employed by Procter and Gamble to act as a displayman on an American-style merchandising campaign introducing Fairy Soap and Oxydol to the West Country.

I particularly enjoyed calling on the village shops. The countryside was softer than in the North and the lanes seemed to beckon one amidst tall hedgerows. I loved the country inns where I would go for my lunchtime break. I remember one day sitting at a large wooden table in the cobbled courtyard of the George at Norton St Philip, my eyes fixed on the great oak doors as if half expecting some troopers from Cromwell's Army to come striding in. Now all these years later I am writing this in my home at Monkton Combe, which is only a few miles away and close to Bath.

I really liked Bath from the moment I walked across the little footbridge which then existed between the railway station and the Royal Hotel and I was soon sending picture postcards to my friends.

Of course, the lovely stretch of open parkland right in the centre of the city, affectionately known as the 'Rec', drew me like a magnet. I loved to walk across it and then along the riverside. Looking back on the city was like viewing a sensational theatre backdrop on a big scale.

There were those Saturdays – alas, far too few – when I would go to the rugby ground, itself part of the Rec, and see the famous Rugby Club, known, incidentally, as Bath Football Club, in action. Founded in 1865, it ranked amongst the world's oldest rugby clubs and the passion for the game was an eye-opener to me, coming as I did from soccer-mad Tyneside. Crowds of some 4,000 seemed to be regularly expected and on one Saturday when I was there, the place was invaded by a thousand or more coming by train from the Welsh valleys. I seem to remember it was a game against Newport. I think the Bath captain was M.V. Shaw and the hon secretary was the long-serving Eddy Simpkins, a master at Oldfield Boys' School, who was to have a remarkable spell in this office from 1908 until 1958. I remember seeing the great R.A. Gerrard, a powerfully built centre, who could run like a stag and was to win fourteen caps for England and, two years later, carve a famous partnership with the great Prince Alex Obolensky, to whom he fed the passes which enabled him to become part of rugby legend by scoring two famous tries.

It was about eightpence to get into the ground, one shilling into the enclosure, one shilling and eightpence into the north stand and it would knock you back all of two shillings into the main stand. To cries of 'Feet! Feet!' from the crowd, I was delighted to see that the Bath pack was adept at taking the ball forward at their feet, something at which we in the North, and particularly of course in the Scottish Borders, excelled. I little thought how actively I would be involved with the famous club in the years ahead.

I made a point of going to the Theatre Royal, of course, and was much impressed with it. There was another theatre in Bath at that time – the Palace. Always loving a stage show, I went along for a typical vaudeville theatre programme. It was just opposite the Theatre Royal and is now a bingo hall. Harry Barstow, in his well-researched book *Gladiators of a Roman City*, recalls Bath nights at the Palace. Apparently it was the custom for managers at the Palace to occasionally invite Bath rugby players along to a show. This would occur on a training night with the idea that by the time the lads got to the show they would have expended much energy training and be fairly quiet. But this proved to be rather wishful thinking, as it happened, for after the showers the lads were soon fresh again and, of course, had only a short jog to the Palace. Then the fun would really start. Comedy is what the audience was seeking and comedy certainly came thick and fast. Actresses were wooed and often won with, at times, nothing more romantic than a helping of fish and chips. The whole place erupted into a riot of cheers and counter cheers on these occasions, with the poor old orchestra solidly in the line of fire as a barrage of onions was directed at the stage.

In more recent years we were to be represented on stage at the Theatre Royal by that great Bath Rugby Club character, Coochie – or Mr Chilcott to you! His appearances were in the true tradition of pantomime and for the complete season as a professional in a well-staged show. Back in the wild days of the Palace, however, it was something quite different, though threatening to bring the house down perhaps more realistically. On such an evening, with many of the audience taking shelter from onions flying in every direction, but mostly between the Rugby boys, the *Bath Evening Chronicle* reported that, 'It was enough to make the local cricket fraternity green with envy.'

That was during my stay of only a few months, but what brought me closer to Bath was when after the War I met Eric Hall at the home of Viscount Swinton. Eric and I were enthusiasts for the Conservative Party and I remember when later we attended the Party Conference at Llandudno, Ted Leather, MP for North Somerset, electrified the gathering with a remarkable speech. I think he later became Governor of Bermuda.

I often stayed with Eric at the family home in Southstoke, near Bath. His mother, Vera, and I hit it off at once. After all, she was a Geordie. He had two delightful sisters, Diane and Hazel, whom I christened 'Di and Fry' for some reason I can't remember. Eric's father, Basil, ran Bath Garages which extended down most of one side of James Street West next to the old Green Park Station. They were agents for many leading makes which included Morris, Wolseley, Riley and MG.

And so developed my love affair with Bath. Weekends often found me driving down the 90 miles from London. Our favourite eating place was The Hole In The Wall. There was more elegance than now. In the summer we would often be down at the Halls' family cottage at Ringstead Bay and on their yacht which was berthed at Weymouth. Around this time Roddy Llewellyn ran a commune locally and Princess Margaret was sometimes to be seen visiting the commune's shop at the foot of Milsom Street.

Strange to relate, Bath at one time was quite black and grimy. I remember around, I think, 1955 or 1956 seeing signs saying,

'Clean up Bath!' In fact, Jane Austen refers to the grimness of its appearance in the 1800s. One of her characters, Anne Elliott, reported, 'She caught the first dim view of the extensive buildings smoking in the rain without any wish of seeing them better.' In 1961, however, Alistair Cooke in his 'Letter from Bath' wrote,

> The first time I was in Bath after the war, the Roman Baths, the great Abbey, the crescents built by John Wood and his son were black with grime and pitted with rot, but in the last year or two Bath has wakened up with a bang to what is unique about its heritage: an eighteenth century town built in a single style out of local stone that abounds in nearby quarries. As they have done in so many old towns they have blasted away the centuries of dirt that had added more grime than bloom and today you can see the two great crescents and the circus as they were in the seventeen-sixties and seventeen-seventies. Great lyrical arcs of a light biscuit colour, gay and graceful as they were meant to be.

Bath stone is, of course, a beautiful building material, but like all natural materials it needs to breathe.

To return to Eric Hall. By 1964 he was able to acquire 'big money' and buy 51 per cent of the shares of Bath Garages, which acted as a kick-start to him building up a substantial chain of motor dealers in the West Country. Concurrently he was busy merging a yacht chandling business with a new company building life-rafts and dinghies which was named 'C-craft'. It proved to be most successful and he later sold it to Dunlop. His charm of manner and business acumen were an effective combination. We often met in London during this time and I remember on one occasion we saw David Frost putting on one of his first appearances as a cabaret artiste. Some years ago Eric and his wife Jo went to live in the Channel Islands.

More recently I have seen Lionel Jefferies when he appeared in *The Wild Duck* by Ibsen at the Theatre Royal. Eileen and he joined me in a good reunion at the Bath Spa Hotel. It was much earlier, I think in 1969, when I had spent the weekend at their home near London, having watched the Cup Final on TV on the Saturday afternoon, that he was eagerly looking forward to directing his first film, *The Railway Children*, and there was the suggestion that I might be asked to be Production Manager.

'You could do that all right. Just look how you got bamboo stages built and made things happen in all sorts of strange places in Burma,' I remember him saying with a laugh. It was, however, early days and I didn't hear further from him on this, but he certainly made a good job of directing the film.

One day soon after it was released I had a phone call that at first startled me. It was a woman's voice and I thought she said, 'This is your wife'! I soon realised, though, that it was 'This Is Your Life.' The BBC arrange these programmes superbly. Secrecy is carefully maintained. On the night it was huge fun. Charlie Lines, who ran the band in my show in Burma, was there. He was then a senior official in HM Customs. There were stars galore making their appearances. Of course, *The Railway Children* was well represented by Jenny Agutter and Dinah Sheridan.

I was awaiting my call to go on when suddenly Ingrid Bergman arrived. She had dashed over from a West End theatre and somehow just had time to make an appearance. 'Do I follow you on?' she asked me after our introduction. Did she follow me on? She was only the World's Number One Box Office Star at the time! So beautiful and mesmeric, it was a delight to meet and talk to her, even for the few minutes whilst we waited.

It all went off well. I accordingly did my stuff as I had briefly rehearsed it. Afterwards John Mills teased me. 'Truly Shakespearean,' he said laughing. There was a lot of leg pulling and I spent much of the time with Dick Emery, my favourite comedian. No, he did not say to me, 'You are awful, but I like you!' Actually he was keen for me to do some promotional work for him.

I must say, the BBC do themselves proud. The hospitality was superb.

I suppose we all have our own trophies about our home. They bring back memories. The Japanese officer's sword went to the Regimental Museum long ago, but I have a superb casting in bronze of Monty, head and shoulders, presented to me as a reminder of the great Alamein Nights. It's on the mantelshelf of my 'pride and joy', an Adam fireplace which I bought at an auction at Frimley Hall, Surrey many moons ago, and has moved around with me ever since. The centre of it should never really be dusted for sentimental reasons. I can see the very spot where Bobby and Samantha Moore leaned backwards, drinks in their hands, with half the England team sat around in the lounge of my house in Victoria, London.

Then there is the one-and-a-half-foot head of the Masai warrior. He is adorned with long earrings and his expression is proud and fearless. This is a reminder of a wonderful visit to Africa viewing big game within sight of the snow-capped peaks of Mount Kilimanjaro and hearing the distant rumble of lions.

I brought the head home safely held on my knees on the aircraft. Next to me, Katie Boyle told me how she had loved Africa and how she was so relaxed that she loved to run naked with the jungle on one side and the ocean on the other. At Entebbe we were joined by Princess Marina, who was seen off by President Dr Milton Obote of Uganda. She came and sat opposite me across the gangway. To come home next to two beautiful and talented women was a bonus indeed.

Hanging on the hall stand is a light-grey fedora. It's a kind of talisman I usually wore at the rugby matches. When that highly respected correspondent, Stephen Jones, kindly did a foreword to my book *Triple Triumph*, he wrote that he would not take a fee, but suggested I sent a donation to the 'Society for Ageing Fedoras'! Incidentally, in that piece he also wrote, 'Bath have been the most innovative as well as the most successful team in Britain.'

It was given me by Christy's, the makers, and was first worn by Shaun, my photographer when Pat Phoenix and he were dressed as Bonny and Clyde, complete with violin case, for a celebrity visit to open a new supermarket. It was a great success, but I remember what a rush it was en route collecting Pat at her cottage outside Manchester in time to meet the police motorcycle escort who awaited us on the outskirts of Stoke on Trent. We just made it in time, which was fortunate as a big crowd was in place when we arrived outside the store. It had been quite hilarious collecting Pat. It was about nine o'clock when we called. She must have

Opposite: *Pat Phoenix as I saw her on the set in action as Elsie Tanner in* Coronation Street. *(Picture compliments of Granada Television)*

been partying the night before and I remember how we helped to get her ready. Pat raced around semi-nude! There were knickers hanging on lampshades in her bedroom. Somehow it all got sorted out and we were off. She was like that. Always game for a laugh.

I remember how she slipped away from the civic reception party as soon as it was polite and I found her with a group of workmen in a back room swapping stories and having a high old time. That was Pat all right. She had a wonderful touch with people: and she really was Elsie Tanner. She knew all about the highs and lows of life and she was certainly in need of a bit of luck when she first read for the part in *Coronation Street*. She talked to me a lot about it; but what a huge success she made of it all. We met a few times in the Film Exchange, a club which was then opposite the old Opera House in Manchester. Many of the *Coronation Street* cast came there. How she used to joke about *Crossroads*, the rival soap. She used to call it 'The Repertory Company'.

Pat's umbrella will always remain unfurled in my entrance hall. It came into my possession when I had a flat in Cheltenham. On Gold Cup days for two years running I booked a hospitality tent on behalf of a client company, a former member of my scout troop in Newcastle upon Tyne, Geoff Longstaffe, was getting together the British operation for the company, the leading Scandinavian paint manufacturers, and he asked me to handle their UK Public Relations. I had a very enjoyable visit to Stockholm to finalise matters. The name of the Company was Beckers.

My arrangements for the Gold Cup were at a time when this kind of hospitality was in its infancy. My flat was quite spacious and we were able to entertain some twenty guests, mostly commercial paint buyers. First there was a kind of late breakfast spread served professionally and then two Rolls Royces ferried the guests to the course, which was a couple of miles away. I had invited Pat, who loved racing, but in the end she was unable to come and Tony Booth came instead, having borrowed her umbrella for the occasion as the weather was very undecided.

It was a hugely successful day. Denis – by then Sir Denis – Hamilton and Olive also joined us. Lunch was served superbly. In the gathering darkness, long after the races had ended, we were safely back at the flat, but no Tony Booth! Shaun went searching for him. We eventually got Tony back, though he was, of course, in no state to remember Pat's umbrella when he finally went on his way. She would never let me return it to her. I last met them when Tony and she were appearing together at the Theatre Royal in Bath in *The Spider's Web* by Agatha Christie. They were staying at the Old Mill Hotel near the toll point at Bathampton. I thought she looked tired so purposely I saw very little of her. A year or two later when playing in Scarborough she collapsed. It was diagnosed as cancer. Tony and she were married not long before she was given the Last Rites.

Then on a nearby wall hangs an entirely different memento. It's a group picture of the Bath Football Club (Rugby Union) Management Committee 1995–96. There are twenty on the picture including 'yours truly'. I enjoyed working with them. They represented a wide span of business, legal and academic interests and were, in my opinion, far removed from Will Carling's 'old farts in blazers'. I always particularly enjoyed going off on 'The Committee Coach' to away fixtures.

I became involved when just before one match I was asked to call in at the office of the late Clive Howard, the much-esteemed Honorary Secretary, who was manager of the Bath branch of an insurance company. He told me that dealing with the press was amongst his many duties. In fact, they appeared to invade his office on match days looking for somewhere to work and use the telephone. There was very little space to move in the place as a result. He invited me to meet the committee who asked me to take on the duties of Hon Press Secretary, a position the club had never had previously. There was not, I found, a true understanding in some quarters of the value of the press, most of whom had to arrive very early in order to find a decent seat, to say nothing of finding a car space. I even heard it suggested, though I hasten to add only by an individual or two and not by the club, that newspapers should be asked to pay for the seats they occupied. The first signs of the arrival of television cameras plus crews and vehicles were to send a shudder up some of these same people.

But with patience the value of good media relations became better appreciated and the need for a Press Box was accepted and an estimate of cost agreed. I have to say that I tried good

The new press box at the Rec, Bath's famous rugby ground.

humouredly to speak of my trials and tribulations in all this at a general meeting of club members, who appeared to enjoy it, except one member who to this day has never spoken to me.

In his excellent book, *Ace of Clubs*, Brian Jones, who was Editor of the *Bath Chronicle* in the 1960s, writes,

> And indeed it is the press, week in and week out, rather less fickle than national radio and television, that keeps clubs and their followers up to date with trends and teams in a sport moving rapidly into big money [with all the headaches that will bring!].
>
> That dramatic shift in the game was visibly manifest to visitors to the Rec at the start of the 1992/93 season: part of the roof of the main stand was missing. The gap was to be filled by the new press box.
>
> It was a few weeks late in arriving and cost around £80,000, rather more than originally envisaged, but its excellent facilities for press, radio and television meant that few would argue with the boast of the club's ebullient press officer, Ken Johnstone. 'It is the best press box in the game as befits a club that has more column inches written about it than any other.'

That last point was worth making. Bath benefitted from its frequent exposure from BBC Rugby Special and HTV and in that extensive coverage from the quality dailies and Sundays, in particular, whose column inches must have equalled the felling of a few forests.

I developed a high regard for the denizens of the press box, including the radio and TV men, of course, and I always enjoyed their excellent co-operation. They were a great bunch. Rugby correspondents usually have to leave on tour soon after a busy season. Travelling in another country, often in small aircraft, may sound attractive, but it can be uncomfortable and there is always pressure to meet deadlines with little relaxation. Soon after returning home the new season is upon them.

Incidentally, I know where one hard-working rugby correspondent is able to cool his fevered brow. It's the home of Robert Armstrong of the *Guardian*, and it's an idyllic setting. The cottage is named Wildacre and you find it at the end of a leafy lane not a stone's throw – and I mean just a few yards – from the waters of Ringstead Bay in Dorset. With his wife, the artist Merete Bates, busy painting and arranging exhibitions, his daughter Galina – surely the most gorgeous looking of veterinary surgeons – and young Adam, a very bright teenager, it's an ideal spot to at least attempt to wind down.

The football correspondent, however, does not have the same kind of touring to cover, but he is almost always involved with news of the movement of players and the huge sums of money the game now attracts, so there is little respite, especially with the big international tournaments like Euro 2000 and the World Cup.

Newspapers, too, are changing in a subtle manner. Unlike North America, where there is no cheque book sports journalism, here one can find a player so tied up with another newspaper that it curtails interviews. There is increasing pressure and direction from editorial desks as space for sport increases – there can be up to twenty pages of sport in a Sunday newspaper. Take the month of July, when there is championship golf, cricket and the second week of Wimbledon – plus early news of domestic football. There appears at times to be emphasis on conflict stories, particularly in football. Conflict between players and clubs, between players and players, between players and wives or girlfriends, and so on.

Then there are the photographers, who really do a splendid job. At Bath we were the first to provide a service which enabled pictures to be wired direct into newspaper offices, which at the time was, I believe, something Twickenham did not have.

Improving the match programme was an immediate task for me, and we won an award for this. An eight-page newspaper, 'The RECorder', which I wrote and produced, was very well received.

I enjoyed 'stirring up the scene' a bit with some old-fashioned 'razamataz' from time to time. For example, the *Western Daily Press* of Tuesday, 22 October 1996 ran a two-column story entitled 'In a flap over French cockerels' by Wendy Best. (This was picked up nationally.) It went, 'French rugby fans risk ruffling the feathers of the RSPCA chiefs when they visit Bath this weekend and release six cockerels onto the pitch before the match.' And it went on to say that on Saturday Bath would play Dax in a crucial game and needed victory to go on to the quarter-finals of the Heineken European Cup. All very true, except the bit about the cockerels, I am afraid. I kept the story running and running. The Dax papers joined in and had pictures of cockerels in pens, presumably being prepared for the invasion – '*Bath redoute les coqs dacquais!*'

It became quite hilarious and marvellous publicity. The French press loved it. The RSPCA advised me that they had special nets and would willingly help train our stewards how to catch cockerels with them and the Ministry of Agriculture even contacted me to say that they would be keeping a sharp lookout at Channel ports. More of the media picked up the story and it became the spin of the week. When he saw some of the press stories, Ed Goodall, the club Chief Executive, appeared to be quite startled. Everyone involved enjoyed the joke afterwards.

I received a letter about a month after I took on the job, asking me if I needed an assistant. It came from Joan Budge, a very enthusiastic club member. I found her to be charming. She worked at Bath University and was within a year of retirement. Joan loved her rugby and was extremely knowledgeable. Thus began a most enjoyable partnership. The new press box now had improved fittings and we arranged more press dossiers, telephone connections and developed the use of the sports pavilion apart from one room for the St John Ambulance section. This meant that press photographers had their own facilities and phone connections.

Everything went swimmingly, but about a year later on one very hot day when we were both on our feet for about ten hours attending pretty well non-stop to the whole squad and dozens of media, dealing with group pictures, individual interviews for TV, radio and press and so forth, plus a full-scale press conference, I could see that she had become desperately tired. But Joan would not ease up. I felt sure that she was not well and asked her to rest. She lived alone and unfortunately collapsed and died a few days later.

I think our visit to Bordeaux on Friday and Saturday, 30 and 31 January 1998 was to me one of the most enjoyable of all my rugby occasions. On the night previous to the big clash between Bath and Brive in the European Cup Final I was in a restaurant sitting at a long table relaxing with some twenty members of the sports press. We ate and we drank and we sang and I was in my element. And the next evening – on the eve of the match – we were off by coach to a superb banquet at a chateau some twenty miles away as the guest of Heinekens. Some of the very best wines of Bordeaux were served. Next to me at dinner was one of the most respected members of the Press, Colin Price of the *Daily Mirror*, and I was so sorry to hear of his death little more than eighteen months later.

The atmosphere next day was electric. After our brilliant heart-stopping win, Bath supporters celebrated far into the night. Many had already received pre-match hospitality from Brive supporters en route. It was all in absolutely marked contrast to the quite awful scenes of our unspeakable football hooligans in Belgium at the 2000 Euro Cup games. The Government had seemed powerless to get control of the situation. The chances of our staging the World Cup were surely harmed beyond repair.

If I may recount one amusing anecdote concerning a press report. A North Country team were playing Bath at the Rec. I had promised to phone in a few lines at the end of the game to a Manchester newspaper, but by the time the game came round I was already in the local hospital, the RUH, having had a hip replacement. I suddenly remembered my assignment, but fortunately the excellent Hospital Radio Service was, as usual, relaying a commentary from the ground. I accordingly listened to it and passed on my brief report by telephone. I was asked to complete it a few minutes later with the final score. Just when the final moments of the game took place and I awaited the score on the hospital radio, the trolley with the telephone on it was whisked away down the ward.

'Hi,' I shouted, without my cry being heeded. 'Hi there! I want my trolley back!'

With that I suddenly got moving in my wheelchair, my leg up in the air, and propelled myself frantically after the departing trolley. On reaching it, I hurriedly dialled the Manchester number and gave the score, startling the poor nurse almost out of her wits.

May I recount another anecdote? Just one more, I promise you.

We were at Cardiff for the semi-final of the 1996/97 European Cup. There was, of course, a full press attendance of some thirty correspondents, all of whom were in the press room about an hour before kick-off. Suddenly I received some news of the Bath team that I wished them all to know so I jumped in the lift up to the press room, which I then entered, called for attention and made the following announcement:

'Jon Sleightholme will not be playing for Bath this afternoon. He is not well due to something he has eaten. There will be a full report on the whistle.'

I can vouch for the enormous roar of laughter that followed this!

Not all my ideas came to fruition. When Federico Mendez, the Argentinean international, joined the club, I planned to have him met at the airport and on reaching Bath he was to be transferred to a smart horse-drawn carriage festooned in the Argentine colours with an outrider dressed as a gaucho. The media would be on hand as they trotted up to the clubhouse.

John Hall, hearing of my plans, was aghast and hurriedly contacted me asking me not to go ahead with the idea.

The club certainly made news when we arranged to play Wigan under Rugby League rules at Maine Road, Manchester on 8 May 1996 and then in a return match under Rugby Union rules on 25 May 1996 at Twickenham. It was known as The Rugby Challenge

1996 and it meant some feverish organisation. Many of our ladies did a splendid job manning a phone-in booking office at the ground. Those much to the fore in our match arrangements included Danny Sacco, who ran our Bath mini team, Colin Gale, our Hon Treasurer, and John Hall.

Among those stalwarts of either code who were fascinated by it all was the playwright Colin Welland who wrote to me,

> I have been dreaming of this game for as long as I can remember. Raised in the heartland of Rugby League, yet playing Union all my life, I sat through childhood as the arguments raged above and around, thirteen v fifteen, pros against dabblers, the 100 years war. All were safe in the comfort of hot air, both evincing the merits of their code confident in the fact that the showdown would only kick-off in cloud cuckoo land.
>
> Well, wherever, whenever that dream time is, it is upon us. Wigan, whose successive heroes I've lauded to London ears since journeying south 30 years ago, are finally to test the skill and resolve of the mightiest Union side of the decade.
>
> How will the cherry and whites cope with rucks and mauls? How will Bath match the fitness of full time pros whose livings depend on speed of hand and fleetness of foot? A fascinating prospect and one which, after all these years, is to pass me by – a family wedding. Still I will be with you in spirit and watching on the box.
>
> Good luck to both teams and may you all witness a feast of running rugby. In Wigan's case, at least, it won't be for the want of trying.

I won't go into the scores and scorers. Suffice to say that as expected, the home team in each historic game, playing under its own rules, won handsomely, but I would like to add that we at least scored a splendid Rugby League try up at Maine Road – the home of Manchester City Football Club – in the dying minutes by none other than our very own Jon Callard. There was, I remember, a marvellous poster displayed showing Edwards, the Wigan Captain, and Phil de Glanville, our Captain.

When at Manchester I was intrigued to listen to some of the vigorous lobbying that was going on all around me on the part of Rugby Union committee men, not from Bath, but several other clubs. It was the same at Bordeaux after our great victory in the

European Cup. Leading club officials in the game moved restlessly from group to group in the Reception tent afterwards, all engaged in a seemingly endless dialogue, plying their views and plans for the future of the game. Inexorably the professional era loomed ahead and one became almost fearful for the outcome in the face of such apparent discord and crude carpetbagging.

I have enjoyed meeting and working with the Bath players and have always received the utmost co-operation and courtesy from them. They are a great bunch. When *The Rugby Club*, the BBC TV production, came out, a number of them called out their congratulations, particularly following one notable episode in which I appeared. (Incidentally I heard from places as far apart as Israel, Cyprus and Portugal from friends who had seen it!) That piece of filming, shot in Venice by the BBC, had the crowds massing on the side of the canal. 'You Dirk Bogarde?' enquired one happy Japanese snapper.

I was delighted to have an invitation to visit HMS *Illustrious*. This was because Doug Ryder, one of the old Bath Rugby committee had developed an association between ship and club which resulted in exchange visits with members of the ship's rugby XV and ourselves.

The Supporters' Club now numbers some 900 members, which is a good proportion for a ground with a capacity of some 9,000. The move to professional mode has been smooth enough, once its inevitability was accepted, and Andrew Brownsword, the club's owner, is very approachable. It was our big success at Bordeaux that seemed to relax him and it was a huge incentive for his foresight in backing us.

A history of the club is being prepared. It's a formidable task, of course, for a club which started in 1865, but those two great stalwarts, Colin Gale and Peter Hall, are tackling it with a will, though its completion will, of necessity, take considerable time.

Perhaps the most exciting development at the club has been the expansion of an enlightened youth development programme. As for young players reaching stardom, the brilliant Matt Perry and Iain Bailshaw are outstanding examples. What is so impressive, also, is that both have retained their personal charm amidst their success.

It was always a great satisfaction to me that Jack Rowell, a former captain of my old club, Gosforth, had become the inspiration of Bath Rugby from the time he took over as coach in 1978–79. The teams that Jack built became the marvel of the game. He is unquestionably one of my real heroes.

When you phone the Callard household the answer buzzer says, 'This is Jon and Gail here!' What a team they are, together with Georgia, 5 and Francesca, 2. They first met in training college at Cheltenham and both became teachers. Unquestionably my favourite rugby player and now Head Coach at Bath, Jon was born at Leicester on 1 June 1966. We have always been very good friends. He, too, is one of my heroes. Character has always been one of his greatest assets. He had to patiently wait his time when he first joined Bath, playing in the United because Jonathan Webb was first choice full-back, but when he retired it was Jon Callard who took over and also, incidentally, as full-back for England, kicking a match-winning penalty in the last minute of a most exciting game at Murrayfield in the 1994 Five Nations Championship (15 points to 14). Since that day Jon has given us all such wonderful moments on the field, both for club and country. Who will ever forget his triumph at Bordeaux?

Everyone enjoys a rugby tour and the West Country is a favourite. I came here forty odd years ago with a XV from Westcombe Park, a club in Kent near Orpington and Petts Wood. I remember a particularly enjoyable game at Bathampton against the Old Edwardians. We made our headquarters in an inn on the river near Bradford-on-Avon. What a party it was! It usually ended with someone swimming fully clothed.

It was, however, pretty well my swan-song as a player. A knee I wrenched badly during an impromptu knockabout in Burma on a piece of ground as hard as concrete began to play up. Incidentally, I did not report sick when it happened as I did not want to risk being flown out to India as next day we were moving into Prome on a mopping-up exercise. Instead I went in on the back of an elephant, which prompted the Commanding Officer to observe, 'I thought this was the Infantry, not the bloody Cavalry!'

My village of Monkton Combe is about four miles from Bath. It shares its ecclesiastical benefice with Combe Down and Southstoke.

When the vicar, Paul Langham had his fortieth birthday we gave him a wonderful surprise by luring him on a false pretext to the nearby Rockery Tea Gardens. There were some three hundred of us, children and adults, all on tiptoe with excitement hiding in the bushes!

The wife of a visiting Canadian ecclesiastic told me that in all their trip around England, she thought one of the loveliest sights was the view one suddenly gets when coming out of the bend at the top of Brass Knocker Hill, the valley where I live.

The village is also reached by three narrow and twisting lanes running down from Combe Down and the lower end of Brass Knocker Hill itself. These lanes are in places no wider than the width of a car and more suited to horse and carts but it helps to sustain the rustic feeling, if sometimes a bit of a challenge in winter.

At the foot of Brass Knocker Hill there is the last remaining stretch of the old Somerset Coal Canal now thankfully restored and in the summer months quite busy with pleasure craft some of which are equipped for lengthy trips joining up with the upper reaches of the Thames. My old General, the late Sir Hugh Stockwell, who lived nearby, officially opened the new stretch of canal and remarked that having had quite a lot to do with a very famous canal he thought it fitting to open this one! He was referring, of course, to when he was in command of British Land Forces at the time of the Suez Canal crisis in 1956. The village has its pub but there are few houses and cottages other than the dozen or so occupied by the excellent Monkton Combe School as additional dormitories to the main buildings of the school. There is a fine Country Club on the high ground behind the village.

The Monks' Retreat where the monks apparently grew produce to take to the Abbey at Bath is now a very tastefully designed Retirement Home. Next to it is the Church of St Michael and All Angels which was mentioned in the Domesday Book of 1086. I am a somewhat irregular attender but when I slip into my pew seat next to Nan and Peter Kelly they nod and smile with warmth as though I had never been absent.

Our village hall has its branch of the WRI and there are other occasional meetings on various interesting subjects. I am rather keen on barn owls and I was terribly disappointed to miss a splendid talk on this subject but I certainly did not miss the Millenium Party. That was a knockout!

I have a very comfortably designed flat in St Michael's Court, a group of two-storey buildings converted from farm property by the Bagnall-Oakeley family.

A hundred years ago a student at Monkton Combe School wrote:

Immediately outside the dormitory windows on one side were meadows sloping upwards from the road, with cows almost level with our windows; on the opposite side they looked across the valley to the wooded hills. We were embosomed in the purest unspoilt country. I do not think it was fancy; but the influence of our surroundings there affected us deeply.

In those days there was absolute freedom to walk and wander. In our dormitories the country looked at us, we smelt it as soon as the window opened, the doors leading to it stood open, nothing hindered picking wild roses or sweet violets in their seasons in a few odd minutes. Regularly at one time between breakfast and school I wandered up a lane with hedgerow on one side, field on the other, up the hill and, when the bell rang, dashed headlong down the drung to be in time for school. Flowers were everywhere, hedgerow flowers, meadow flowers, wood flowers ... how I revelled in them. Little wheeled traffic came our way; only occasionally on nearby roads the great teams of horses dragging loads of Bath stone ... I have a vivid impression of lush meadows laid up for hay. And alas we sometimes took short cuts, at which the poor old farmer Wicks threatened us, if he ever caught sight of us. But we never did it unless we were in a hurry! I cannot remember any arable land. It was all wood, meadow and plenty of water; the Brook with a fine bathing pool in Freeman's field (how we scurried to get our towels after afternoon school in summer); the Avon and the two lovely canals with water lilies, white and yellow, and the barges, brightly coloured, creeping along them towed by horses.

On half holidays for reasons given and approved we could go into Bath. It was the School custom that, if we won a School match in

Bath, the team had a brake out; otherwise they had to foot it! ...
There was a farm connected with the School, and in mid-morning
there were great jugs of milk with hard biscuits, and we might drink
as much as we liked. I do not remember any epidemic; nor was
there an infirmary. I do not remember doctor's visits either. If we
said we had a headache, we were allowed to spend the morning in
the garden, *quietly*.

A hundred years ago!

I must say that most days in the summer my heart rejoices when
I pull back my bedroom curtains and look down the valley which
stretches away and out of view some two miles distant; and there
is the tumultuous dawn chorus from a great copper beech not fifty
yards away. The welcome softens into sweet intermittent calls from
jackdaws and robins, aided by the lively calls of the blue tits and
the long coo of the wood pigeons. Sometimes pheasants march in
single file across my lawn. It is all a thrilling overture to the day
and, just to complete the picture, there's a river stocked with trout
and, yes, a castle on the horizon!

Across the valley the woods are a rich assortment of oak, ash
and larch with some maple also in attendance; all as a background
to trim fields with cattle grazing on the lower slopes within sight
of the farmhouse. The church clock strikes the hours and you can
almost see what time it is through the branches of the oak tree
on the other side of the wall.

May I just add my favourite piece, 'Those men whom I have
seen succeed best in life were men who went about with a smile
on their face and hope in their heart believing that good times,
all times will pass away.'